The Carolinas

Gardener's Guide

The Carolinas
Gardener's Guide

Toby Bost & Jim Wilson

COOL SPRINGS PRESS
A Division of Thomas Nelson Publishers
Since 1798

Published by Cool Springs Press, a Division of Thomas Nelson, Inc., P. O. Box 141000, Nashville, Tennessee, 37214.

Bost, Toby.
    The Carolinas gardener's guide / Toby Bost & Jim Wilson.— Rev. ed.
      p. cm.
    ISBN 1-59186-049-0
    1.Landscape plants—North Carolina. 2. Landscape plants—South Carolina. 3. Landscape gardening—North Carolina. 4. Landscape gardening—South Carolina. I. Wilson, Jim. II. Title.
    SB407.B5859 2005
    635.9'09756--dc22

                                    2004021666

First printing 2005
Printed in the United States of America
10 9 8 7 6 5 4

Managing Editors: Billie Brownell and Bryan Norman
Designer: Sheri Ferguson, Ferguson Design
Horticulture Editor: Dr. Bob Polomski
Production Artist: S.E. Anderson

On the Cover: *Iris ensata,* caprician butterfly, photographed by Jerry Pavia

Cool Springs Press books may be purchased in bulk for educational, business, fundraising, or sales promotional use. For information, please email **SpecialMarkets@ThomasNelson.com**.

Visit the Thomas Nelson website at **www.ThomasNelson.com** and the Cool Springs Press website at **www.coolspringspress.net**

Dedication and Acknowledgments

Dedicated to the Master Gardeners of the Carolinas for their great work in helping other gardeners grow.

Practice is the gardener's path, and science is the light to the path."
—Anonymous

We would like to thank the County Extension Agents of the Carolinas who freely give their time, knowledge, and passion for the education of gardeners and the benefit of communities. Without their substantial contributions, gardeners throughout the Carolinas would be deprived of new plant management techniques, trends in horticulture, gardening shows, workshops, newsletters, and seminars. Your contributions help make the Carolinas truly great.

Also, Cool Springs Press is long overdue recognition. Their sensitive state and regional books meet the diverse needs of gardeners throughout the country who occupy different hardiness zones and face various geographical challenges. Your books guide gardeners toward the results they desire and in turn a life-long love for gardening. Further, we'd like to thank our editors, Billie Brownell and Bryan Norman. Their commitment helped make this book comprehensive, accurate, and beautiful and guided it as it grew from a list of dos and don'ts to a consistent, accessible, friendly tool for gardeners throughout the Carolinas.

Photography Credits

Thomas Eltzroth: pages 20, 26, 27, 28, 29, 31, 33, 34, 35, 36, 39, 44, 45, 47, 50, 52, 55, 61, 63, 66, 67, 68, 70, 71, 72, 80, 82, 83, 86, 87, 88, 89, 95, 96, 98, 99, 100, 101, 102, 103, 105, 106, 107, 109, 112, 114, 116, 122, 123, 126, 134, 135, 138, 139, 140, 142, 146, 147, 148, 150, 151, 152, 153, 157, 159, 160, 161, 169, 170, 171, 172, 173, 180, 186, 188, 191, 193, 198, 199, 201, 204, 205, 218, 226, 230, 234, 247, back cover photographs

Liz Ball and Rick Ray: pages 49, 54, 58, 60, 69, 73, 76, 97, 104, 124, 137, 141, 143, 149, 164, 182, 187, 194, 200, 202, 208, 210, 212, 222, 223, 224, 229, 232, 233, 235, 242, 244, 248, 249

Jerry Pavia: the front cover, and pages 12, 16, 23, 30, 32, 38, 41, 42, 43, 46, 48, 53, 59, 64, 77, 85, 90, 91, 129, 133, 144, 145, 154, 155, 156, 158, 163, 166, 168, 184, 185, 192, 196, 203, 206, 209, 211, 213, 214, 216, 237, 241, 243, 246

Pam Harper: pages 37, 74, 75, 78, 79, 215, 225, 228, 238, 239, 240, 245

Dency Kane: pages 94, 236

Toby Bost: page 189

Dave MacKenzie: page 207

Lorenzo Gunn: pages 181, 197, 226

Laura Coit: pages 108, 231

Cathy Barash: pages 65, 190

Lee Anne White: page 130

Dr. Mike Dirr: pages 136, 251

Andre Viette: pages 10, 131, 176

Peter Loewer: pages 119, 120, 121, 125

Neil Soderstrom: page 118

William Adams: pages 40, 113, 115, 117, 127, 217

Felder Rushing: pages 13, 21, 22, 51, 57, 62, 93, 110, 128, 174, 178, 219, 220, 250

Ralph Snodsmith: pages 56, 81, 195

Mark Turner® Turner Photographics: page 176

Charles Mann: pages 14, 84, 162, 167, 175, 183

Karen Bussolini: pages 24, 92, 165

Robin Conover: page 15

Bill Kersey: all illustrations

Table of Contents

Featured Plants

Welcome to Gardening *in* *the Carolinas*

At one time the United States was a loose union of thirteen colonies operating as separate countries. "Carolina" included not only today's North and South Carolina, but also an immense hunk of country stretching to the Mississippi River. There is precedent for combining North and South Carolina into one book about gardening. After all, they share the same hardiness and heat zones and generally the same soil types. Prevailing southwest to northeast winds warm and cool both states and the hurricanes brush both shores. Both South and North Carolina have a strong cadre of Master Gardeners trained by Cooperative Extension agents to help you.

During much of the 20th century, it is fair to say that only two of the four seasons were fully utilized by flower gardeners in the Carolinas. They had azaleas and rhododendrons in the spring and camellias in the fall and a long stretch of green in between. The spring and fall seasons also brought food gardening, though with little more than okra, black-eyed peas, and sweet potatoes

That's all changing now. Thanks to heat-and humidity-resistant flowers, landscapes can glow with color during the summer. Rock-hardy winter annuals can brighten the dark winter days. Raised beds with new perfect drainage are making all-season food gardening not only enjoyable but gratifyingly productive.

But let's be honest about gardening in the Carolinas. Except high in the mountains, summertime gardening is an early morning and late evening activity. Midday gardening is not fun; the risk of dehydration, heat stroke, and skin cancer is real. That's why experienced Carolina gardeners plant shade trees as a first order of business. They know from trial and error that when books say, "grow in full sun," that plants will grow just as well with afternoon shade, and that the same shade is a great place for a comfortable seat and a glass of sweet tea.

Though the sun can be your enemy, you can make your gardening friend, unlike some pesky critters. Dog and deer ticks lurk on plants waiting for you to come along; stinging caterpillars take refuge under tattered foliage; yellow jackets bore holes in inconvenient places. Slather Avon Skin-so-Soft® from head to toe before venturing into your summer garden to deter the ticks. Wear leather gloves in perennial gardens in late summer to protect your hands from stinging caterpillars. Products with DEET® repel mosquitoes. And a hornet-wasp killer aerosol sprayed into their entrance at dusk will prevent unsuspecting passers-by a lot of pain. Well, you didn't really expect four season of good gardening weather to come without a downside, did you?

Once you get into the swing of gardening in the Carolinas, you can make the trying weather and intractable soil your servant. Gardeners moving to the Carolinas from up north often complain about the sun "not being in the right place for the time of day." Summer days in the Carolinas are shorter, nighttime comes with a rush, and winter days are significantly longer. And they complain about "that awful clay." Give it a chance and it will grow beautiful plants when adequately modified with soil conditioners.

A Perennial Garden

Toby Bost and Jim Wilson lecture frequently, and both have heard the same request many times: "I wish you could come by my house and tell me what I'm doing wrong." They wrote this book to honor that request. Study this guide filled with years of experience, and gardening will be more enjoyable and productive. You will look forward to spending time in your garden rather than dreading the prospect. With each passing year you will gain skill and confidence. You could even become that person that all the neighbors turn to for advice—a "gardening guru."

Good luck with your Carolina garden!

The Benefits of Organic Matter

Organic matter is a component that increases a soil's water-holding capability while giving it a dark, earthy appearance. It is found in manure, compost, aged leaves, sawdust, and decomposing mulch.

Peat moss is readily available to gardeners and is suitable for amending sandy soils and for use in container gardening. In Piedmont clay soils, finely-ground composted pine bark is one of the best amendments. (Its general particle size should be one-half inch or smaller.) Tight clay soils can be improved if thirty to fifty percent (by volume) of pine-bark soil conditioner is tilled into the garden (spread a three-inch layer over the bed and spade or till six inches in depth). Other good amendments are leaf compost, granite screening, small pea gravel, and Perma-Till™. Hardwood bark should not be used as a soil conditioner; however, aged hardwood bark makes a fine landscaping mulch.

"Black Gold"

Compost is biologically active organic matter that can be made at home by nature (humus or "woods dirt"). No gardener should be without a compost bin. Stir a little compost into the top few inches of soil, and your plants will flourish. (Compost does for plants what steroids do for athletes—but safely, of course!) Gardeners gloat over their compost. Some even call it "Black Gold." The billions of living creatures found in compost help plant roots absorb water and nutrients. Every organic gardener knows that you feed the soil, not the plants.

Making compost is simple. Just layer "green and brown" organic yard wastes, maintain moisture content, and turn a few times. In six months or so, you will have a high-quality organic material that can be used as a soil amendment. Toby says, "I make compost quickly using two trash bags of shredded hardwood leaves combined with one bag of grass clippings." There are numerous recipes and instructions for composting available at any County Cooperative Extension Office or public library. You will need two cubic feet of compost for every eight square feet of garden bed you plan to amend.

How to Prepare a Bed

Poorly drained clay soils are the norm throughout much of the state. When preparing a new bed for planting, several tricks will help you avoid "wet feet" and subsequent root rot. The simplest method is to borrow topsoil from one area and add it to the new bed. Rototill the bed and rake it smooth. Adding a few inches of topsoil can have a profound influence on whether a plant lives or flounders.

Landscape timbers or ties, rock retaining walls, and steel edging materials are frequently used to facilitate bed preparation. Or you can create berms for planting, using another technique that involves sculpting high mounds of amended native soils that serve a dual purpose as planting bed and privacy screen. If sand is used in clay soil to improve drainage, the volume of sand must exceed seventy percent.

Finally, where soil drainage is questionable, install a "French drain." This project is best performed with a backhoe. Lay slotted drain tile in the bottom of a two-foot-deep trench that has a two-percent slope to daylight. Surround the drain pipe with a bed of crushed stone and then backfill with a loose soil mix. This is the method often used for preparing beds for roses and rhododendrons.

After all is said and done about bed preparation, many gardeners will continue to dig a planting hole and throw a few inches of gravel into the bottom. Though they may feel good about this effort, it is a total waste of time and will more than likely worsen soil drainage. Digging a hole in a poorly drained site is something like constructing a pool or creating an in-ground aquarium—only riparian plants thrive under such conditions.

When in doubt, check soil drainage before planting. You can do this with a posthole digger or shovel and a bucket of water. Dig a hole one foot deep and fill it with water. Let it drain cleanly, then refill with water. If the water is still there the next day, don't plant until you install drain tiles or create berms.

Just a Numbers Game

Although seventeen essential nutrients are required for plant growth and development, only three are important to remember when gardening in the Carolinas. A healthy plant will consume the largest amounts of three nutrients, nitrogen (N), phosphorus (P), and potassium (K). These elements are

A Meadow Garden

A Rose Garden Lining a Path

the main ingredients in fertilizer and are expressed in terms of a percentage weight. For example, a general garden fertilizer labeled 10-10-10 contains 10 percent nitrogen, 10 percent phosphorus, and 10 percent potassium. The other seventy percent is filler or clay.

Each nutrient serves a function in the overall health of a plant. Nitrogen promotes vegetative or foliar growth; higher nitrogen percentages in a bag are beneficial for lawns or evergreen plants. Phosphorus enhances root and flower development; "starter" fertilizers and "bloom-boosters" are rich in this nutrient. Potassium is important for the overall health of a plant; "winterizer" fertilizers have a high percentage of potassium and may help a plant tolerate drought, cold, or disease. (A general rule of thumb when applying garden fertilizers is to use one to three pounds of actual nitrogen per thousand square feet. That's equivalent to one gallon of 10-10-10 for every thousand square feet of garden area.)

The soil's pH determines the availability of the plant nutrients; acidic soils starve plants by locking up vital nutrients, thus creating deficiencies. Monitor the soil pH by soil testing. Limestone neutralizes acidic soils and helps fertilizers work. Acidic soils can waste more than half the nitrogen fertilizer applied, and wasted fertilizers are an environmental hazard.

Though selecting the right fertilizer can be a bit frustrating, it's really just a numbers game. Compare the costs of fertilizer products by the amount you are paying for each pound of nitrogen or other dominant nutrients in the package. Slow-release fertilizers generally cost more, but they have some distinct advantages over common garden fertilizers. They release nutrients slowly to plants and are less likely to burn roots from high salt concentrates. For best results, apply a fertilizer with at least forty to fifty percent of its nitrogen in the ammoniacal or urea form. Slow-release fertilizers are an ecologically sound way to supply nutrients since excess nutrients will not leave the garden after a heavy rain. It is prudent to clean up after granular fertilizer and pesticide applications. Sweep hard surfaces, like drives and walks, to keep these materials from entering storm drains and polluting our water. Last but not least, fertilizers need not be applied more often than once or twice each season, freeing the gardener for more important tasks.

The Importance of a Soil Test

When it comes to soil-testing kits, you get what you pay for. The inexpensive chemical kits and probes are acceptable for a "ball park" analysis. If you test this way, we still recommend the services of a professional laboratory every few years, especially for major garden installations. In the Carolinas, either the Department of Agriculture's Agronomic Services will analyze your soil or you can contact a County Cooperative Extension Office for a free soil test kit. Many large farm-supply stores offer their customers a similar service.

No amount of fertilizer will compensate for a soil pH that is out of kilter. More than half the problems identified by the Plant Disease Clinic at North Carolina State University were caused by fertilizers—too much, in most cases. The optimum pH for most lawns and gardens is 5.5 to 6.5. (Remember that a pH below 6.9 is acidic and a pH above 7 is considered alkaline.) The addition of limestone reduces the acidity of soil and raises the soil pH. How much limestone you need depends on the type of soil, amount of organic matter, residual nutrients, and other factors.

The Best Defense

The conditions that make our gardens flourish also make for a happy homeland for insect and disease pests. Mild winters and wet, humid summers favor healthy populations of bugs and blights each growing season. Quarantines for gypsy moths and fire ants are currently in place in North and South Carolina. We are holding our breath in hopes that these and other garden pests will not become widespread throughout the Carolinas.

A prudent axiom to garden by is, "The best defense against pests is a healthy plant." Most gardening plants can tolerate moderate amounts of leaf injury before a pest-control strategy should be implemented. Natural predators often lurk on the garden fringes, waiting to help when problems arise. Second only to a vigorously growing plant is variety selection. The strength of this book is in its plant variety recommendations. The industry has made great strides over the last three decades in the selection and breeding of genetically superior plant varieties. Choose these plants, and you will have an ally in the fight against pests.

Integrated Pest Management

Our approach to pest control in the lawn and garden incorporates the principles of Integrated Pest Management (IPM). Proper identification of the pest and of the host plant is of paramount importance in the IPM system. This may appear to be a slow, painstaking course of action, but it does make more sense than the "Spray and Pray" philosophy of some gardeners today. In one situation, pruning a diseased twig may solve the problem. In another case, a fungicide application may be justified. Removal of a certain plant variety may be required in another situation. IPM is here to stay—learn more about it.

Weed Control

Ask any gardener what he or she dislikes most about gardening, and nine out of ten times the response will be "weeding." Gardeners and professionals alike go to great lengths to keep weeds under control. The most ecologically sound approach to weed control is mulching landscape beds and gardens. Organic

Irises Bordering Roughly Hewn Wood

materials such as bark, compost, and pine needles are good choices for mulch. On steep banks and slopes, use shredded hardwood bark or pine needles; on flat surfaces, use bark nuggets, which won't float off in a rainstorm. The rule for mulches is to apply to a depth of one to three inches, and don't heap the mulch up against the trunks of trees. Landscape fabrics can be useful in areas where irrigation is not an option.

There are some excellent pre-emergent herbicides for keeping crabgrass out of beds; apply these in late February or March. To get the grassy weeds out of shrub and perennial borders, handweed or apply a grass killer that contains setnoxydim, such as Vantage™. Finale™ and Roundup™ (glyphosate products) are excellent for clearing a new bed prior to planting. If you spot-spray with glyphosate products, be sure they don't contact the green tissues of any garden plant because they kill everything green.

The Need for Water

Unless you incorporate drought-tolerant plants into your garden design (a practice called Xeriscaping), irrigation will be necessary. There is no substitute for water in gardening! Plants cannot produce their own food via photosynthesis without sufficient water.

While lawns consume a lot of water, herbs and groundcovers prefer drier conditions by virtue of their native habitats. Most regions of the Carolinas receive thirty-five inches of rainfall each year, and some have twice this amount. The wet periods are interspersed with dry seasons, and supplemental irrigation can play a vital role in garden survival.

Most plants in our gardens need at least one inch of water a week, whether measured with a rain gauge or a tuna fish can. That's the equivalent of six hundred gallons of water a week for a twenty- by fifty-foot garden. It would take several hours to apply this amount with a handheld garden hose, so it is best to buy sprinklers of some type.

Supplemental watering is a must during the first season. With the use of sprinklers, handwatering, or more elaborate permanent systems that have time clocks, the garden can be kept in good health. In clay soils where soils absorb water slowly, drip irrigation in combination with mulch is the preferred method for watering woody ornamentals. An inexpensive water timer and a few soaker hoses can be the gardener's best friends.

Many gardeners prefer to water "on demand," especially in established gardens. Given time and experience, even the novice can take this approach. You must learn to recognize the symptoms of water stress before irreparable harm is done to the garden because of negligence or oversight.

Sunlight Requirements

For the best results, plants need to be placed where they will receive the proper amount of sunlight. We have indicated the amount of sunlight suitable for each plant's growing requirements.

Hardiness Zones

Zone maps rate how much cold a plant can endure, giving an idea of its survivability at low winter temperatures. The most common map in current use is the United States Department of Agriculture (USDA) Plant Hardiness Zone Map. Each ten-degree drop in average minimum winter temperature places a region in the hardiness zone with the next lower number. In North Carolina, gardeners in the mountain regions are in Zone 6, while gardeners near Charleston and farther south live in Zone 8b.

Remember that these are averages, and seasonal extremes of cold will limit what grows in your garden. Another map available from Rutgers University accounts for rainfall and sunshine, two other important climatological factors that determine a plant's hardiness in the garden. The newest map developed by the American Horticultural Society (AHS) determines which plants will survive summer's hottest days. The AHS Plant Heat-Zone Map divides the country into twelve zones; each zone corresponds to the average number of days each year with temperatures over 86 degrees Fahrenheit. The Piedmont region is in Heat Zone 7 and averages sixty to ninety days above this temperature.

What's in a Name?

Although common names are easier to remember and pronounce, a scientific or botanical name allows you to communicate with a gardener in China or a horticulturist in Argentina. The new world opening up to us via the Internet makes knowledge of plant nomenclature even more essential.

Both common and botanical names are used throughout this book. A plant's botanical name consists of a genus and a species epithet, both italicized. For example, all hollies belong to the genus *Ilex*. The epithet identifies a specific kind of holly: *Ilex cornuta* is a Chinese holly. To identify a plant even more closely, a cultivar name describes a special feature or tells the name of the person who selected the plant. The cultivar name is set off by single quotation marks. For example, the needlepoint holly's botanical name is *Ilex cornuta* 'Needlepoint'. Some plants that occur naturally in the wild may be denoted with the abbreviation "var." and another word following the epithet.

Knowing these straightforward rules of taxonomy will be of use as you search catalogs and websites for new and interesting garden varieties.

Gardening Made Simpler

The turfgrasses and garden plants described in this book are time-tested and durable in Carolina gardens. The plant list is by no means complete. It was necessary to exclude some fine ornamentals, but the plants on these pages are readily available at the major wholesale and retail nurseries in our states. Landscape professionals will recognize most of the plants from the required plant lists provided by their trade associations for the Contractor's exam and Certified Landscape Technician credentials. Certainly the list is a good starting point for creating a new garden or revitalizing an existing one in the Carolinas.

In a recent national survey, sixty-eight percent of the respondents stated that they wanted gardening simplified. This book makes an attempt to meet the wishes of this majority. Gardening is America's Number One "Leisure" activity—it should not be drudgery. Likewise, gardening books should be enjoyable to read.

We hope the *Carolinas Gardener's Guide* will accomplish its goal of taking the mystery out of gardening in our states. This book offers a wealth of information gathered through networking with home gardeners and professionals alike. It contains the latest research findings on plant varieties, practical gardening techniques, and "how-to" suggestions set in an easy-to-read format.

How to Use the *Carolinas Gardener's Guide*

As coauthors, we worked together to ensure that the information in this book can be applied throughout both states. Each entry in this guide provides you with information about a plant's particular characteristics, its habits, and its basic requirements for vigorous growth as well as our personal experience and knowledge of it. We have tried to include the information you need to realize each plant's potential. Only when a plant performs at its best can one appreciate it fully. You will find such pertinent information as mature height and spread, bloom period and seasonal colors (if any), sun and soil preferences, planting tips, water requirements, fertilizing needs, pruning and care, and pest information. Each section is clearly marked for easy reference.

Sun Preferences

For quick reference, we include symbols to represent the range of sunlight suitable for each plant. "Full Sun" means a site receiving 8 or more hours of direct sun daily. "Part Sun" means a site that receives direct sun about 6 hours a day, or partial sun all day. "Part Shade" means a site that receives afternoon shade. "Full Shade" means a site that is in dappled or even in deep shade all day. Some plants grow successfully in more than one sun exposure, which will be indicated by more than one sun symbol. Note: Afternoon sun is stronger than morning sun, and this exposure is more apt to stress certain plants.

Full Sun　　**Part Sun**　　**Part Shade**　　**Shade**

Additional Benefits

Many plants offer benefits that further enhance their appeal. The following symbols indicate some of the more notable additional benefits:

 Attracts Butterflies

 Attracts Hummingbirds

 Produces Edible Fruit

 Has Fragrance

 Produces Food for Birds and Wildlife

 Drought Resistant

 Suitable for Cut Flowers or Arrangements

 Long Bloom Period

 Native Plant

 Supports Bees

 Provides Shelter for Birds

 Good Fall Color

Companion Planting and Design

In this section, we provide suggestions for companion plantings and different ways to showcase your plants. This is where many people find the most enjoyment from gardening.

Our Personal Favorite

This section describes those specific cultivars or varieties that we have found to be particularly noteworthy. Or, we sometimes suggest other species that are also good choices. Give them a try ... or, perhaps you'll find your own personal favorite.

USDA Cold Hardiness Zones

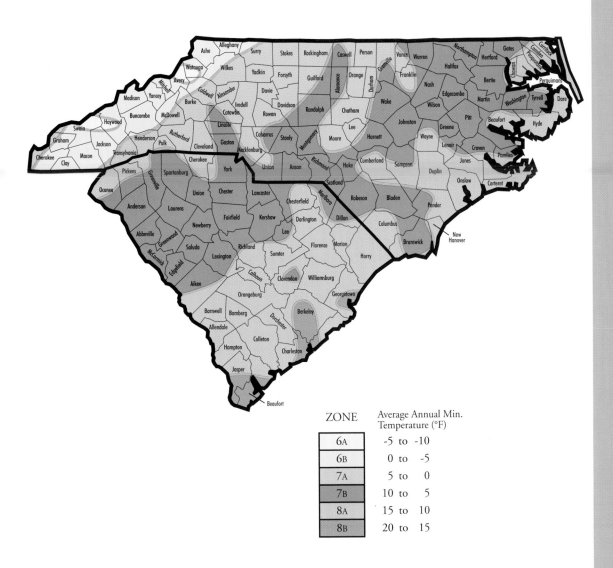

ZONE	Average Annual Min. Temperature (°F)
6A	-5 to -10
6B	0 to -5
7A	5 to 0
7B	10 to 5
8A	15 to 10
8B	20 to 15

Hardiness Zones

The United States Department of Agriculture (USDA) developed the cold-hardiness zone designations. They are based on the minimum average temperatures all over the country. Each variation of 10 degrees Fahrenheit represents a different zone, indicated by colored bands on a zone map. Because perennial plants, whose roots survive winter, vary in their tolerance for cold, it is important to choose those plants that are suitable for the zone of your region. Consult this map to learn in which zone you live. Most of the plants in this book will perform well throughout the area. Though a plant may grow in zones other than its recommended cold-hardiness zone, it is best to select plants labeled for your zone, or warmer.

Annuals *for the Carolinas*

Annual flowers are garden plants that complete their life cycles in one growing season. These jewels, also called bedding plants, are cheerful workhorses of the landscape. They transform uninteresting spaces into colorful flower beds. Many kinds bloom continuously from spring until a hard frost in autumn blackens their foliage and terminates the bedding plant season. Annuals are the backbone of the summer garden and are important for supplying early color in perennial beds. Most are sun lovers, though a few are appropriate for lightly shaded landscapes. Petunias, pansies, dianthus, and wax begonias dazzle your eye with lovely color. Annuals are easy to plug into otherwise bleak gardens that are just waking up from their winter dormancy.

The Versatility of Annuals

Most gardeners buy seedlings in pots or cell-packs from local garden centers for planting out after danger of frost has passed. Many quick-sprouting annuals, however, lend themselves to direct-seeding in the garden. New gardeners may feel uncomfortable with seed germination at first, so it may be better for them to stick with the greenhouse-grown transplants. For the more experienced starting the newest annual introductions from seeds in February, a sunny windowsill equipped with fluorescent lights can provide a diversion from the winter doldrums.

Annuals can be massed in beds for color impact. Some gardeners find monochromatic plantings of annuals to be effective, such as a "white garden" that consists of white periwinkle, white petunias, and white marigolds or zinnias. Most southerners like to celebrate with garden color and find it difficult to stay with a single color scheme. Stylish color combinations are seen along every residential street, but you will seldom see the stereotypical "petunias in old tire planters." Heat resistant annuals in containers as large as half-barrels provide color accents.

Gardeners with a sharp eye for color tend to look at the color of their house and garden accessories before choosing flower colors. Dark colored homes in green surroundings may look somber and can benefit from bright flower colors. Light colors will make a small garden space appear larger.

Proving the Winners

The South has a dynamic plant evaluation network in place. Every year residents and tourists alike enjoy the wildflower beds planted along our highways, courtesy of the fine work of the Highway Departments. The staffs of the state Botanical Gardens in Chapel Hill and Clemson work hard learning how to

A Bed of Geraniums

propagate and preserve our native flora, both annuals and perennials, and to use them in highway and public garden plantings. Annuals are evaluated years ahead of general availability by horticulturists at both North Carolina State University and Clemson University. The J.C. Raulston Arboretum at Raleigh conducts extensive trials of annuals. This program benefits commercial flower growers who must select the best varieties to purchase for the upcoming season.

The garden seed and plant industry also operate a number of programs to evaluate and promote promising new annual and perennial varieties. The oldest (est. 1932) is All-America Selections. Newer marketing consortiums include Proven Winners, Flower Fields, Simply Beautiful, and Athens Select. A venerable seed company, Park Seeds at Greenwood, SC, opens its flower trials to the gardening public the third week in June of every year. While seed and plant breeders provide valuable services, field trials in the Carolinas are still needed to evaluate new varieties under the soil and climate conditions peculiar to the Tar Heel and Palmetto states.

How-to advice and cultural information is available from the horticulture departments' websites: http://www.ncstate-plants.net   http://hgic.clemson.edu

Annuals Are Hard to Beat

For the display of color you will get for your expenditure and effort, annuals are hard to beat. Keep in mind the two groups of annuals. The ones with tiny seeds should be sown indoors six to ten weeks before the planting season in order for them to develop and flower on time. This is especially important where short growing seasons prevail, such as in the mountains. Also, there are the quick sprouting annuals that will bloom rapidly from direct-seeding in the garden. Some of these will "self-sow," which can be a blessing or a curse. Toby planted 'Flamingo Feather' celosia some years ago, and it soon became a nuisance, providing far too many seedlings every spring in his flower beds. However, he does count on volunteer seedlings of impatiens and globe amaranth every year to use as filler flowers in borders.

The Possibilities Are Endless

Hundreds of varieties are available, and there is no shortage of opportunities for creating stunning beds of annuals in Carolina gardens. Some annuals, such as cosmos, dahlias, and sunflowers, are perfect for cutting gardens. Peruse the seed catalogs for the newest flower selections for sowing at home or buy healthy, compact transplants at the garden shop each spring. Tall, long-stemmed varieties for cutting are easier to find in seed catalogs than in displays of started plants. Homegrown seedlings can be planted out in the garden in April or May after the chance of late frost is past. Annuals are easy to grow and require attention only to routine fertilizing, irrigation during dry periods, and control of weeds that can spoil the floral display.

Planting Tips

Most kinds of annual flowers with freshly opened blooms are offered for sale as bedding plants. Some are in tiny, two-inch cells; others are in three- or four-inch pots. A few may be for sale in larger pots but at much steeper prices. Consequently, many gardeners buy flats of three to six dozen individual colors in cell-packs, while others with smaller gardens settle for six-packs or individual pots.

Some gardeners, having experienced mediocre success in transplanting small plants of annuals directly to the garden, routinely pot up small annuals into four-inch pots and grow them for two or three weeks before setting them into the garden. In good grade potting soil, the plants develop more substantial root systems and survive the rigors of transplanting with little loss of momentum.

Whether you transplant small annuals directly to a flower bed or container, or grow them in a larger pot, consider what veteran gardeners call "butterflying" their rootballs. Root systems can become so congested that they encase the rootball in a solid mat of rootlets that are reluctant to strike out into the surrounding soil in flower beds or containers. This condition is described as "potbound." Butterflying the rootball consists of pushing or tapping the rootball out of the cell or pot, grasping it with both hands, and, with your fingertips across the bottom of the root system, cracking the rootball. New feeder roots will grow out of the crack and into the surrounding soil to take up water and nutrients.

Before butterflying or shifting up annuals to larger pots, prepare your soil. Ideally, you should have submitted a sample of your flower bed soil to your County Cooperative Extension Agent's office for testing. If you lack test results, liming is called for on all Carolina soil types except for a few near the coast. As a general rule, top-dress and work lime into the soil prior to planting. On sandy soils apply one-half pound per ten square feet. On clay soils (the heavy, sticky stuff), apply one pound per ten square feet. Use pelletized dolomitic limestone that supplies both calcium and magnesium, and work it in thoroughly. Liming soils helps in two ways: it counteracts excessive acidity in the soil, and it supplies calcium and magnesium. Both elements are secondary but necessary plant nutrients.

Work up your soil by spading or tilling before spreading limestone. Remove roots of perennial grasses or weeds. For consistency of coverage, divide the recommended application of limestone into two parts. Broadcast half while walking in one direction and the other half while walking across your initial path. This is a good opportunity to add organic soil conditioner as well: aged pine bark, mushroom compost, or peanut compost, etc. Spread it in a two-inch layer. Finally, spread fertilizer to add the major plant

Coreopsis, Salvia, Celosia, and Other Annuals

nutrients nitrogen, phosphorus, and potassium. One of the controlled-release fertilizers will do the best job; it will feed your annuals through most of the growing season. Spade or till these amendments into the soil.

Read the descriptive label that came with your plants. If it calls for full sun all day, you can be assured that the plant will benefit from afternoon shade. Most sun-loving annuals can endure full sun all day long, but they will need more frequent watering. If the label calls for shade, set your plants where they will get light shade or high shade during much of the day. Few flowering annuals will do well in moderate to deep shade; foliage plants fare better because their broad leaves can trap the limited light that bounces into shaded areas. Follow the between-plant spacing recommended on the label. On large flower beds leave "sneak paths" behind two or three rows of plants. Run the path across the line of sight and make it just wide enough to traverse without stepping on plants.

Now you can "set out" your plants into your flower bed or into a container of at least seven gallons capacity. Use inexpensive white plastic labels to mark temporarily where each plant is to go. Keep a filled watering can handy. Don't add water-soluble fertilizer to the initial watering. Dig individual holes with a trowel and butterfly the rootballs just prior to transplanting. Position the plant so that the top of the rootball is level with or slightly above the surface of the surrounding soil. Pull the excavated soil (backfill) around the rootball and firm it down slightly. Water the plant before moving on to the next. Collect the marker labels as you go.

Don't pinch the tops out of annuals when planting. This cruel and unusual punishment is a holdover from the days when most annual flowers grew tall. Now, most are bred to grow into compact forms. After completing the planting, set a sprinkler to wet down the entire bed. Let it run for an hour. Leave it in place because you will need to water your new flowers every morning for three or four days. Once they begin looking happy, you can reduce watering to every three days, then to weekly.

Now What?

Keeping your flower beds free of weeds is most important. If you build a flower bed, weeds will come. The best way to minimize weeding is to spread a two-inch layer of mulch. Pine or hardwood bark works well. Don't pull the mulch up close to the stems of annuals; it can hold moisture and cause plants to rot. Pine straw is difficult to work in between plants of annuals and is usually reserved for larger perennials and shrubs.

Broadleaf weeds and grass will find a way to emerge. Take a dandelion digger with you to pry out the entire root system with minimum soil disturbance. Collect the weeds and dump them in your compost heap. If you recognize the terrible weed called "Florida betony," take a spray bottle of a non-selective herbicide with you. Set a tin can (bottom removed) over the weed before spraying, to avoid spray drift. This tough customer may try to regrow. Spray it again in three or four weeks. Any of the aggressive spreaders such as chameleon plant or culinary mint can be eradicated in this way.

Rigging a drip irrigation system is the easiest and most responsible and efficient way to water a flower bed during dry periods. Flowers like about one inch of rainfall or irrigation per week, twice that on sandy soils, which tend to dry out faster. "Leaky hose" is the simplest drip irrigation system. Serpentize the porous hose through the flowerbed so that no plant is more than nine to twelve inches from the hose. Connect the leaky hose to a water faucet and let it run for an hour twice a week during dry weather. Some gardeners object to the industrial look of leaky hoses snaking among their flowers and conceal them beneath mulch. That can lead, of course, to damaging the hose with a hoe or dandelion digger. If you leave the hose on the surface, the annuals will soon spread and cover it.

Deadheading annual flowers can be a dreaded task or a way to calm your turbulent mind while doing no-brainer work. Either way, deadheading leads to a second flush of color and to neater looking flower beds. A few annuals such as coreopsis, cosmos, and sunflowers can provide food for finches and are often allowed to go to seed.

Starting Annuals from Seeds

If you have a sunny south or west-facing windowsill, you can sprout seeds of annuals successfully and grow them to transplanting size. Even better is a fluorescent light fixture that can be lowered to within two inches of the tops of seed pans. Better yet are the metal halide lamps that come even closer to imitating the full spectrum of sunlight and can deliver the footcandles needed by plants when placed further away than fluorescent tubes.

Cosmos

Most flower seeds will sprout (germinate) at soil temperatures of 60 to 65 degrees Fahrenheit. Some species that have a tropical provenance sprout more rapidly at 70 to 80 degrees Fahrenheit. Such warm temperatures can be produced atop a hot water heater or by using a horticultural heating pad with an adjustable thermostat. It is most important that you move the seed pan to a somewhat cooler area just as soon as you see green seedlings emerging. Some gardeners cover seed pans with clear plastic wrap to maintain high humidity; covers must be removed as soon as you see green.

Plastic meat trays about three inches deep make good seed pans. Use an ice pick, auger, or a large nail to punch six to eight drainage holes. Fill pans to within $1/2$ inch of the rim with "Seed Starting Mix" which is formulated from fine Canadian sphagnum peat moss and fine particles of Vermiculite or Perlite. Use a short length of board to firm down and level the mix. Moisten the starter mix by setting the filled pan in a tray of warm water. Capillarity will pull water up into the mix and saturate it.

Gardeners usually plant the contents of a standard seed packet in a single seed pan. Some prefer to scatter the seeds evenly over the surface; others prefer to plant the seeds in three or four straight lines or "drills." The best topping to cover seeds is "milled sphagnum moss," which is produced by grinding the ropy moss from the surface of peat bogs. It has biological properties which greatly reduce the incidence of "damping-off," an infection that kills seedlings at ground level. A very thin topping of seed starter mix will work nearly as well. Certain species require light to sprout, but enough light can penetrate a thin topping to initiate germination.

Gardeners usually start seeds six to eight weeks prior to the spring frost-free date, earlier on species that can tolerate light frosts and later on fast sprouting, fast growing species. The initial bottom-watering should suffice to sprout the seeds, especially if the seed pan is covered with clear plastic wrap. Over-watering seed pans is a fast track to damping off, especially if the germinating area cools to 50 to 60 degrees Fahrenheit at night.

The rate of growth of seedlings depends greatly on the size of the seeds. Large seeds produce robust seedlings with enough stored carbohydrates to nourish them for up to three weeks. If they're given adequate light and the proper range of heat, you can almost hear them grow. Tiny seeds, on the other hand, produce seedlings almost too small to see. They grow excruciatingly slowly until they can produce enough surface area of foliage to trap a significant amount of light.

When seedlings develop four to six leaves, they can be transplanted to individual two- to three-inch pots filled with high quality potting soil formulated for bedding plants. They can be "pricked out" (pried out) of seed pans with a Popsicle stick or a similar tool. Hold seedlings by their leaves, not by their stems, to avoid crushing the tender stem tissue.

Poke a planting hole in the center of the filled pot and lower the seedling into it so that the top of the root system is level with the surface of the soil. Pinch the potting soil to firm it around the root system. Set the potted plant aside for bottom-watering when all the seedlings have been transplanted. Certain species such as lobelia and begonia have such tiny seedlings that they are customarily transplanted in small clumps, grown on for a few weeks, then divided into individual plants for transplanting into pots.

Invariably, first-time seed starters are surprised, even overwhelmed, by the geometric increase in space needed at transplanting time. You can go, say, from fifty seedlings in a small pan to fifty individual pots of two- to four-inch diameter. All of a sudden, the area lighted by two forty-eight-inch fluorescent tubes must strain to hold the plants from one seed pan. Advanced gardeners often keep a "coldframe" handy, lighted by the sun and perhaps warmed with grounded electric light bulbs, to handle the overflow of plants.

Your reaction to these directions may be to ask, "Why bother?" If you like to try the very newest annuals, you can usually buy seeds a year or two before started plants become widely available. Also, the tall varieties of annuals that are preferred for cutting gardens are rarely available as started plants because they take too long to show color and grow too tall in the process. Neither growers nor retailers like to handle them. Starting from seeds gives gardeners a way to propagate heirloom varieties that are no longer grown by seed companies and to produce plants at a lower unit cost than is possible with purchase of bedding plants. Last but not least, starting from seeds is the mark of a good gardener. It isn't easy to balance light intensity, temperature, and soil moisture to the needs of each species. Prior to World War II, starting from seeds was the only way to grow. If millions of gardeners could master the technique without using fluorescent or halide lamps, surely you can, too.

Angelonia
Angelonia angustifolia

Although known in botanical gardens for many years, angel flower plants only recently began to appear in garden centers. Now it has become a major player in the South. In semi-tropical countries, angelonia grows as a perennial, but in the Carolinas its sensitivity to frost means growing it as an annual. Heat and humidity don't faze it. Angelonia gets its common name because it begins blooming when snapdragons take a summer break. Its medium length, curving spikes are somewhat reminiscent of snaps. Seed breeders have recently expanded the color choices to include pastel shades and bicolors and are developing dwarf strains that stand up to beating rain. Angelonia is gaining popularity for container gardens and for flower arrangements. It will bloom reliably, if somewhat late, in relatively cool, upper elevations.

Other Common Names
Angel Flower, Summer Snapdragon

Bloom Period and Seasonal Color
Deep violet blue, white, pink, lavender, and bicolors summer through fall.

Mature Height × Spread
16 to 24 in. × 16 to 24 in.; half that size in dwarf varieties.

When, Where, and How to Plant
Wait until two weeks after the spring frost-free date before setting out started plants. Grow in fertile, moist soil. Angelonia thrives in full sun. Near the coast or on hot, sandy land, it thrives in afternoon shade. Refer to "Planting Tips" in the introduction for soil preparation and planting instructions. Space 18 inches apart, wider if you intend to intersperse filler flowers. If you need lots of plants at low cost, start seeds indoors eight to ten weeks before the frost-free date.

Growing Tips
Drip irrigation works best for angelonia; watering with a sprinkler can beat down the spikes. Although angelonia has narrow leaves that give it drought resistance, the production of blooms suffers without weekly water. Mulching reduces soil-splash which can mar spikes. Mix an extended-release fertilizer with the backfill at planting to feed for most of the season. For faster response, use a water-soluble plant food formulated for flowers.

Care
Deadhead spent spikes when they begin to look shabby. In late summer, shear back all the plants to half-height and drench the soil with a shot of 1-2-2 ratio water-soluble fertilizer. Angelonia is by nature a bit "floppy"; some of its branches tend to recline then straighten up, making them an asset to flower arrangers. Harvest spikes frequently for flower arrangements; new flowers will form quickly. Angelonia is so new to the Carolinas that pests and plant diseases have yet to discover it.

Companion Planting and Design
Use it to fill beds between low edgers and tall background flowers such as cleome. Or try enclosing a bed of mixed color angelonia and blue sage between an edging of dusty miller or curry plant for the calming influence of silver. A background of mandevilla vines on low trellises looks good with lavender or purple angel flower. When mixing angelonia colors in beds, use only one bicolored variety with perhaps three separate colors to highlight the show-stopping bicolor blooms.

Our Personal Favorites
Jim likes the original deep violet blue. Toby leans toward 'Angel Mist Light Pink'.

When, Where, and How to Plant

Wait until all danger of frost is past to set out container plants. Do as farmers used to...take your shoes off and walk on the soil. If it feels warm to your soles, it is prime time for planting salvias. Few gardeners start salvia from seeds because they require ten to twelve weeks from seed to garden-ready plants. Dwarf varieties need well drained, fertile soil; the tall types are more adaptable. This chapter's introduction will help with soil preparation and planting. Space plants of vigorous varieties 2 feet apart, dwarf varieties 1 foot apart. Full sun to part shade (in coastal areas or sandhills) is fine.

Growing Tips

For optimum bloom and dark foliage color, apply liquid fertilizer monthly or work controlled-release fertilizer into the soil prior to planting. Water twice weekly during dry spells. Watch for drooping foliage; it can be telling you that you need to let the sprinkler run longer to soak deeper. Two to 3 inches of mulch can trap water so that it soaks in rather than running off.

Care

If you give salvia moderately fertile soil and good drainage, there isn't much you can do to help it, except to snip off spent flower spikes and to supply about 1 inch of water per week during dry spells. The plants will look sparse from deadheading but will grow new spikes. Few pests bother salvia.

Companion Planting and Design

The blazing scarlet and intense reds of annual salvia beg for blue, silver, or white companions to temper the visual jangling. The scarlet color looks good in patriotic red, white, and blue combinations. The purple shades blend nicely with golden or orange marigolds. Be sure to save and read the labels to assist you in selecting companionable heights. Some of the dwarf varieties will not grow much higher than they were when you purchased them and could be overwhelmed by more robust neighbors.

Our Personal Favorite

'Flare' matures at 18 inches in height and is quite heat-resistant. Its intense scarlet color is visible some distance away.

Breeders have brought down the mature height of annual salvia to one foot or less and have added new colors beyond the familiar blazing scarlet or dark red. This has opened up new uses for annual salvia as filler plants for large beds and as a staple for container gardens. The robust medium-height varieties still have an edge on the vertically challenged selections because the big guys have large plants that can support prolonged bloom. When the little plants are loaded with blossoms and are hit by drought and extreme heat, they really have to struggle to survive. Yet, if you tend to their needs and whack off spent flower spikes, even the extreme dwarf sizes can recover and continue to bloom. See the Perennials chapter for another species of salvia.

Other Common Name
Scarlet Sage

Bloom Period and Seasonal Color
Dark red, scarlet, purple, pink, and white in early summer through midsummer.

Mature Height × Spread
18 to 36 in. × 12 to18 in. for the old-fashioned tall varieties
10 to 18 in. × 6 to 12 in. for dwarf varieties.

Begonia

Begonia semperflorens

If you need a colorful, durable annual to dress up an entrance bed, wax begonias may be the right choice for you. Plants show their colors at small sizes and are often sold in cell-packs, which translate to a relatively low price per plant. Do not confuse this plant with the wimpy tuberous begonias used in states north of the Carolinas or with the fine pink perennial Begonia grandis that is often seen in shade gardens. Wax begonia varieties with colorful, bronzy foliage are wonderfully tolerant of sun and heat, and they like afternoon shade. Varieties with green foliage tend to scorch in full sun unless watered faithfully. Planting can take place any time during spring or summer for an instant show of flowers and foliage.

Other Common Names
Wax-leaved Begonia, Fibrous-rooted Begonia

Bloom Period and Seasonal Color
Pink, coral, white, red, or bicolored blossoms against green, red, or bronze foliage all summer.

Mature Height × Spread
6 to 12 in. × 12 in., taller on large-leaf varieties

When, Where, and How to Plant
Begonias can be injured by late frosts, but planting is safe across the Carolinas by mid-May. Mix organic soil conditioner into your flower bed for both water-holding capacity and good drainage, and wax leaf begonias will thrive. They will do even better if mulched. Set plants 12 to 18 inches apart. Choose your sites carefully; bronzeleaf varieties can withstand full sun but, except in highland areas. Lustrous greenleaf varieties prefer afternoon shade. Begonia seeds are like dust and can be a challenge to handle; use started plants for faster, more predictable results.

Growing Tips
Water twice weekly if no rain falls; begonias are shallow rooted and can drop leaves if neglected. Liquid-feed begonias monthly; always soak the soil before feeding. Leave a few open, mulched patches in beds so you can step in to spread granular flower fertilizer in midsummer.

Care
If begonias grow leggy by midsummer, prune them back halfway. Shape plants into mounds rather than giving them "flattops." Small caterpillars may try to wrap leaves into tubular hideaways; spray them with non-toxic *Bt*. Crowded beds may lead to leaf diseases, so leave room between plants for wind passage and for easy weed removal without mangling the brittle plants. Tip cuttings of 2-inch lengths will root in moist potting soil, an inexpensive way to expand plantings.

Companion Planting and Design
Wax-leaved begonias make choice plants for containers because of their relatively small, free-flowering plants. They are effective in mass plantings, grouped with other summer annuals, or around mailboxes. Grow begonias as an edging with taller salvias or perennials or in drifts of separate colors to fill beds. The heat resistant 'Dragon Wing' begonias are impressive in container gardens alone or in combination with lower-growing or trailing summer annuals in full sun or afternoon shade. They can grow twice as large as wax-leaved begonias.

Our Personal Favorites
Cocktail and Pizzazz hybrids are superior in flower power, but Jim is in love with the 'Dragon Wing'.

Butter Daisy
Melampodium paludosum

When, Where, and How to Plant
Wait until frost danger is past before setting out the plants. Butter Daisy can withstand full sun across the Carolinas, but near the coast or on hot sandhills, afternoon shade reduces the chance of leaf scorch. You can grow butter daisies in unimproved soil, but they will grow more uniformly and reward you with more color if you mix in organic soil conditioner prior to planting. Space dwarf varieties 12 inches apart; 18 inches for tall varieties. For container gardens, choose the dwarf varieties; tuck them in among other low growing annuals. Young plants are so rugged that, though they are smaller than a teacup, they don't stall out but resume growing and flowering shortly after transplanting.

Growing Tips
Butter daisy can get by with infrequent watering, perhaps a deep soaking every two weeks, but the foliage looks better if the plants are watered weekly during dry spells. Go easy on feeding dwarf varieties; the plants are so small that they can't use much fertilizer.

Care
Butter daisy is "self-covering," meaning that new foliage grows to cover spent blooms. The plants don't need deadheading or pruning. Just let them do their thing. White flies have been known to infest the tightly branched plants, but insecticidal soap should keep them in check.

Companion Planting and Design
True blues or violet blues are hard to find, but they make ideal companions. Look into balloon flower, blue salvia, bellflower, *evolvulus*, *Aster × frikartii*, and the dainty blue flower called "Swan River Daisy." For tall background flowers, consider *Salvia guaranitica* or *Salvia azurea*. If you are feeling bold, consider one of the heat-resistant foliage plants called *alternanthera* or Jacob's coat to interplant with butter daisy. Try one of the boldly bicolored, burgundy/tan Jacob's coat cultivars with willowy, wiry leaves as a companion.

Our Personal Favorites
We like 'Million Gold' and 'Lemon Delight', but they have tiny flowers. We are watching for one with larger flowers that virtually hide its foliage.

Butter daisy has impressive resistance to heat and humidity. It first hit the mass market about twenty years ago, but burdened by its jawbreaker botanical name, it got off to a slow start. Then someone came up with the appealing and appropriate name of "butter daisy," and plant breeders began rectifying a problem. The original butter daisy had lanky, sparsely flowered plants. Breeders developed compact varieties to give gardeners more bang for their buck, more flowers on smaller, denser plants. Now, butter daisy can be seen in gardens all over the South, quite an accomplishment for a flower that offers only one blossom color (golden yellow) and light green, rough-leaved, rather nondescript plants. It's a jungle out there in gardens, but this little heat-resistant edging flower doesn't let it intimidate her.

Bloom Period and Seasonal Color
All-summer light golden yellow blossoms without letup.

Mature Height × Spread
24 in. × 12 in. for the original
12 in. × 12 in. for dwarf varieties

Celosia
Celosia sp.

Over much of the South, celosias were long considered too "common" for elegant gardens. Celosia sets prodigious crops of oily seeds that can live for years in garden soil and germinate when suitable light, heat, and soil moisture conditions prevail. Every old farmstead or small city bungalow hosted dozens of tall celosia plants: sometimes the plume type, sometimes the convoluted crested or cockscomb type, or rarely, the tasselated "wheat" type. The flowers of old-fashioned celosias turned brown and looked tacky by late summer, but the newer plume varieties hold their color for weeks on end and keep on adding fresh new plumes. Now, so many variations, not only in plant size but also in colors and blossom forms, are available that celosias are once again "in."

Other Common Names
Plume Celosia, Cockscomb, Prince's Feather, Wheat Celosia

Bloom Period and Seasonal Color
All-summer bloom; plumes, tassels, or cockscombs in deep red, scarlet orange, deep gold, yellow, pink, or white.

Mature Height × Spread
Standard varieties 18 to 30 in. × 12 to 18 in.
Dwarf varieties 8 to 12 in. × 8 to 12 in.

When, Where, and How to Plant
Set out blooming plants after frost danger is past. Celosia needs full sun or, near the coast or in the hot sandhills, afternoon shade. Celosia has proved that it can grow on almost any soil with minimal care. However, its flowers will be larger and will look good longer if you grow celosia in well drained soil. Space dwarf varieties 10 inches apart, standard varieties 24 inches apart. Celosia can be direct-seeded in warm garden soil but will bloom forty-five days later than transplants already in bloom when set out. Mulching is especially important with dwarf varieties that can be marred by soil splash.

Growing Tips
Celosia will grow with little water but looks much better when watered weekly. In midsummer, scatter 1-2-2 ratio flower fertilizer and water it in.

Care
Normally, none of the celosias attract serious plant diseases or insects. Root rot may occur on heavy clay soil during rainy spells. It can cause quick death of plants, with no lingering. Pull out affected plants if you suspect root rot. Deadhead faded flowers every two weeks. Plumes, combs, or tassels of standard-height varieties can be cut when young and dried in the dark to retain color. When your garden soil has warmed to about 75 degrees Fahrenheit, volunteer seedlings will begin to grow from last year's seed crop. If you delay thinning until the plants show their colors, you can pull out and discard wishy-washy shades and keep the sharp, vivid colors.

Companion Planting and Design
Purple heliotrope next to a golden or orange celosia makes a bold combination. Butter daisy is a great mate for edging taller celosia, or try old-fashioned portulaca in mixed colors or a straight color selected to complement your shade of celosia. Wheat celosia grows taller than most other varieties and is usually placed as a background for shorter annuals.

Our Personal Favorite
'Fresh Look' is a medium-height, All-America Selections winner that comes in dark red and golden yellow shades. It forms fresh plumes throughout summer and never looks faded.

When, Where, and How to Plant

The tall varieties are usually direct-seeded, and seeds are not expensive. The dwarf varieties are "cute" but not as rugged as the big ones. Set out seedlings or direct-seed anytime after spring frost danger is past, and through midsummer. Grow cosmos in full sun; they don't need special soil preparation. Plants should stand no more than 2 feet apart to have them grow into a solid mass with each plant holding up its neighbor against wind and rainstorms. Topping common cosmos by pinching or shearing when plants are 2 feet tall can force them to branch out and become less prone to blowing over during rain and windstorms. See the chapter introduction for more planting guidelines.

Growing Tips

Watering with a sprinkler can cause cosmos to lean or fall over. Instead, trickle water around the plants or serpentize a soaker hose among them while they are young and widely spaced. Midseason fertilizing is needed on sandy soils or depleted clay.

Care

Thin volunteer seedlings to stand 24 inches apart. Shearing, feeding, and watering will bring exhausted plants back into flower production. Do wild birds, especially finches, a favor by leaving some seeds for them. While gleaning seeds, they will devour the occasional insect as well. Aphids on tender stems are about the only problem suffered by this rugged plant.

Companion Planting and Design

Face down the tall varieties of common cosmos with the slightly shorter plants of 'Sparkler' spiderflower and wrap an edging of Mexican heather around the flower bed. Sulphur cosmos calls for red, mahogany, blue, or white flowers. You can find complementary colors among the many varieties of periwinkle. They bloom in season with cosmos.

Our Personal Favorites

'Gazebo' has much larger flowers than the old-fashioned common cosmos. In the sulphur cosmos, consider the All-America Selections winner, 'Cosmic', in yellow or orange shades.

Its ferny, airy leaves give this species of cosmos a delicate look. How deceiving! Cosmos can endure all sorts of weather while continuing to open its candy-colored blossoms. This species has long stems which bend with the wind and are delightful in country-style bouquets or when bouncing from the antics of hungry finches seeking cosmos seeds. Another and somewhat more heat-tolerant species, Cosmos sulphureus, has yellow, golden, or light orange blossoms on rough-leaved plants and is even more heat resistant. Both species are often seen in highway median plantings, direct-seeded in July for late summer and fall color. Both species grow quickly and easily from seeds. You can start your own cosmos from seeds sown indoors eight weeks prior to the spring frost-free date. Usually only the quick-blooming dwarf varieties are available as started plants.

Other Common Name
Common Cosmos

Bloom Period and Seasonal Color
All summer in pink, magenta, crimson, white, and lavender.

Mature Height × Spread
4 to 6 ft. × 2 ft. if spring-seeded; somewhat shorter if direct-seeded in midsummer.
12 to 18 in. × 12 in. for dwarf varieties.

Dusty Miller
Senecio cineraria

Plants from four different genera are sold as "dusty miller": chiefly Senecio cineraria, but also Chrysanthemum ptarmicaeflorum, Centaurea gymnocarpa, and Artemisia stellarana. These silver plants are so popular that garden centers often sell out of them early. While the many forms of "dusty miller" are usually grown as annuals in the Carolinas, some species will winter over in well-drained soil. You can choose dusty millers with lacy, ferny, deeply cut, or ruffled leaves. Some have a green tinge to their basic silver color, while others with downy leaves are so bright that they seem to reflect the sun. Dusty millers have long been used as edging plants or plugged into sandy or rocky slopes. Lately, they have become an essential part of container garden combinations, quelling disagreements between conflicting colors with their cool, calm demeanor.

Bloom Period and Seasonal Color
Dusty millers flaunt silver foliage from the day you set out the plants until winter. Foliage is their strong suit.

Mature Height × Spread
Artemisia stellarana: 2 ft. x. Spreading
Other species: 12 to 18 in. × 24 in.

When, Where, and How to Plant
Hardened-off plants can be set out a week before the spring frost-free date. Most plantings are started from plants in cell-packs or pots in a full-sun location. Since all species prefer dry soil, consider mixing a 2-inch layer of play sand and a 3-inch layer of ground pine bark into heavy clay soil. A raised bed standing perhaps 3 inches above the surrounding soil should result. Alternatively, work up the soil and spread 2 to 3 inches of cracked gravel atop it. Scrape the gravel aside, set the dusty miller plants in place, and pull the gravel up around the root balls. *A. stellarana* responds particularly well to growing in gravel-topped beds that simulate its native habitat.

Growing Tips
Thorough but infrequent watering will help the young plants strike new roots. Once the transplants perk up, water only when plants begin to look wilted. One or two feedings with water-soluble 1-2-2 ratio flower fertilizer should suffice for the season. Wait two weeks after transplanting before feeding. When planting in potting soils, go easy on watering. Mix controlled-release fertilizer into the potting soil used for container gardens, unless the label says it is already included.

Care
Dusty millers have no plant pests. Their only serious problem is root rot that can come from soil that stays wet. You may have to pinch plants in containers to keep them compact. Thin volunteer seedlings to stand 24 inches apart.

Companion Planting and Design
What a perfect plant for container gardening! Jim reports that when he does container gardening demonstrations he often looks first for one of the dusty millers then builds combinations around whichever species he can find. Stick with other drought resistant plants when designing plant combinations for flower beds or containers. Portulaca, purslane, creeping zinnia (*Sanvitalia*), lantana, blanket flower, any of the fleshy-leaved sedums, Mexican bush sage, dahlberg daisy, and *Zinnia angustifolia* would qualify.

Our Personal Favorites
Jim likes 'Cirrus' for its large, silver, wavy-edged leaves. Toby likes 'Colchester White.'

When, Where, and How to Plant

Set plants in garden beds after the last spring frost. Afternoon shade is preferred, but given water when needed, geraniums can thrive in full sun. Potted plants can be set out anytime during the growing season, but peak bloom time is from late spring through midsummer. Geraniums need good air circulation. To improve soil drainage, plant in slightly raised beds amended with bark soil conditioner. Do not use fresh manure! Information in the chapter introduction will detail how to improve your soil.

Growing Tips

Geraniums establish quickly with very little care. In fact, too much water in spring rots the roots. Keep foliage dry during watering by using a water wand to wet only the soil. Drip irrigation also moistens the soil without wetting the leaves. Geraniums respond well to fertilization, particularly if they are grown in soils lacking a ready source of nitrogen. Small yellow leaves are an indication that additional fertilizer is needed. Water-soluble fertilizer (the "blue stuff") is suitable for bimonthly applications.

Care

During the dog days of summer, geraniums may stop blooming. If so, cut the plants back slightly, feed and water them; also, cooler weather should bring them around. Don't hesitate to prune leggy geraniums; they will respond with more flowers. Wet summers can lead to geranium leaf diseases. Always remove diseased or yellowing foliage when deadheading. When wet summer weather arrives, apply a fungicide twice, at an interval of one week, to prevent leaf spot and flower diseases. Good air circulation helps prevent leaf spot fungi. Be sure to leave sneak paths among your geranium plants to access them for deadheading. Geraniums can look awful when loaded with spent flowers.

Companion Planting and Design

Geraniums make stunning container or patio plants. Use them to create color beds with tall annuals such as salvias or sun coleus used in the background or in containers combined with bacopa and variegated ivy.

Our Personal Favorites

The Oglevee and Orbit series has intensely-zoned foliage and large flower clusters on compact plants.

"If a window or a garden could have but one plant, that plant would likely be a Geranium," wrote the great American horticulturist Liberty Hyde Bailey. *Gardeners can buy blooming plants or sow seeds of hybrid geraniums indoors in winter to grow dazzling new seedlings in myriad colors and leaf variations. In the Carolinas, geraniums are grown as annuals unless a thrifty gardener digs the plants and takes them inside before frost. Bright blooms are arranged in ball-like clusters above the foliage. Round leaves have wavy edges and, when bruised, emit a characteristic odor. The plants we call "geraniums" in North America are actually from a different genus, Pelargonium. True geraniums are quite different woodland edge perennials. Trying to correct this long-standing misnomer would be as productive as pushing rope, so let's go with common usage.*

Other Common Name
Zonal Geranium

Bloom Period and Seasonal Color
Summer blooms in red, salmon, pink, white, orange, coral, magenta, and bicolors, single and double.

Mature Height × Spread
20 in. × 12 to 20 in.

Gerbera Daisy
Gerbera jamesonii

Long before gerbera daisies became a major bedding plant, thousands of long-stemmed blossoms were air-shipped from California to florists each year. In home gardens, gerberas were mostly seen in mild winter areas. What pushed them into the bedding plant arena and into more northerly states was the development of shorter stemmed, earlier blooming varieties. Breeders are working for greater uniformity in height and larger-diameter blossoms from second-generation seeds saved from hybrids. They are also developing many fanciful blossom forms. Gerbera plants in bloom are still rather expensive, and one seldom sees them massed in sizable beds. Instead, they are often planted near the front door of a home, in ground beds, or in containers. In these intimate settings, uniformity isn't important. Near the coast and occasionally further inland, gerberas act as perennials if grown in well drained soil or containers.

Other Common Names
Gerbera, Transvaal Daisy

Bloom Period and Seasonal Color
Intermittently through the summer primarily in red, orange, yellow, and gold but also pink, salmon, and white.

Mature Height × Spread.
12 to 18 in. × 12 in.

When, Where, and How to Plant
Plant from late spring through midsummer. Once hardened off, gerbera plants can withstand a few degrees of frost. Gerbera daisies are technically half-hardy perennials, but it is prudent to delay setting out plants until frost danger is past. Select a site in afternoon shade near the coast, full sun elsewhere. Prepare well-drained beds and scatter dolomitic limestone per soil test directions. Gerbera daisies resent wet feet. Set potted plants in prepared beds or containers so that the tops of the rootballs are level with the surface. If you want the old-fashioned, long-stemmed kinds for cutting, you will need to order seeds, start them in fall, and grow them under lights through winter.

Growing Tips
Gerberas like a moderate, sustained level of soil fertility. They respond well to controlled-release fertilizer (CRF) worked into the soil. Top-dressing CRF is not recommended, as the beads of fertilizer need to be surrounded by soil for optimum release of nutrients. Water gerberas every seven to ten days between rains. Run water on the soil; don't wet the foliage.

Care
The blossoms of gerberas are so large that they sap a plant's energy. Cutting them for arrangements encourages more blooms to form. Slugs are the worst problem. Gerbera's large-leaved rosettes provide shelter and nourishment if you allow it. Scatter the type of snail bait that is harmless to pets and wildlife. It will also kill earwigs and pillbugs (roly-polys).

Companion Planting and Design
You won't often see gerberas growing among other flowers. They are so special that few gardeners wish to divert attention from them. Yet, they do work smoothly in container gardens. Combining them with aggressive vines like ornamental sweet potatoes should be avoided. The slow-growing gerberas could easily be swamped by thuggish vines.

Our Personal Favorite
Curiously, gerbera plants on sale at garden centers are rarely identified by variety. You can choose between large-flowered types with a single layer of ray petals or somewhat smaller blossoms with long, thin, twisted petals.

Globe Amaranth
Gomphrena globosa

When, Where, and How to Plant

Plants are sold in plastic cell-packs, or you can try your hand at sowing seeds of the new cultivars after the soil warms. Globe amaranth needs a sunny location and well drained soil; even a dry spot in the garden will do, and a pH level of about 6. Seeds can be sown in the garden, but they require darkness to sprout and must be covered with soil or newspaper to keep out light. Remove the cover when the first sprouts appear. Small potted seedlings are a better bet for beginning gardeners. Plant after danger of frost has passed, or anytime through summer. More information on soil preparation and planting is in this chapter's introduction. Don't "bury" started plants; the top of the root ball should be barely covered with soil.

Growing Tips

Water newly sown beds daily until seeds germinate. Water 3 times a week until vigorous growth begins. Water established plants every ten days. Apply a water-soluble flower fertilizer every six weeks. A one- to two-inch layer of mulch minimizes the need for irrigation.

Care

Globe amaranth thrives on neglect. Prune plants by 1/3 if they get leggy. To dry the flowers, cut when the flowers are half-open. Hang them upside down, attached with clothespins to a coat hanger. Leafhoppers are known to spread viruses, though rarely. Avoid poorly drained soils, which lead to root rot. Voracious black and gray blister beetles may strip foliage late in the season. Don't handle these critters; they can irritate your skin.

Companion Planting and Design

Plant in large beds as an accent or grow dwarf varieties in container gardens. The medium texture of globe amaranth will be most enjoyed in front of a hedge or wooden fence. Good companions are annuals that can endure dry, hot soil: lantana, creeping zinnia, iceplant, sedum, portulaca, and verbena for example.

Our Personal Favorites

Gnome series sports compact, free-flowering plants; 'Lavender Lady' is most appealing.

Dependable and durable even during hot and humid weather, globe amaranth ranks at or near the top of the list of plants for low-maintenance flower gardens. Its one-inch-round flowers resemble fluffy clover heads. This plant tolerates wind and searing sun and keeps right on blooming. Some cultivars are short and stocky and keep on flowering in containers until frost. The standard, old-fashioned varieties, while growing only knee-high, billow out to fill beds with solid masses of color. Gomphrena requires very little care; spent blossoms tend to shatter and be covered by new foliage and flowers. Varieties range in height from ten to twenty-four inches. The variety 'Lavender Fields' bears one- to two-inch lilac blooms that make wonderful cut flowers for both fresh and dried arrangements. 'Strawberry Fields' dries to a deep red.

Bloom Period and Seasonal Color
Spring until frost with white, mauve, lilac, orange-red, and salmon flowers.

Mature Height × Spread
10 in. to 24 in. × 10 to 20 in., depending on variety; taller with abundant soil moisture.

Impatiens
Impatiens walleriana

Incredibly versatile impatiens, including the sun-tolerant New Guinea species, are the top- selling bedding plant. When established in a moist bed, they will frequently self-sow, returning the next summer for a floral display. Grow them in filtered light or light to moderate shade and watch that area glow! Impatiens comes in a wide range of colors, most of which can be mixed effectively. They are among the most shade-tolerant of annual flowers, and the color they provide to the garden does not stop until the first killing frost. Some impatiens varieties are bred to grow low, but too much water and fertilizer (and too little sunlight) can make them grow tall and lanky. Some have wee blossoms and are best suited to container gardens. Certain New Guinea cultivars have wildly variegated foliage or flowers.

Other Common Name
Busy Lizzie

Bloom Period and Seasonal Color
Spring through fall in colors ranging from white and palest pink to deep red and bright orange.

Mature Height × Spread
10 to 24 in. × 15 to 30 in.

When, Where, and How to Plant
Set out transplants in spring after the danger of frost has passed. Impatiens in packs or pots can be planted anytime during the warm months. Plant in slightly acidic, moist, well drained soil. Keep the soil moist and the new varieties of impatiens can take morning sun. Even sturdy New Guinea impatiens, if planted in full sun, will look wilted by mid-afternoon but will recover by nightfall. Impatiens loves humus-laden soils. See the chapter introduction and follow instructions for planting azaleas. They have similar needs for organic matter. Incorporate fertilizer (1-2-2 ratio) into the soil. After setting out transplants, water with a liquid starter solution to ensure quick establishment then mulch lightly to conserve moisture and control weeds. In large beds, mulch *before* planting.

Growing Tips
Newly planted impatiens are quite succulent and wilt readily if soil dries out. Keep the bed moist for the first month then maintain a consistent, moderate level of soil moisture throughout the growing season. A midsummer supplemental feeding with dry granular flower food will provide nutrition for extra growth and color.

Care
To get bushier plants, cut new seedlings back 1/3 two weeks after planting. When frost threatens, cover beds with a floating row cover. Slugs may be a problem in the damp, shady environment that suits impatiens. Reduce slug infestation by not watering at night or use one of the baits that are safe for pets and wildlife.

Companion Planting and Design
Plant white flowers as a foil for brilliant varieties of impatiens. White also shows up well at night. Impatiens make a fine edging when used with foundation shrubs planted on the north or east side of a house. Mass in drifts by color or in mixed borders. Tuck into corners by entranceways or grow in windowboxes or hanging baskets.

Our Personal Favorite
'Victorian Rose' hybrid is a great semidouble selection for beds and containers. The 'Blitz 2000' and 'Bruno' hybrids are best for heat- and drought-tolerance.

Indian Blanket

Gaillardia grandiflora

When, Where and How to Plant

Indian blanket grows quickly and easily from late spring planting. Give gaillardia full sun or late afternoon shade. Digging in organic soil conditioner won't help performance greatly, but a light application of granular fertilizer worked into the soil will promote fast growth. Blanket flower is accustomed to fending for itself in poor, dry soil. Despite its drought tolerance, transplanted gaillardia needs watering every two or three days for two weeks after planting. Direct-seeding gaillardia is an inexpensive way to grow plants for sizable beds.

Growing Tips

Once seedlings of blanket flower take hold there isn't much more you can do for them except water weekly between rains. Annual blanket flower is one of the few fast-growing flowers that will tolerate Carolina seacoast conditions, even surviving light salt spray. Gaillardia will thrive in containers that can't be watered more than 2 or 3 times weekly. Additional feeding is unnecessary.

Care

Deadheading, feeding, and watering late in the season can bring a second flush of blooms. Pests and plant diseases don't seem to bother it, but butterflies are drawn to the open-faced varieties with daisy flowers. Leave a few spent flowers of colors you especially like. They will form seeds that will drop and give you volunteer seedlings for the coming season.

Companion Planting and Design

Imagine Texas and Oklahoma roadsides in June and July and you will get the picture. Think blue or yellow when selecting companion plants: blue daze (*Evolvulus*), Mexican heather, blue salvia, and petunia. All bloom at the same time. Red or yellow plants also go well with blanket flower: scarlet sage, marigolds, lantana, million bells, celosia, and Jerusalem sage are good examples.

Our Personal Favorites

It would be hard to find a fancier blanket flower than the All-America Selections winner, 'Arizona Sun'. Yet for its variegated daisy flowers that nourish butterflies, our vote would go to 'Painter's Palette'. 'Goblin' is a fine compact one.

Of the native American annuals, Indian blanket may be the most tolerant of hostile surroundings. You can see it along dry Texas roadsides, and you can find it here and there among dunes overlooking southern seacoasts. Yet, it hasn't placed in the hit parade perhaps because it is available only in warm colors. Plant breeders continue to dress up this country cousin by converting its natural daisy-like form into round lollipops and whittling notches into its petal tips, but the color palette remains in the near-red, mahogany, golden, and orange spectrum. More blossoms are bicolor than are solid shades. The plant itself has furry, silvery gray leaves as befits a drought-resistant species. Blanket flower will often drop seeds and volunteer the following year but never becomes invasive.

Other Common Name
Blanket Flower

Bloom Period and Seasonal Color
Light and dark colors in the warm spectrum ring the reddish central disk all summer until hard frost.

Mature Height × Spread
12 to 14 in. × 10 to 12 in. for dwarf varieties
14 in. × 14 to 16 in. for standard varieties
18 in. × 24 in. for the perennial species

Lantana
Lantana camara

This showy member of the verbena family is valued for its profusion of blooms over a long season. Southern gardeners have found lantana drought-resistant, easy to grow in average soils, and a magnet for flocks of butterflies. It is grown as a tender summer annual in most climate zones of the Carolinas. Flattened bloom clusters are borne on coarse, upright to arching woody stems covered with rich green, three-inch, leathery leaves. Each flower cluster may contain thirty or more tiny blossoms that may change colors as they mature. Some varieties are naturally shrub-like while others are low-growing and spreading. The latter growth habit is valued for containers. All lantanas release a pungent odor when handled. Spring-planted lantana may perennialize in southerly reaches of the Carolinas.

Bloom Period and Seasonal Color
Summer to fall in vivid colors of yellow, orange, and red to peach.

Mature Height × Spread
2 to 4 ft. × 3 to 5 ft. for bush types
1 ft. × 2¹/₂ ft. for spreaders

When, Where, and How to Plant
Plant in spring or early summer. Starting from potted plants is preferred to growing from seeds, particularly in Zone 7. Plants begin blooming when quite small and never let up until killed by frost. Lantana likes hot, sunny locations. It is fabulous in planters and container gardens but will need consistent watering since it is a rampant grower. Use it as a bedding plant in ordinary soil without amendments, but avoid soils that are poorly drained, or incorporate bark soil conditioner to improve drainage. Water twice weekly for several weeks.

Growing Tips
Lantana is care-free as long as it gets a little water in hot, dry periods. Mulch flower beds to extend the time between waterings. Apply a water-soluble flower fertilizer monthly to keep lantana happy. Use controlled-release fertilizers in container gardens instead.

Care
There are no pests or diseases. Prune occasionally to keep lantana dense and loaded with flowers. It is not important to deadhead blooms, but heading back rangy shoots will help maintain symmetry. Lantana will perennialize if it's not cut back at the end of the season. A deep mulch of pine needles will give added winter protection in Zone 8 gardens; remove mulch and prune back in early spring. This plant comes with a warning for children: The porcelain black berries are poisonous when eaten! Use in the background so children won't notice the fruit. Wear gloves when handling lantana plants; the leaves have hairs that can irritate skin.

Companion Planting and Design
Lantana is as content in a landscape bed with annuals as it is in a hanging basket or container. Grow in a sunny perennial garden or with companions like globe amaranth, melampodium, narrowleaf zinnia, and ornamental grasses.

Our Personal Favorites
The hot colors of 'Dallas Red' and the profuse blooming of 'New Gold' make them special. 'Miss Huff' and 'Mozelle' are the most winter hardy of all.

Marigold

Tagetes spp. and hybrids

When, Where, and How to Plant

Sow seed outdoors or set out transplants in spring after all danger of frost has passed. Plant in full sun in ordinary garden soil. Marigolds will grow with afternoon shade but will tend to stretch. Do not plant in rich, high-nitrogen soil; this will produce foliage at the expense of flowers. Marigolds grow quickly and easily from seeds. Before planting seeds, read the instructions on the seed packet. The seeds should be planted at a depth of $1/3$ inch. Covered with play sand, they will germinate in seven to ten days at soil temperatures of 65 degrees Fahrenheit and higher. For early flowers, use transplants. Space African (*T. erecta*) types 18 to 24 inches apart—French (*T. patula*) varieties 9 to 14 inches apart. Keep seedbeds moist until the seedlings are well established.

Growing Tips

Water weekly, more often during droughts. Some water should drain from containers with each watering to avoid a buildup of salts. Avoid the overstimulation produced by high-nitrogen fertilizers. After setting out plants, drench the soil with a water-soluble flower fertilizer (bloom-starter type) or scatter a 1-2-2 ratio fertilizer. Keep it 3 inches from the stem to avoid injury. Always water well before feeding plants.

Care

Remove spent blooms to promote continuous flowering. Stake taller varieties for support. When using marigolds as cut flowers, clip off the leaves. Leafhoppers may attack marigolds; watch for spider mites in dry weather. Systemic insecticides or soap sprays will take care of most pests. No serious diseases occur except where the soil drains poorly.

Companion Planting and Design

Marigolds are awe-inspiring when grouped in large mass plantings and are an excellent choice for edging hot, dry beds. Welcome visitors by planting bright marigolds in an entrance bed or by a mailbox. Blue summer flowers such as blue daze and ageratum look good with marigolds.

Our Personal Favorite

The 'Inca' hybrids have it all—big 4-inch blooms, compact erect plants, and heat resistance.

Marigolds are one of the most popular annuals in the Carolinas. Though they are native to Mexico, some are incorrectly called "African" or "French." Marigolds come in any height needed for gardens and in various flower forms. With carnation-like or domed blooms up to four inches in diameter, "African" hybrids make fine cut flowers and can be planted at the back of a border. "French" types are low growing and make superb edging and container garden flowers. Signet types have small flowers but loads of them. Marigolds grow well in poor soil even during the hot summer months but may sulk during August in Zone 8. The single flowered French marigolds such as 'Dainty Marietta' draw more butterflies than types with convoluted double flowers.

Other Common Names

African Marigolds (*Tagetes erecta*), lately called "American" Marigolds, French Marigolds (*Tagetes patula*), Signet or Gnome Marigolds (*Tagetes tenuifolia*)

Bloom Period and Seasonal Color

Spring through fall, in colors ranging from yellow and orange to maroon, white, near-red, and bicolors.

Mature Height × Spread

African (and American) marigolds: 14 to 36 in. × 20 in.
French marigolds: 8 to 12 in. × equal spread
Signet marigolds 24 in. × 24 in.

Million Bells

Calibrachoa sp.

At first glance, you might think that million bells are small-flowered, little-leaf petunias. Not so; million bells is a different species and a relative newcomer to American gardens. It quickly made a good name for itself in container gardens and window boxes where it spreads and trails. In garden beds, it hugs the ground. In a container filled with good potting soil, million bells will continue blooming without letup until fall frost. It prefers the good drainage and aeration of sandy garden soils because on heavy soils the dense mat of foliage tends to trap water. Consistently moist foliage tends to mold. The blooms on million bells are flared like the "bells" of trumpets and are positioned on the stems where you can look right into them.

Other Common Name
Calibrachoa

Bloom Period and Seasonal Color
All summer in shades of blue, pink, lavender, and coral.

Mature Height × Spread
4 to 8 in. × 12 to 24 in.

When, Where, and How to Plant
Million bells is almost always grown from started plants in 3- to 4-inch pots, with first blooms showing to validate the color. Calibrachoa plants go on display as much as a month before it is safe to set them into your garden or in a container. Wait until frost danger is past to avoid losing your baby plants. Grow in full sun or afternoon shade. Two types are available—mounding and trailing. The tiny flowers of million bells are best enjoyed close up in containers or, if in garden beds, on raised berms or planter boxes to maximize visibility. On heavy soils, mulch around your million bells with 1 inch of play sand to keep the surface dry. See the general introduction for information on building berms for improved drainage.

Growing Tips
Go easy on feeding million bells. Heavy feeding with nitrogen-rich plant foods can overstimulate the plants and result in sparse blooming. In good quality potting soils, there is no need to worry about over-watering, so water every day or two. They are designed to drain off surplus water and attain a good level of aeration within minutes of watering. Irrigate ground beds weekly during periods of drought.

Care
Million bells are nearly care-free. The mounding types planted in the landscape are subject to stem and root rot in poorly drained, clay soils. Remove diseased plants promptly or remove dying twigs. Leaf-eating caterpillars can be controlled using a spray of *Bt.* or handpicking. Keep the foliage dry to avoid fungal molds like *Botrytis*. This puppy is self-cleaning and branches freely.

Companion Planting and Design
In large containers, where combinations of tall, mounded, and trailing plants are used, consider combining million bells with bacopa (*Sutera*), wax-leaved begonias, and blue salvia or dracaena. For continuous color, interplant million bells among perennials, which go in and out of bloom rather quickly.

Our Personal Favorites
Jim's personal favorite is 'Terra Cotta'. Its coral color deepens to deep bronze with age. Toby's favorite is the Superbells™ series.

Nasturtium
Tropaeolum majus

When, Where, and How to Plant

Set out started plants at the spring frost-free date, and cover them if a freak frost is predicted. Nasturtiums are easy to start early indoors from seeds soaked overnight in warm water and planted two seeds per pot in 3- to 4-inch pots. Grow seedlings for eight weeks and transplant them to the garden or to large containers soon after frost danger is past. A fall crop can be direct-seeded in the garden in late August. Grow in afternoon shade near the coast; in full sun elsewhere. Dig flower fertilizer into your soil at the rate of 1 pound per 100 square feet to provide nutrition for the life of the crop. Thin or set plants on 2-foot centers.

Growing Tips

Don't water nasturtiums unless they show signs of wilting. Too much water will force unwanted vegetative growth, as will heavy fertilization.

Care

When hot weather begins to fry your spring nasturtiums, let the heat take them. Watch out for imported cabbage worms. The loopy green worms can be killed with *Bt* without poisoning your edible crop. Control aphids on new growth with insecticidal soap, but wait a week before eating flowers or foliage. Harvest blooms regularly to keep them from setting seeds. Eat blossoms after soaking them in cold water to flush out insects. Young leaves are also quite palatable; a little nippy, but a good addition to other salad greens.

Companion Planting and Design

In containers, plant nasturtiums by themselves so they can be yanked out with the onset of warm weather and replaced with durable summer flowers. In gardens, they can be planted in front of garlic chives and edged with ornamental strawberries such as 'Pink Panda'.

Our Personal Favorites

'Alaska' has everything going for it: a great variety of blossom colors, intricately folded and doubled forms, flowers held above its cream and green variegated leaves, and uniformity of plant size. The old-fashioned ramblers are still available from seeds; they are often called "climbing nasturtiums."

If you have ever visited cool coastal California and have seen nasturtiums rambling up and over fences year-round, you might get the wrong impression of how they might do in the Carolinas. Our cool spring and fall seasons are so short that we have to settle for quick crops timed to escape the heat of summer and the cold of winter. Also, we grow "bush" varieties that form rounded clumps with quite short runners. On these improved varieties, blossoms are "exerted" above the foliage. In other words, the flower stems are longer than the leaf stems. This results in a vastly improved show of color; there is nothing shy about these new nasturtiums! To top it off, breeders have doubled the blossoms with more rows of petals, folded intricately into an amazing variety of forms.

Other Common Name
Indian Cress

Bloom Period and Seasonal Color
Spring or fall in orange, golden, yellow, and white blossom colors and either blue-green, purple, or cream-mottled leaves.

Mature Height × Spread
Ultra dwarf varieties 8 in. × 6 in.
Standard varieties 12 to 14 in. × 12 to 14 in.

Nicotiana

Nicotiana sanderae

Breeders have produced several shorter, day-blooming varieties of flowering tobacco that bloom early and produce so many flowers that you can hardly see the leaves. They were unable to include a strong trait for fragrance until recently, but good gardeners don't let that stop them. They grow a few plants of N. alata, the tall white, fragrant species, and place them near the back of their flower beds. The day-blooming nicotiana looks somewhat like a bush petunia, with flaring trumpet-shaped blossoms that face out or up, making the plants very colorful. The mound-shaped plants fit nicely into flower beds. On a heat-resistance scale of one to ten, nicotiana would rate about a seven. It puts on quite a show for sixty days and would then decline if not sheared and brought back into bloom.

Other Common Name
Flowering Tobacco

Bloom Period and Seasonal Color
Late spring through late summer, longer if sheared, in red, pink, yellow, lavender, and white.

Mature Height × Spread
24 in. × 12 in. for standard-height varieties
12 in. × 12 in. for ultra dwarfs
36 in. × 24 in. for tall whites

When, Where, and How to Plant

Nicotiana is usually started from plants in packs or pots. Plants are frost-tender and should not be set in the garden or in a container until frost danger is past. Afternoon shade will prolong bloom for a week or two longer than a full-sun situation. You can increase your chances of good performance if you follow the suggestions for soil preparation and planting in the chapter introduction. Set started plants in limed and fertilized soil that has been aerated by the addition of organic soil conditioner.

Growing Tips

Nicotianas are so highly bred that fertilization and watering have to be done sparingly to avoid encouraging too much vegetative growth or starving them into premature decline. Shear standard varieties after peak bloom; feed and water to speed reblooming.

Care

Nicotiana needs little care. The plants tend to remain erect and don't flop. The dwarf varieties do not have sufficient vigor to recover from shearing. Aphids may collect on tender new growth. Control them with insecticidal soap. Caterpillars may try to wrap leaves around themselves, which is more of a cosmetic problem than life-threatening. Spraying with *Bt* should take care of most leaf feeders. Root rot may occur in poorly drained soils. Mulching with aged pine bark or hardwood bark will prolong the bloom span.

Companion Plants

Read the label to learn the height of your selected variety at maturity. You can stairstep progressively taller nicotiana varieties of complementary colors or mix nicotiana with other summer-blooming annuals of compatible height. It is often interplanted with late-blooming tender perennials such as Mexican bush salvia or pineapple sage that can take over when the nicotiana has bowed out. Angel flower and pentas make good buddies for nicotiana in flowerbeds and in containers.

Our Personal Favorite

Reportedly, the new mixed color Saratoga hybrid nicotianas are fragrant, but we have yet to try them. A cool day will reduce fragrance.

Pansy

Viola × wittrockiana

When, Where, and How to Plant

Begin setting out started plants in late August and continue through late fall. Group them in large containers or in ground beds. Plant in spring when the soil is dry enough to work. Grow in full sun during the winter, afternoon shade if spring planted. Amend poor soil with several inches of compost, cow manure, or bark conditioner. Where soil drainage is suspect, build up beds 4 inches or more above the surrounding soil. Pansies are easy to work with and will "catch" if you settle them in with a thorough soaking.

Growing Tips

Water new plantings every two or three days and weekly after new growth starts. When daffodils are in full bloom, scatter a granular slow-release fertilizer made for flowers or a general fertilizer that is high in phosphorous (some shops sell a product called Pansy Food®). Wash off foliage within a few minutes following application.

Care

If plants grow leggy and floppy, prune them back halfway to encourage branching and flowering. Mulch with 1 inch or more of fine pine bark scattered between plants in spring. Deadhead and cut back leggy plants in mid-spring. Leaf spot and stem rot diseases can occur in poorly drained or crowded beds; remove blighted leaves promptly. Sprinkle pine straw over pansy beds if temperatures are forecast to fall into the teens. In the western Carolinas, mulch beds heavily and plant through the mulch to delay freezing of soil. Deer love pansies, so be prepared to use a repellent.

Companion Planting and Design

Use in rock gardens, containers, and mass groupings. Many public gardens interplant pansies with Darwin tulips so that the pansies serve as a ground cover. It is hard to beat the sight of red tulips poking out of a bed of blue 'Crystal Bowl' pansies—wow! Try pansies or violas with cold-tolerant ornamental kale and cabbage.

Our Personal Favorites

The old-fashioned 'Maxim Blue' with the "clown face" is our preference. All-America Selections winner 'Ultima Morpho' is a free-flowering bicolor.

What would we plant for color in our winter landscapes if we didn't have pansies? No other flower can deliver consistent color during fall, winter, and spring from fall planting. Come out on an icy morning and see pansies face down, apparently in distress. Return later when the sun has warmed the plants and they will be perked up, no worse for the wear. A spring-planted crop is also possible except in the cool mountains, but only a few weeks of color will be realized before summer heat and humidity takes the starch out of your plants. Pansies are loved for their bright velvety faces and their numerous colors. Landscapers value them for their relatively low cost and versatility. In the horticultural industry, pansies with slightly smaller flowers and often with solid colors are usually labeled "violas."

Other Common Name
Viola

Bloom Period and Seasonal Color
Fall through June in blue, rose, purple, maroon, red, yellow, orange, white, and tricolor.

Mature Height × Spread
5 to 9 in. × 10 in.

Pentas

Pentas lanceolata

Pentas had to wait for widespread popularity until breeders developed shorter, earlier-blooming varieties. When the new varieties appeared on bedding plant displays, they were an instant hit, and when they showed southern gardeners their durability under heat and humidity, they pushed ahead of more delicate annuals. Now they rank among the top twenty annuals in the Carolinas. One common name given pentas, star cluster flower, certainly fits them. The plants support tight two- to three-inch wide clusters of small, star-shaped flowers in a great range of pastel and dark colors. Butterflies like the secure footing and nectar provided by the clusters, especially the swallowtails. The clusters look up at you, which in a flower with a short frame, is a visual plus.

Other Common Name
Star Cluster Flower

Bloom Period and Seasonal Color
All summer long in red, pink, lavender, and white.

Mature Height × Spread
10 in. × 8 in. for ultra-dwarf varieties
20 in. × 15 in. for standard varieties

When, Where, and How to Plant
Buy plants of pentas and set them into flower beds or containers after frost danger is past. Grow them in full sun, or near the coast or in the hot sandhills, in afternoon shade. Read the labels to be sure you are getting the right height plants for your particular landscape situation. Improving your soil can prolong the span of bloom and help pentas maintain good condition through periods of dry weather. The chapter introduction will tell you how.

Growing Tips
Pentas respond to controlled-release fertilizer (CRF) mixed into the soil. Apply according to directions. Read the package label carefully on potting soils. The premium grades contain enough controlled-release fertilizer to feed plants until August. At planting time, swirl a supplementary amount of CRF into the surface of the potting soil to maintain robust growth and flowering until frost kills the plants. Alternatively, feed every two weeks with water-soluble fertilizer diluted per directions. Water pentas deeply and weekly during periods of drought and just before fertilizer feedings.

Care
Pentas send up so many flower clusters that they place a drain on the vigor of plants, especially the dwarf varieties. When you see spent clusters begin to turn brown, deadhead the plants. Use pruning shears; the stems are tough. Rabbits will nibble pentas; deer repellent usually works for rabbits as well. Pentas are seldom bothered by insects or diseases. Leafhoppers occasionally appear, but pentas recover on their own.

Companion Planting and Design
Pentas are such fun to work with because you can pick and choose just the right colors from bedding plant displays. They combine beautifully with blue salvia, kangaroo paw, nicotiana, and petunias. You might wish to avoid the fast spreading varieties of petunias or ornamental sweet potatoes as they tend to overgrow pentas.

Our Personal Favorite
The 'New Look' series has small plants and colors ranging from deep red through the pastels and white. No blue, but you can bring blue in from some other species.

Periwinkle
Catharanthus roseus

When, Where, and How to Plant

The many color choices of periwinkle help it display well on garden center plant stands, and most gardeners opt for started plants. Delay planting until the soil is warm and danger of frost is past. Periwinkle grows easily from seeds sown indoors eight to ten weeks prior to the spring frost-free date, or a crop for midsummer planting for late bloom can be direct-seeded in warm garden soil. Plant in full sun or, near the coast, in afternoon shade. Periwinkle, despite its adaptability, grows much better in soil amended with a 2-inch layer of organic soil conditioner, or in sandy soil. It isn't happy in cold, soggy, slow-draining clay. Periwinkle is susceptible to black root rot on poorly drained clay soil. Improve aeration by mixing in 2 to 3 inches of organic soil conditioner. Space plants about 18 inches apart to have them grow together by midsummer. Refer to the chapter introduction for helpful planting hints.

Growing Tips

Granular flower garden fertilizer and limestone worked into the soil prior to planting will get periwinkle off to a fast start. Alternatively, cottonseed meal incorporated at 5 pounds per 100 square feet will provide ample nutrition. Water sufficiently to thoroughly wet the root zone in drought.

Care

There isn't much you can do to help periwinkle "do its thing," except to keep weeds pulled before they go to seed. Its spent flowers obligingly drop off. Shear off seedheads in late summer. Remove wilted plants promptly (soil with roots) to eliminate soil-inhabiting fungi. Periwinkle seldom attracts pests except the occasional spittle bug.

Companion Planting and Design

Periwinkle is a good neighbor to many kinds of heat resistant summer annuals. Pentas look good with periwinkle of a compatible color, as does sun-tolerant coleus selected for color agreement.

Our Personal Favorite

'Jaio Dark Red' deserves the award it received from All-America Selections. Dark blossoms such as these, the contrasting white eye notwithstanding, display better if set off by white or silver plants such as white periwinkle or dusty miller.

Often mistakenly called "vinca," periwinkle has only glossy, dark green leaves in common with the blue flowered, spreading vinca vine. Periwinkle has dense, upright bushes covered with open-faced blossoms in many pastel shades plus orange, red, and white. Modern varieties offer much larger flowers than those sold only a few years ago. Periwinkle is one of the most popular heat- and humidity-resistant flowers for the South. It is tough, adaptable, reasonably drought resistant, and troubled by few pests. It would be an all-purpose flower except that it is of little use as a cut flower. One of its attractions is the ease with which dust and urban grime can be sluiced off its foliage, leaving it shiny and squeaky clean. Periwinkle will occasionally overwinter in protected coastal gardens.

Other Common Name
Madagascar Periwinkle

Bloom Period and Seasonal Color
Nonstop until fall frost blooms red, plum, blueberry, pink, apricot, coral, and white.

Mature Height × Spread
12 to 14 in. × 18 to 24 in.

Persian Shield

Strobilanthes dyerianus

Persian shield, once considered a house plant, has won a place for itself in container gardens and as a dramatic foliage plant in flower beds. No other easily grown tropical plant has such exotic leaves, light purple overlaid on green, air-brushed with silver, and laced with dark veins. The plant is rather lanky but responds willingly to shaping by pinching or pruning. You'll find yourself unable to resist exerting a little control each time you pass by it. Don't wait for flowers; the short violet spikes come late and are upstaged by the foliage. The size of the leaves of Persian shield indicates its state of nutrition. When planted in good soil and fed and watered regularly, leaves can reach six to eight inches.

Bloom Period and Seasonal Color
Deep purple, silver, and green begin at planting time and increase as plant matures.

Mature Height × Spread
1 to 2 ft. × 2 ft., larger in Zone 8

When, Where, and How to Plant
Don't expose this tender tropical to cold weather. Even better, hold your plants indoors until the soil feels warm to your bare feet or until neighborhood boys brag about skinny dipping. Persian shield is usually sold in 4- to 6-inch pots, at about 1 foot in height, and grows rapidly in containers or ground beds. Set plants in light or dappled shade in the hotter Zone 8 region; elsewhere, full sun is fine. Amend garden soil generously with an organic soil conditioner, and mulch around the plants to maintain a consistent soil moisture level. Water the transplanted Persian shield well and repeat the watering every two or three days until leaf buds break into new foliage. Persian shield is nearly fail-safe, but if more information will reassure you, see the chapter introduction.

Growing Tips
Persian shield is a "natural" for growing in containers with premium grade potting soil and watered every two or three days. Where planted in sunny borders, leaves may parch unless watered twice weekly. Liquid feeding every two weeks will produce spectacular foliage.

Care
For specimen plants, pinch off just the tip leaves of branches. Buds further back on the branch will break into new leaves. In garden beds, group 3 to 5 plants closely and let them develop as nature directs. Root cuttings of the plant in autumn to have starts for the next year. Supplies are often limited in garden centers. Neither of us has seen insect or disease problems on Persian shield.

Companion Planting and Design
Persian shield makes a great plant for adding height and substance to container gardens. You will need to prune it accordingly, perhaps even espaliering a plant on a short trellis. Silver plants (artemisia, dusty miller, curry plant) look good with it, as does heliotrope, petunia, sun coleus, or million bells in compatible colors. Group summer annuals around it to hide its lanky legs.

Our Personal Favorite
This is easy: only one kind is on the market.

When, Where, and How to Plant

Hold off planting petunias until the soil is warm and the chance of frost has passed. Petunias need lots of sun to thrive and show off their brilliant color. Good soil drainage and air circulation is a must for disease prevention. Amend beds with compost or bark soil conditioner. Add limestone to soil with a pH level below 6.0. The chapter introduction will help you prepare soil that would grow roots on a broomstick. Space seedlings or rooted cuttings 10 to 24 inches apart, depending on the cultivar. Petunias need to be thoroughly watered after planting.

Growing Tips

Once they begin to grow, petunias are drought tolerant and need only occasional irrigation. Water every third day for two weeks, then weekly and as needed to prevent wilting. Slow-release flower fertilizers or organic plant foods will give you nutrients balanced for flower production. If you use a water-soluble product, fertilize every three or four weeks, using a 1-2-2 ratio nutrient source.

Care

Water in the morning to reduce the incidence of leaf diseases and blossom blight. Mulch plantings early in the season for weed control and to prevent soil splash; a 1- to 2-inch layer will do. Pinch or shear back petunias any time they ramble too far. Root and stem rot diseases are common in poorly drained clays; rotate with other annuals periodically. 'Purple Wave' petunias are exceptional but are not immune to problems related to over-watering. Wilted and yellowing foliage spells trouble; call your County Cooperative Extension Agent.

Companion Planting and Design

Petunias are great plants to follow pansies; plant them when the pansies fade out in late May. Group petunias in drifts for a color impact or interplant with perennials to provide color when other annuals are taking time out. The cascading habit of 'Wave' or 'Cascadia' petunias makes them ideal for planters or as ground covers.

Our Personal Favorites

The 'Wave' petunias continue to score high marks. Jim's favorite color is 'Misty Lilac Wave'.

Some gardeners cooled on petunias when they became garden clichés, but new colors and plant habits are winning back the disenchanted. Petunias are summer garden workhorses, sturdy annuals that come in myriad colors and either spreading or compact plants. They produce masses of trumpet-shaped blooms on drooping branches. An edging of 'Fantasy Pink Morn', a pale pink milliflora type will stay low and compact. What a contrast with the 'Wave' series which has ground-hugging branches up to 2 feet in length! They can be planted in a window box or can serve as a ground cover on a hot, steep bank. Millifloras have especially dense plants with quarter-size flowers. Petunias grow beautifully in containers—the cascading types in hanging baskets, and the compact types as filler plants in container gardens.

Bloom Period and Seasonal Color
All summer in shades from white and palest pink to brilliant red, yellow, mid-blue, and dark purple.

Mature Height × Spread
$^1/_2$ to 1 ft. × 1 to 3 ft.

Polka-dot Plant

Hypoestes phyllostachya

The leaves of polka-dot plant are covered with wee, white or cream colored spots over a green, pink, or dark red base color. Its flowers are inconspicuous. Why, then, would anyone bother to plant it? Polka-dot plant is one of the few richly colored ornamentals that will grow well in light to medium shade while standing up to hot, humid weather. Also, it shows its characteristic colors from seedling stage through maturity. Southern gardeners have found many uses for polka-dot plant: as a mound-shaped ornamental for containers gardens, as a colorful bedding plant for lightly shaded areas, and as an edging for medium-height shade plants. Using brightly colored foliage plants to light up shaded areas is nothing new, but polka-dot plant expands the narrow range of choices for such difficult sites.

Other Common Names
Freckle Face, Measles Plant

Bloom Period and Seasonal Color
Color impact begins with seedlings and intensifies throughout the summer; green, pink, and dark red base colors generously flecked with small white spots.

Mature Height × Spread
1¹/₂ to 2 ft. × 1 to 1¹/₂ ft.

When, Where, and How to Plant
Polka-dot plants are usually sold in 6-packs or 2- to 3-inch pots. Wait until frost danger is past before transplanting them to container gardens or to flower beds. Site in beds that will receive after-noon shade or light shade all day. Mix in a 2-inch layer of organic soil conditioner and granular 1-2-2 ratio fertilizer, and spread a 1- to 2-inch layer of aged pine bark or hardwood bark mulch. Scrape the mulch aside and dig individual planting holes 12 inches apart. Set the plants in place, pull the amended soil around the root ball, and spread a shallow layer of mulch over the root ball.

Growing Tips
Be faithful in watering. Spritz new plantings mornings and afternoons until you see signs of new growth, usually within seven to ten days. Later, reduce watering frequency to twice weekly during dry weather. If you allow the plants to dry out enough for leaves to parch or discolor, they will need two or three weeks of intensive liquid feeding and watering to produce enough new growth to hide the results of neglect.

Care
Polka-dot plants are forgiving of pinching. They tend to shoot out the occasional ungainly branch, but a hard pinch on branch tips will result in reserve buds breaking into new foliage. Near the coast, polka-dot plants may live through mild win-ters. No serious plant diseases or pests have been noted.

Companion Planting and Design
Use mondo grass or bunch-type liriope as edgings for beds of polka dot plants, and a backdrop of Persian shield or caladiums. In container gardens for shaded sites, choose a foliage color that agrees with other plants in your design. Pink is the liveli-est color. The white on green combination has a formal look and the red on green is a bit heavy. The effect can be lightened by adding white impa-tiens to the design.

Our Personal Favorites
The 'Splash' series of three-color combinations is outstanding.

When, Where, and How to Plant

Rose moss flourishes in heat, drought, and full sun but will languish in wet, clay soil. Set out plants soon after spring frost danger is past and the soil feels warm to the touch. Plant seeds to get lots of seedlings at low cost. Work up a bed about 2 feet × 2 feet and cover it with a 2-inch layer of play sand. Wait until early May and make shallow furrows across the sand. Trickle seeds down the furrows and cover with the barest sprinkling of sand. Water with a fine mist, twice daily. When they put on 6 to 8 leaves, pry out seedlings with a knife and transplant them on 12 inch centers in prepared soil or into 2-inch pots to grow on before transplanting.

Growing Tips

Grow with only light applications of plant food when preparing the soil and another when you cut back the plants. No wet feet, please! Let the plants get by on nature's bounty. Leave sneak paths in beds; portulaca and purslane are brittle and easily damaged.

Care

Don't be afraid to pinch them when they look leggy. Rose moss blooms so prodigiously that it wears itself out by the dog days of August. Shear the plants to half-height, and feed and water them lightly to stimulate a late show of color. Rose moss is usually free of plant diseases and damage from insects. Performance is always improved by growing it in raised beds covered with 2 in. of play sand or in sandy, dry soil.

Companion Planting and Design

Combine rose moss with other drought-resistant plants such as Indian blanket, Mont Blanc *Nierembergia*, sedum, hen and chicks, creeping zinnia (*Sanvitalia*), and dusty miller. The related purslanes, which have plump leaves larger than rose moss, trail better and can be combined with rose moss in containers. Rock gardens are enhanced with mixed color plantings.

Our Personal Favorites

'Sundial Hybrids' are good portulacas, as are the 'Yubi' and 'Hotshot' color series in the purslanes.

Few flowers can match rose moss for brilliance, partly because its petals are so thin that they are backlighted by sun for part of the day. At one time, rose moss was notorious for closing its flowers, reacting to changes in cloud coverage and time of day. Now plant breeders have selected for flowers that remain open during most of the day and during sunny or partly cloudy weather. Few flowers are more drought resistant, although drought-stricken moss rose can look pretty shriveled until its leaves plump up with renewed soil moisture. Modern varieties have been purged of virtually all "single" blossoms, leading to fancy, fully double, many-petaled blooms in a delicious range of colors. Modern varieties also have considerably larger blossoms than "your grandma's rose moss."

Other Common Names
Portulaca, Moss Rose, Purslane

Bloom Period and Seasonal Color
Early to midsummer in red, pink, yellow, peach, and white plus an encore if sheared and fed. Mature portulaca takes on a bronzy-rose tint.

Mature Height × Spread
4 to 10 in. × 16 to 24 in.

Snapdragon
Antirrhinum sp.

At one time, most varieties of snapdragon produced tall plants with stately spikes that needed staking. During the past several decades, plant heights have been steadily decreased as have the days from planting seeds to "first color." The individual blossoms have been made larger and more ornate. Recently introduced varieties with lax branches take on a semi-trailing form to give snapdragons more utility in hanging baskets and container gardens. Experienced gardeners still start tall varieties of snaps from seeds indoors to produce inexpensive plants for their cutting gardens. Regardless of the décor of one's home, an arrangement of tall snaps, perhaps mixed with late-spring-blooming spikes of larkspur, attests to the skill of the grower. Yet, the modern trend is toward beds of the shorter varieties of snaps.

Other Common Name
Snaps

Bloom Period and Seasonal Color.
Shades of red, pink, yellow, purple and white bloom in early summer through midsummer.

Mature Height × Spread
Tall snaps, 24 to 30 in. × 12 in.
Intermediate, 12 to 16 in. × 12 in.
Ultra dwarf, 8 to 10 in. × 8 in.

When, Where, and How to Plant
Many gardeners like snaps so much that they start seeds indoors in late fall to have seedlings ready to set out in early spring. Once hardened off by gradual exposure to cold winds, the seedlings will weather light frosts. In coastal areas, seeds can be started in pots or flats out of doors in late summer and set into the garden in October. Other gardeners opt for seedlings in packs or pots, just showing color. Plant snaps in well drained soil, in a sunny site. Afternoon shade won't hurt them. Be sure to leave room between plants for air passage when they mature. Space tall varieties 24 inches apart, intermediate varieties 12 inches apart and the ultra dwarfs 8 to 10 inches apart for good air circulation.

Growing Tips
Weekly, flow water on the soil between plants or use drip irrigation to avoid wetting the foliage. Mix controlled-release flower fertilizer into the soil prior to planting to feed all season.

Care
Watch for aphids (you can see them clustering on spikes) and thrips (they are hard to see; you know they may be there if blossoms are distorted.) Aphids are relatively easy to control with sprays of insecticidal soap; thrips are difficult and may call for a combination fertilizer/systemic insecticide. Snaps are vulnerable to foliage diseases. Keep an appropriate fungicide handy for spraying on plants when a hot spot breaks out. On heavy clay soils, try spreading a mulch of play sand between your snapdragon seedlings to keep down the soil splash that spreads some foliage diseases. Slow draining soil can encourage root rot. Deadhead spent spikes.

Companion Planting and Design
Snaps come in myriad colors. They make excellent cut flowers. Gardeners often mix colors in beds edged with other cool weather ornamentals such as dianthus, pansies or violas, or ornamental kale or cabbage.

Our Personal Favorites
Jim likes the 'Butterfly' snaps for their fancy flowers. Toby prefers the tall Rockets.

Spiderflower
Cleome hassleriana

When, Where, and How to Plant

Cleome seeds germinate so readily and grow so strongly from direct-seeding in sunny, warm flowerbeds that it may give you the confidence to try sowing other flowers. No elaborate soil preparation is necessary. Work the soil early, let it sit until frost danger is past, and scrape off the weeds with a sharp hoe. Cut a short, shallow furrow and scatter the seeds down its length. Cover with 1/4 inch of play sand. When the seedlings have developed 6 or 8 leaves, carefully transplant them 18 inches apart in flower bed soil amended with organic soil conditioner. Water immediately and daily for the next few days. You can buy spiderflower plants already started, but they are usually still in the green stage, days from flowering. Medium-height selections rarely lean from wind and rain, especially if planted close together for mutual support.

Growing Tips

Once your transplants have set anchoring roots, feed them with water-soluble flower food diluted per directions. Cleome needs little supplemental water except during severe drought. Handle the plants carefully; they have many sharp thorns.

Care

Little is needed in the way of care except for weed pulling. When the plants bush out enough to touch each other, they will shade out most weeds. Remove seedpods if self-sowing is not wanted. Spider mites are one of the few pests that affect spiderflowers. Most miticides have been pulled off the market, but insecticidal soap gives good control of these sap-sucking pests. Follow directions carefully to avoid burning foliage in hot, summer conditions.

Companion Planting and Design

The four colors of the Sparkler series look good together when mixed and massed in flower beds. Blue flowers and silver foliage plants make good edgings for beds of cleome. Try one of the medium-height sunflowers with numerous small blossoms as a background flower.

Our Personal Favorite

Toby and Jim agree 'Sparkler' is the best thing since sliced bread and running water.

Old-fashioned spiderflowers grew so tall that their heavy flower heads bent with rain and wind and stay bowed as if in obeisance to the storm gods. The common name comes from the spidery look of the long, thread-like flower stems, wispy blossoms, and filamentous stamens. Seedpods form after the spent petals fall. Upon drying, they uncurl and fling seeds, guaranteeing a generous crop of seedlings for years to come. Unfortunately, the color range in the old varieties included only dark pink and purple, with white accents. Now, plant breeders have shortened the height of spiderflowers to three feet and have added new colors. This stocky, sturdy new variety, 'Sparkler', is not nearly so likely to bend in the rain. One of its colors, 'Sparkler Blush', won an All-America Selections award.

Other Common Name
Spider Plant, Cleome

Bloom Period and Seasonal Color
Early summer until fall frost, with peak color in midsummer. Pink/white, purple/white, salmon/white bicolors.

Mature Height × Spread
Tall, 6 to 8 ft. × 1 1/2 ft.
Midsize, 2 to 3 ft. × 1 ft.

Spreading Zinnia
Zinnia angustifolia

This zinnia species is for gardeners who dislike the care required by many annuals. For years, only golden, orange, or yellow colors were available. They were used for dry, hot sites that receive little attention. Now you can enjoy 'Crystal White', an All-America Selections introduction, a compact plant that grows to ten inches in height and has a somewhat wider spread. Its single pure-white flowers are over an inch in size. Recently, the hybrid 'Profusion' series, with Z. angustifolia as one parent, also garnered AAS awards and added cherry to the color range. Their small, narrow, medium green leaves are resistant to powdery mildew disease, unlike the standard garden variety (Z. elegans). Spreading zinnias are exceptionally tolerant of the heat and humidity of the Carolinas.

Other Common Names
Narrowleaf or Willowleaf Zinnia, Classic Zinnia

Bloom Period and Seasonal Color
Late spring through fall frost; small but numerous white, orange, yellow, gold, or cherry flowers.

Mature Height × Spread
12 to 16 in. × equal spread. The original narrowleaf species grows taller and wider.

When, Where, and How to Plant
Set out plants or sow seeds well after the danger of frost has passed. Zinnias prefer full sun and well-drained soil in garden beds or containers. If you start with plants it is best to select stocky transplants that have few blooms. Sow seeds in lightly fertilized soil, tilled to a depth of 4 to 6 inches, and raked smooth. Cover seeds lightly with 1/3 inch of soil and firm them into the soil with the back of an iron rake. Water the bed thoroughly, using a watering wand or a nozzle designed for misting seedbeds. Keep the bed or row moist until the seeds germinate. Space plants or thin seedlings 18 inches apart so the plants can develop their natural shape.

Growing Tips
For container gardens, read the potting soil label. If it is not fortified with controlled-release fertilizer, mix in 1 tablespoon per gallon of pot capacity. In ground beds, fertilize the plants monthly by broadcasting 1-2-2 ratio fertilizer (for example, 5-10-10) between the plants to keep them healthy and blooming. Irrigate established plants for the first month with about an inch of water per week. Avoid wetting the foliage late in the day.

Care
In late summer, spreading zinnias can be sheared to rejuvenate the planting. If the seedlings were not thinned properly, plants may become crowded, which can contribute to mildew susceptibility during wet summers. They have no pests and are low maintenance annuals. It is not uncommon for seedlings to reappear magically the next summer.

Companion Planting and Design
Spreading zinnia is often used to fill large beds and in containers. In areas that can't be watered frequently, this is the zinnia of choice. For highest visibility at dusk, plant the yellow or white-blooming varieties. Spreading zinnias can be used in mass groupings with blue ageratum and 'Wave' petunias.

Our Personal Favorite
'Profusion Cherry', a hybrid, gets rave reviews from serious gardeners.

Sun Coleus
Solenostemon scutellariodes

When, Where, and How to Plant

Set out plants in spring when the soil temperature warms to 55 degrees Fahrenheit and after fear of spring frosts passes, or at any time through late summer. Moisture-retentive soils are advised for full-sun locations and result in less maintenance in partial sun or dappled-shade locations. (See the chapter introduction for soil preparation and planting instruction.) Space large cultivars 30 inches apart and small-leaved types 18 inches apart. Vigorous, large-leaved cultivars grow so large that they are usually planted alone in containers and grown as eye-catching specimens. Leave sneak paths among plants in ground beds. Coleus plants are quite brittle and can be damaged by foot traffic during watering or weeding.

Growing Tips

Sun coleus demands moist soil to perform. Use soaker hoses or water by hand to irrigate roots weekly and deeply during hot weather. A 1- to 2-inch layer of mulch helps to retain water and suppress weeds. Use controlled-release fertilizer in container plantings. Apply water-soluble fertilizer to ground beds monthly, more often in sandy soils.

Care

Pinch or cut leaders to make coleus dense and bushy, with a mounded habit. To keep foliage vigorous, remove flower spikes before they elongate. Sun coleus is pest free, except for slugs and snails that decimate small plants. Control slugs with baits or saucers of beer. Additional plants can be produced by rooting tip cuttings in potting soil. Take tip cuttings in September to pot up for next year's plants and to enjoy indoors during winter.

Companion Planting and Design

Use sun coleus as a background for lower annuals, such as wax begonias, angelonias, 'Blackie' sweet potato vines, or lavender-blue fan flowers to hide their ankles and knees. Mass plants for best effect. In shade gardens, combine with evergreen ferns and caladiums. The light-colored cultivars show up better in shaded sites.

Our Personal Favorites

For a fall show with mums, 'Alabama Sunset' has burgundy-tipped leaves with gold centers. The unusual leaf shapes of the 'Duckfoot' series of colors are novel and amusing.

Coleus has been the backbone of annual shade gardens for generations, but it is has broken out into the sun. The new vegetatively propagated sun coleus selections offer brilliant garden color that never stops, and if you water them frequently, they will thrive in full sun. In the Carolinas, this tropical is grown as an annual. In moist or irrigated beds, its vibrant, nonstop color will attract favorable attention from spring to fall. Sun coleus is ideal for container gardens or borders to create significant color accents. There has never been an annual easier to grow in our Piedmont clay soil. Some garden centers offer two dozen or more choices in bicolors, solid colors, and leaf sizes and shapes. As compared to old-fashioned, seed grown, shade garden coleus, the sun-tolerant types are slow to produce flowers and need less deadheading.

Bloom Period and Seasonal Color
Late spring through fall, richly variegated foliage ranging from nickel size to more than 6 in. long.

Mature Height × Spread
2 to 4 ft. × 2 to 3 ft.

Sunflower
Helianthus annuus

Sunflowers are hot! Visit a farmers' market in midsummer to see prominent displays of sunflowers cut at the peak of their bloom. Visit Europe and see flower stands with buckets of mid-sized, long-stemmed sunflower blossoms for sale. Gigantic flower heads steal the show at state fairs. Available either in single- or double-flowered forms, tall or short varieties, sunflowers never become tiresome. "Mammoth" varieties boast heads that reach a foot or more across. The seeds ripen in early fall and attract feeding birds. Sunflowers grow reliably when direct-seeded in garden soil or in a tub for a patio show. Toby reports that one of the fondest memories of his agricultural career was standing in a seemingly endless field of sunflowers in North Dakota during the 1980s, a spiritual experience for a floriculturist!

Bloom Period and Seasonal Color
Summer blooms in shades of yellow, burgundy, red, gold, and white.

Mature Height × Spread
2 to 8 ft. × 1 to 4 ft.

When, Where, and How to Plant
You can start with plants, but growing from seeds is easy. Plant in warm soil at least two weeks after the last frost date in your hardiness zone. Ordinary garden soil is adequate for growing this annual, provided it is well drained, tilled, fortified with 1-2-2 ratio fertilizer and limestone, and raked smooth. Cover the seeds with 1/2 inch of soil and keep them moist. In heavy clay soil, create a 4-inch-high raised row or mound to ensure adequate drainage and to warm the soil. Keep the soil moist. Thin dwarf varieties to 18 inches apart. Space larger varieties 3 to 4 feet apart.

Growing Tips
Water new seedlings and transplants weekly until they begin strong growth. Sunflowers tolerate heat and drought well. Once established, they should be watered only during extended dry spells. Side-dress with a granular garden fertilizer once during the growing season to prolong the production of blossoms. Scatter 1/2 cup on the soil around each plant; keep it 10 inches away from the stem.

Care
The large-headed varieties that are grown for bird-seed or for showing at fairs should be staked for support using an 8-foot, 2-by-2-inch wooden stake or steel fence post with canvas straps. No pruning is required. Control worm and beetle pests with approved insecticides. Dwarf varieties will "play out" after the main flower heads develop.

Companion Planting and Design
Plant dwarf or mid-sized cultivars that produce multiple branches and continuous blooms. It's a great plant for bird watchers. The gigantic varieties can overpower your garden. Because the 'Mammoth' types can reach 8 feet high very fast, they can make a quick screen for the garden or along a fence row. 'Teddy Bear' has short stalks and makes a fine cut flower.

Our Personal Favorite
'Ring of Fire', is zoned with contrasting light/dark colors and typifies the new generation of sunflowers.

Sweet Potato Vine

Ipomoea batatas

When, Where, and How to Plant

Purchase potted plants or use last season's stored ornamental sweet potato tubers or rooted cuttings (slips) anytime in spring or summer. Plant in a sunny flower bed when danger of frost has passed and the soil is warm, preferably May or later in most locations. Plants grow best when they are placed in well-tilled soil with lime and organic matter have been added. Sweet potato vines grow as well in clay as they do in sandy loam soils, provided the soil drains quickly. But they grow even better in good grade potting soil. Allow plenty of room for the vines to grow, as they can spread 6 or more feet in a season. Cover tuberous roots with 2 inches of amended soil or set started plants at grade level in a flower bed. Water well and delay mulching until summer.

Growing Tips

Keep the soil evenly moist until foliage matures. Once established, the vines benefit from deep irrigation when they appear wilted. Drench soil around vines with a liquid high-nitrogen fertilizer, such as 20-20-20, at least monthly to keep the foliage healthy.

Care

Prune vines occasionally to keep them in bounds. This is the perfect pass-along plant. Root clippings for hanging baskets and other container gardens. The potato weevil or slugs may eat a few holes in the leaves. Consult your County Cooperative Extension Agent for controls. Before frost kills plants, take cuttings for next year. You may dig the fleshy roots and store them in dry peat moss in a crawl space or basement.

Companion Planting and Design

Plant mixed-color beds of sweet potato vines as bold garden statements. Plant along the front of borders or as a ground cover accent. Good companions are sun coleus, blue sage, zinnia, and ornamental grasses.

Our Personal Favorites

Toby likes 'Margarita' for its unique chartreuse color. Jim likes 'Tricolor' for containers because it isn't as aggressive as the burgundy or chartreuse cultivars.

Now and then, a new variety bolts out of the gate to win the Triple Crown of Color Beds from professional landscapers. This herbaceous annual beats the competition by a long shot. Sweet potato vine grows like kudzu and shares the spotlight with only a few plants of similar foliar attributes. Entire "potato beds" can be seen in commercial landscape installations across the South where colorful foliage adds curb appeal. During the twenty-first century, sweet potato vine has moved from container plant to landscape sweetheart. Commercial plantings are replete with sweet potato vines planted with the red fountain grass for a Kodak moment. The Carolinas are nationally known for edible sweet potato production, thus one could expect that ornamental sweet potatoes would also excel here. They do.

Bloom Period and Seasonal Color

Burgundy, chartreuse, and tricolor cultivars show colorful foliage all summer long.

Mature Height × Spread

1/2 to 1 ft. × 3 to 6 ft.

Bulbs, Corms, Rhizomes, & Tubers *for the Carolinas*

A passion for flowers often begins with a handful of bulbs. Many a beginning gardener has gotten a start in horticulture with a plump amaryllis bulb or a few daffodils. It's rare when a garden shop fails to offer these special plants in season, as they have become a symbol of winter gardening for sun-lovers of all ages. Bulbs, unlike seeds, contain reproductive parts—flowers—as well as undeveloped plants. When given proper growing conditions bulbs will spring to life, with the guarantee of lovely flowers in a short period of time. Bulb culture opens up a whole new realm of possibilities for skilled gardeners as well as beginners.

When we gardeners think of bulbs, what usually comes to mind is Holland, not the Carolinas! There is no doubt that Holland is world-renowned for its tulip tradition and its famous Keukenhof Gardens with ten million flowering bulbs on display. In the Netherlands, bulbs have been grown as an economic staple since the sixteenth century. But with some planning, we in the Carolinas can create a Dutch delight in our yards. You will get the greatest enjoyment from bulbs by planting varieties of both species and hybrid tulips.

Not Just for Spring Anymore

Bulb flowers are not just spring flowers. In the Carolinas, bulbs can bloom twelve months of the year, depending on the species. While the familiar anemones, crocuses, and daffodils are valuable garden bulbs and require little care, they finish their showy performance before spring is over. By Mother's Day, bearded iris, the hallmark of spring bulb season in the Piedmont Triad region, is ablaze, and there is plenty of activity to come in the months that follow.

Indulge yourself with the wonderful woodland varieties like magic lilies and autumn crocus. For vertical accents, scatter a few gladiolus and crocosmia bulbs in a sunny perennial border. The "Oriental" lilies produce large, exquisite, picture-perfect blooms for cutting, while their smaller "Asiatic" cousins are made for color beds. Read the descriptions of the named cultivars; some are deliciously fragrant.

What Is a Bulb?

To set the record straight, not all bulbs arise from the smooth-skinned true bulbs like tulips and daffodils. True bulbs contain fleshy leaf scales, flowerbuds, and stored food surrounded by a papery skin for

A Tulip Landscape

protection. Many of our summer-flowering bulblike plants—such as crocus, iris, and gladiolus—grow from stems called corms or rhizomes; others develop from thick root tissues called tuberous roots or tubers. All of these storage organs are capable of holding food reserves from season to season for the survival of the species. This gives bulbs the ability to "naturalize" (come back year after year) in the garden. Though some bulbs produce seeds after flowering, the seeds are difficult to germinate and may compete for the plant's energy. It is probably best for a gardener to remove the seedpods before

White Irises

they develop, unless of course you are a hybridizer introducing new varieties.

Many of the summer-flowering bulbs bloom when gardens are short on color. On balance, they are better landscape plants than their spring-blooming counterparts. Their foliage as well as their flowers can make a statement in the garden. The bold, variegated foliage of cannas and caladiums provide an exclamation point in a border or in the shadow of a majestic shade tree. If big leaves suit your fancy, gigantic elephant ear plants can be used judiciously as bold foliage accents in color beds and water gardens. The dainty rainlilies, one of our native bulbs, spring to life when a shower breaks a summer dry spell. Cyclamen steal the show in the shade garden as summer comes to an end. Dahlias crank up again and again and produce even better blossoms as State Fair-time rolls around each year.

Preparing the Bed

Successful gardeners prepare bulb beds for the long haul. Unless your planting is for one-season color, as with caladiums, you will want to amend the soil deeply. Studies at North Carolina State University (NCSU) revealed that many bulbs fail to naturalize due to soil acidity and poor fertility. Testing the soil should be a standard practice with new bed installations. Contact your County Cooperative Extension Agent for directions on taking and submitting soil samples. Bulbs will perform well in soils that have been limed to raise the pH to 6.0. Amend poorly drained clay soils with organic matter such as finely-ground bark soil conditioner, or create a raised bed for your bulbs using a quality loam soil.

After NCSU discovered bulbs need slow-release nitrogen more than other major nutrients, they developed a specialty bulb fertilizer. Bulb-booster products supply balanced nutrition and encourage repeat flowering in our gardens. People have commonly used bonemeal at planting time, but this is no longer recommended since bonemeal attracts vermin to the garden and may be a health hazard. The appropriate times for fertilizing spring-flowering bulb beds are in late summer and again in winter when the new shoots are popping out of the ground. These application times correlate to the periods of highest absorption of nutrients. Summer-flowering bulbs can be fertilized with the specialty products in spring as they emerge from their winter rest. But in the warm months, use water-soluble flower fertilizer every six weeks to keep the plants vigorous.

Gardeners complain most about the wildlife they encounter when attempting to grow bulbs. Though squirrels will leave your poisonous daffodil bulbs alone, they may nibble a tulip flower. Browsing deer or pets running through a fragile bulb bed at peak bloom can certainly cause distress. The real menace for lily growers is the presence of pine mice (voles). Fortunately, there are legal ways to control voles, including snaptraps and rodenticides. For the average homeowner in suburbia, a good cat or amending the soil with gravel or VoleBlock™ goes a long way.

Specialty bulb catalogs and garden centers offer many bulb options for gardening year-round. For every sunny garden or shady nook, you can find just the right bulb. Some bulbs may be left in the ground for years, producing flowers for your enjoyment. Others will need to be lifted following the first frosts of autumn. Many of them are capable of surviving harsh storage conditions because they naturally go dormant until they receive an environment conducive to a normal growth cycle. You won't be disappointed with your bulb choices when you find the perfect places for them in your garden.

Amaryllis
Hippeastrum × hybrida

Most Dutch amaryllis are sold to force indoors during the winter months. But in hardiness Zone 8, this bulb can be added to the perennial border or used en masse for a striking display when the spring garden has passed its peak. As its leaves emerge from the ground, this bulbous plant blooms with a cluster of four to six extraordinary trumpet-shaped flowers. Once they establish their permanent root systems, they provide the brilliant color and bold forms that are sorely needed until perennials reach their peak. Amaryllis make superb cut flowers. In cooler parts of the Carolinas, forced amaryllis bulbs can be kept in pots indoors until frost danger is past and then transplanted to the garden. They can be dug before hard frost comes, allowed to dry, then repotted for winter bloom.

Bloom Period and Seasonal Color
White, pink, red, salmon, orange, or striped flowers in late spring.

Mature Height × Spread
To 2 ft. × 1 ft.

When, Where, and How to Plant
For landscape color north of Zone 8, plant amaryllis in spring and handle them as you would dahlias. In Zone 8, plant them outdoors in fall. Though amaryllis can be planted from seeds, divisions, or bulb cuttings, it's best to stick with bulbs! Plant in full sun in rich, well drained soil where the plants will not be disturbed for several years. Their deep, foraging roots should not have to compete with the invasive root systems of shade trees. Prepare the bed by digging deep to break up compacted soil. Mix compost, aged sawdust, or shredded leaves into the bed to enrich and loosen it; this will help your bulbs sink deep roots and increases their chances of survival. If needed, lime the soil to reach the ideal pH of 6.0. Use a bulb-booster fertilizer at the recommended rate when you add organic soil conditioner. Dig a hole 4 to 6 inches deep, cover with the prepared soil, leaving necks at ground level or above.

Growing Tips
When bloom stalks emerge in May or June, water regularly during dry periods. Once beds are well established, they require little attention. Fertilize or apply compost annually to beds.

Care
Do not remove foliage when you are grooming mature plants. When cutting amaryllis blooms for flower arrangements, leave a few inches of stem above ground. It is best to cut the flower stalks when the first buds show color. Remove thrips or aphids by hosing off or by using insecticidal soap. Divide established and crowded beds when foliage turns yellow as the plants go dormant. Maintain a thick winter mulch after frost.

Companion Planting and Design
Plant in a prominent place like an entrance garden, by an ornate garden gate, or in a decorative container. The bulbs naturalize in the warmer regions of the Carolinas, growing larger each year until as many as three stalks of blooms shoot up from each plant in a season.

Our Personal Favorites
'Apple Blossom' is a great amaryllis for planting and forcing. *H. × johnsonii* is reliable outdoors.

Bearded Iris

Iris germanica

When, Where, and How to Plant

The ideal time to plant is in early spring. Late-autumn planting is not advisable because the plants won't have a chance to send down anchor roots. Plant in full sun or at least in strong morning sun. If iris doesn't receive enough sun, it seldom thrives and will produce flowers of inferior size. Well-drained average garden soil is fine. Prepare the bed with bulb-booster fertilizer and lime to a pH of 6.5 to 7.0. When planted properly, the top of the rhizome can be seen above the ground. Be careful not to plant too deep or the plants may not bloom.

Growing Tips

Bearded Irises require an abundance of moisture during the blooming season, but they endure long periods of drought at other times. Water weekly during the flowering period if less than 1 inch of rain falls. Do not mulch iris beds. Fertilize with 5-10-10 in spring before bloom time. A second application one month after blooming is needed to stimulate foliage and rhizome growth.

Care

Overcrowded clumps bloom poorly, so divide them if they become too dense. Divide immediately after flowering. Rhizomes can also be divided while in bloom to ensure the correct flower color is selected. To divide, remove old flower stems and cut the leaves back to 6 inches. Lift the entire clump out of the ground and remove the soil. Cut the clump with a sharp knife so there is a rhizome and a fan of leaves in each division. Discard rhizomes showing signs of decay. The most serious insect is the iris borer. Rake out the pinkish 2-inch larvae from rhizomes at replanting, using a pencil point. The application of foliage sprays in spring is an accepted preventative against borers.

Companion Planting and Design

Interplant with earlier- and later-blooming perennials for a striking textural contrast, or plant an entire bed of bearded iris in a border. Roof iris, *I. tectorum*, shares the season of bloom.

Our Personal Favorite

For plenty of blooms on each stalk, try 'Art Deco', a violet-on-white flower.

These sensational showy plants, named after the Greek goddess of the rainbow, are among the most useful, colorful, and widely grown perennials. The bearded iris flower is made of two sections, an inner section consisting of three upstanding petals called "standards" and three outer drooping or horizontal petals called "falls." The common name comes from the dense, hairy line seen along the midrib of the outer "falls." The leaves of bearded iris are sword-shaped, and the stiff foliage and upright form contrast well with the rounded form of many border perennials. Bearded iris is available in standard and dwarf forms. These lovely late-spring bloomers are easily grown under ordinary garden conditions provided the soil does not stay wet. There are hundreds of named varieties of this marvelous flower.

Other Common Name
German Iris

Bloom Period and Seasonal Color
Wide range of colors in late spring. A few cultivars bloom again in the fall.

Mature Height × Spread
$1^1/2$ to $3^1/2$ ft. × 1 to 2 ft.

Caladium
Caladium bicolor

With their large flamboyant leaves, Caladiums put most other bulbous plants to shame. These beautiful plants prove that foliage can be just as important as flowers in landscapes. These tropical plants come in many shapes, sizes, and color combinations and are generally grown from tubers. They come in two types: fancy-leaved caladiums, which have heart-shaped leaves, and strap-leaved varieties, which have narrow arrow-shaped leaves. Both types are available in a range of color combinations and in sun-loving and shade-loving cultivars. The shade-loving types are more common and are the perfect plants for partial- to full-shade gardens and containers. Forty to sixty percent shade is ideal for most varieties. Though they are not winter hardy, caladiums are a great asset in the summer shade garden. Their brilliant foliage can brighten dark corners.

Bloom Period and Seasonal Color
Boldly-colored leaves in shades of red, burgundy, green, pink, or white from summer to frost.

Mature Height × Spread
1 to 2¹/₂ ft. × 1 to 2 ft.

When, Where, and How to Plant
Plant caladiums outdoors after all danger of frost has passed. Soil must be porous and well drained. Pot up tubers in early spring to force in a warm room. Buy the largest tubers and plant 3 per 6-inch pot. Set 1 inch deep in sterile soilless seed-starting mix and place in a warm, well-lighted room. Water sparingly twice a week. When the pointed shoots emerge, apply a water-soluble fertilizer weekly until the caladiums are ready to transplant in spring. Many garden centers offer pots of pre-sprouted tubers. In landscape beds, caladiums do best in morning sun or dappled shade. Spade in organic matter where soils are sandy or contain clay. Mix in 3 cups of 10-10-10 for each 100 square feet of bed, or use bulb fertilizer per label rate before planting. Place the bulbs 1 to 3 inches deep, and water the beds to encourage sprouting.

Growing Tips
Caladiums love water. Water container-grown plants 2 to 3 times a week in summer and fall. Water bedded plants once a week, more often during the hot summer months. Look for signs of wilting as a watering indicator. Fertilize plants in containers or color bowls with water-soluble 20-20-20 analysis every other week; water monthly in landscape beds. If dry fertilizer is broadcast on top of the soil, water promptly and thoroughly to avoid foliage burn.

Care
Remove the insignificant bloom pods during the growing season. Slugs or snails can spoil new foliage; use a snail bait that is labeled "safe for children and pets." After frost, cut back the leaves, lift the tubers, and dust with sulfur or a similar fungicide before storing them in a dry, cool place for winter. Store tubers in dry peat moss.

Companion Planting and Design
Caladiums make great backdrops for shady borders of impatiens and forget-me-nots. Use them in containers with cascading ivies or in window boxes. The white varieties make a strong visual statement in a shady nook or dull green area of the garden.

Our Personal Favorites
'Florida Sweetheart' is both vigorous and sun tolerant. 'Rose Bud' is dramatic in pots.

Canna

Canna × generalis

When, Where, and How to Plant

Plant rhizomes when soil warms in spring. Seeds of the 'Tropical Red' variety can be sown indoors in late winter. Cannas need sun and well drained soil. The frost-tender rhizomes may not overwinter in the mountain region. Elsewhere, cold-damaged rhizomes can recover and send up sprouts later in the season. Plant cannas in well-tilled garden soil. Mix 10-10-10 fertilizer into the soil at a rate of 2 pounds per 100 square feet or add a bulb-booster plant food during soil preparation. Cover the rhizomes with 2 inches of soil or use 4 inches of well-aged compost for backfill. Firm-in the rhizomes by hand or foot, then water the bed thoroughly. Keep the soil moist until the stalks reach 1 foot in height. Water only lightly until the shoots break the ground.

Growing Tips

Water cannas generously once the leaves are full grown. Use a deep mulch of leaf compost for maintaining large beds. If the plants will be irrigated, fertilize with an all-purpose plant food every six weeks until early September. Too much nitrogen will result in great foliage but few blossoms.

Care

Some varieties are irresistible to Japanese beetles. Shake the foliage routinely in June and catch the beetles in a pail of soapy water. Canna leaf roller caterpillars can distort leaves. Cut off the affected leaf or apply an insecticide. North of Zone 7, dig up the rhizomes in November and store inside at 45 degrees Fahrenheit. If you like to gamble, cover the clumps before winter with a bushel basket stuffed with straw or leaves. Prune off the old foliage and mulch in spring.

Companion Planting and Design

Plant cannas in groups or massed in single colors. Their coarse foliage is a good backdrop for fine-textured perennials and ornamental grasses. Grow as a seasonal screen in a border. Variegated cannas are fabulous accent plants in landscapes or large containers.

Our Personal Favorite

The foliage of 'Bengal Tiger' is extraordinary.

Few herbaceous perennials will catch your eye like cannas. The flowers are large and showy and grow on upright plants that resemble miniature banana trees. Their flowering frenzy lasts until hard frost in November. The biggest canna concern in the western half of the Carolinas is winter hardiness, although these are not finicky plants and are resilient despite weather-related stresses. Cannas reached stardom when numerous mass plantings were done along interstates to prepare for the Olympic Festival in the 1980s. Thousands have been planted since then, beautifying our roadsides. They are spectacular, especially when canna and crape myrtle bloom periods overlap. New canna cultivars have dazzling leaf colors as well as bicolored flowers. Cannas are enjoying a revival and are here to stay!

Bloom Period and Seasonal Color
Red, yellow, pink, or bicolors from summer to first frost.

Mature Height × Spread
2 to 6 ft. × 1 to 3 ft.

Crinum
Crinum sp.

Crinums are great summer-flowering bulbs. Survivors can be found around old homesteads across the South. This member of the amaryllis family is one of the more cold-hardy bulbs and can be safely planted in the eastern mountain regions. The fragrant flowers of crinum resemble those of the common Easter lily but are a bit smaller. Each tubular pink bloom is about four inches long and has a characteristic rose-red stripe on each petal. Up to fifteen flowers are clustered atop each rigid stalk. The South African crinum, C. moorei 'Schmidtii', a white-flowering variety, is especially adapted to the heat and summer rainfall of Zone 8b. You will be delighted with numerous late-summer surprises when you plant crinums in a moist garden spot.

Other Common Name
Milk and Wine Lily

Bloom Period and Seasonal Color
Summer blooms in pink, white, red, and bicolor.

Mature Height × Spread
2 to 3 ft. × equal spread

When, Where, and How to Plant
Plant April through late October. Offsets (suckers or pups) can be removed from the mother bulb for planting in summer. Crinums thrive in sun, provided the soil is moist, or in filtered shade. When planted facing the south sun, the foliage will look rather shabby when the plant goes into summer dormancy. Add large quantities of organic matter (sphagnum peat moss or organic soil conditioner) to sandy or gravelly soils. Bulbs are quite large, requiring a deeply spaded planting hole. Spade up an area at least 1 square foot per bulb and mix in bulb-booster fertilizer as the label directs. Space the bulbs 2 feet apart, planting each with its long neck prominently visible above ground. Watering is not necessary at planting time. Once planted, they should be left undisturbed for many years. If they're planted in a sunny bed, mulch thinly.

Growing Tips
Water weekly during the bloom period if there is a lack of rainfall. Newly planted crinums need a season or two before they begin blooming freely. Apply a flower fertilizer or compost in mid-May each year after the first flowering season. In fall, top-dress plantings with organic mulch or rotted manure to keep them vigorous. Sparse flowering is a symptom of too much shade or planting too deeply.

Care
Crinums have been stalwarts of Southern gardens for generations, since they tolerate ordinary soils. There are no serious pests, just weeds. Use a grass preventer, or hand-cultivate for weed control. Mulch is sufficient for small beds. After four to five years, remove the bulb offsets and replant them to enlarge your collection. Grow crinums in containers in cold regions and take the container inside for winter.

Companion Planting and Design
Swordlike foliage provides a pleasing contrast to finer-textured ornamentals. The species *C. moorei* grows well in a woodland shade garden along with such perennial companions as hosta, ferns, and Japanese aster.

Our Personal Favorites
Deep sea lily ('Milk and Wine') and 'Ellen Bosanquet' are suitable for most gardens.

Daffodil and Jonquil

Narcissus hybrids and *Narcissus jonquilla*

When, Where, and How to Plant

Plant after the first freeze in October or November in full sun to partial shade. While rich, friable soil is preferred, these workhorses will grow amazingly well in some pretty terrible bulb locations. Purchase high quality bulbs—only the largest and firmest—to achieve planting success. Bulbs that have 2 or 3 "noses" (segments) will produce more blooms the first year. Shop early at the garden centers in the fall or buy from mail-order nurseries. Plant as you would tulips, adding lime and phosphate to the soil if needed. Incorporate large quantities of ground pine bark into poorly drained beds. The bulbs should be covered with 2 to 4 inches of topsoil, and mulched.

Growing Tips

Newly planted bulb beds should be watered weekly during dry fall weather. Fertilize the beds in January or when new shoots appear, and again in early fall. When planting, apply 2 pounds of 10-10-10 fertilizer for a 100-square-foot bed or use special bulb fertilizer. Choose proper varieties for forcing.

Care

Remove stems after blooming but not until they have begun to turn yellow. Crowded plantings can be divided at that time. When dividing bulbs, dry them in the sun and store them until fall in a cool, dry location. For cosmetic reasons, some gardeners fold the leaves and secure them with a rubber band, but this is not recommended by experts. Poorly drained soils can result in rot diseases. Daffodils are toxic and are generally avoided by deer, voles, and other furry pests.

Companion Planting and Design

Miniatures such as 'Tête-à-Tête' make stunning rock garden plants. Combine daffodils with pansies, thrift, and candytuft in container gardens; plant bulbs to come up through ground covers.

Our Personal Favorite

'Ice Follies' has been a great performer both in the landscape and for forcing.

These hardy spring-flowering bulbs are quick to naturalize along the margins of woodland gardens. Technically, all are narcissi, but the name "jonquil" is reserved for the species with tubular leaves like chives. Narcissus flowers symbolize spring, and the bulbs adapt to a wide range of climates in the Carolinas. The bulbs grow larger each season and will grow in tight clay soils much better than most other bulbous plants. To have daffodils flowering from late winter until early summer, choose varieties that bloom during different months. If you're looking for fragrance, try the paper-whites (N. tazetta). They are intensely aromatic and are terrific for potting or for planting in borders. Purchase daffodils by the bushel to make inexpensive, magnificent spring floral displays. A Carolina Spring is not complete without daffodils.

Other Common Names
Buttercups, Jonquils

Bloom Period and Seasonal Color
Early to late spring in yellow, white, and bicolored.

Mature Height × Spread
6 to 20 in. × 4 to 8 in.

Dahlia
Dahlia × hybrida

You can choose from more than 1500 dahlia cultivars. Though the iridescent blossoms of dahlia can be as small as a nickel, some grow larger than the biggest dinner plate. This tuberous-rooted ornamental varies tremendously in color, form, and size. Some dahlia flowers are perfectly ball-shaped; others have daisy-like or cactus-shaped blossoms. Their jewel-toned brilliance is unmatched among tender perennials. The stunning blended or bicolor blooms are the result of decades of hybridization. The fast-growing succulent dahlia stems can mature at one foot or top out at over six feet in height, depending on the variety. Dahlias are native to Mexico, so they do well in the warm weather and intense sunshine of the Carolinas.

Bloom Period and Seasonal Color
Summer to fall in every imaginable color, as well as bicolors.

Mature Height × Spread
1 to 7 ft. × 8 to 24 in.

When, Where, and How to Plant
Most tall, large-flowered dahlias are grown from tubers. Quick-growing dwarf varieties are often started from seeds. Start seeds indoors in late winter. Start tubers indoors a month before the last frost date. Place tubers in large nursery pots containing soilless mix. Keep soil semi-dry until the tender shoots emerge. Move pots outdoors to a protected area and keep moist until time to transplant. Tubers can be planted directly in a sunny spot in the garden after danger of frost is past. Dahlias prefer rich, well drained soil but will grow in ordinary loam. Amend tight soils with compost or pine-bark soil conditioner to a depth of 10 inches, then spade in cow manure or slow-release flower fertilizer. Place tubers sideways about 3 inches below the soil line. Do not water before shoots appear!

Growing Tips
To ensure flowers later in the season, water consistently during dry periods. Mulch to conserve moisture. Dahlias are greedy; feed with a 10-20-20 or similar fertilizer every four to six weeks during the growing season. (Always water the day before fertilizing!) Periodically apply foliar applications of a water-soluble fertilizer containing micronutrients.

Care
Pinch shoots soon after the shoots first emerge. Pinch often for more blooms. Tall varieties require support. Combining a wire cage and a stake (like those used for growing tomatoes) is effective. Few pests other than thrips and Japanese beetles bother with this plant; consult your County Cooperative Extension Service for any necessary pest identification and control. Cut the canes back to 3 inches from the ground after frost. Lift the tubers, hose off the clinging soil, and dip in a fungicide. When thoroughly dry, store indoors for the winter in dry peat moss at 50 degrees Fahrenheit. Separate tubers in spring.

Companion Planting and Design
Tall dahlias look best as background plants in group plantings with cannas and fall-blooming perennials. The shorter annual varieties are excellent in borders, windowboxes, and containers.

Our Personal Favorites
Toby likes the dark red, bicolor 'Duet'. Jim likes 'Snowstorm'.

Lily
Lilium spp.

When, Where, and How to Plant

Plant in late fall or spring as soon as the ground thaws. Plant promptly; do not let them sit. Container-grown lilies can be planted even while in bloom. Oriental lilies will tolerate full sun in the western Carolinas, but give them afternoon shade in Zone 8. Provide the white or pastel-colored lilies with dappled shade (preferably away from trees). Grow in well drained, moist, organically rich, acidic soil. Large amounts of sphagnum peat moss or a little sulfur will acidify marginally alkaline soils. In areas where sticky clay soils predominate, lilies do well in raised beds or berms. To ensure good planting conditions, especially in clay soils, incorporate a 2- to 3-inch layer of soil conditioner and bulb fertilizer. Plant bulbs 2 to 4 inches deep. Cover them with soil, water well, and mulch.

Growing Tips

Water weekly during the flowering period, 1 inch of water per week. Keep the soil moist but avoid the overwatering that can rot the bulbs. Provided you enriched the soil with compost, your lilies will not need much in the way of nutrients. Too much nitrogen is harmful; use a bulb fertilizer.

Care

Heat causes Oriental lily flowers to be short-lived. Remember, "head in sun and feet in shade." Mulch well to conserve moisture. Cut the plants back after they bloom, leaving at least half the stem and leaves to nourish the bulb for next year. Remove anthers from cut flowers, since pollen stains fabric. Divide and transplant old established lily beds in fall. Diseases and deer are bigger threats than insects. Lily roots and stems can rot if planted in poorly drained soil. Voles will eat bulbs. After a hard freeze, prune stalks to ground level.

Companion Planting and Design

Plant lilies in groups for the best effect, and use them in containers. For color, interplant lilies with annuals like coleus and impatiens. Use the shorter, more vivid Asiatic lilies in perennial borders.

Our Personal Favorites

'Stargazer' is magnificent—the queen of bulb varieties. Asiatic lily is exceptional in sunny gardens of Zone 8.

"Consider the lilies of the field . . . ." The appeal of lilies is timeless. As far back as 1550 B.C., lilies have been revered for their exquisite flowers and heavenly fragrance. Lilies are fast-growing tender bulbs that produce erect stems and narrow lustrous leaves. During the summer months, Oriental lilies produce up to ten spectacular, often powerfully fragrant, open-faced blooms on each stalk. Oriental hybrids are considered simple to grow. The Asiatic lily is well adapted to the perennial border. Before the 1930s, only skilled plantsmen could revive the desiccated planting stock that was imported from the Far East. Today, with our modern storage capabilities and new hybrid lily varieties, these delightful bulbs are available to all gardeners, all during the planting season.

Bloom Period and Seasonal Color

From May to September in colors ranging from white to yellow, orange, gold, pink, and red.

Mature Height × Spread

3 to 7 ft. × 8 to 15 in.

Magic Lily
Lycoris squamigera

One of the first signs of new life following a mid-July rain-storm is the sudden appearance of the long, green, leafless stems of magic lilies. The flower stems each bear up to seven three-inch, trumpet-shaped, lavender-pink flowers. They are not only visually spectacular but also mildly fragrant as well. Magic lilies are cold-hardy and can survive 20-below-zero winters in states to the north. They may be left in the ground for eight years or more without dividing. Unlike the common red spider lily (L. radiata) that produces fall foliage after blooming, magic lilies sport their leaves in spring. The two-foot-long, dull green leaves wither and die as the warm days arrive. Plant magic lilies where they can be observed frequently as the blooming drama unfolds.

Other Common Names
Surprise Lily, Naked Ladies

Bloom Period and Seasonal Color
Pink blooms in July and August.

Mature Height × Spread
24 in. × 15 in.

When, Where, and How to Plant
Plant bulbs in summer. Magic lilies prefer a deep, humus-conditioned soil, but any quick-draining soil should do fine. Morning-sun locations are perfect. Spade an area 15 by 15 inches for each trio of bulbs. Mix soil amendments and bulb-booster fertilizer to a depth of 10 inches. Place 3 bulbs in the planting hole, spacing them 6 or more inches apart. Cover the bulbs with 4 to 5 inches of easily-crumbled soil. Water well after planting to settle the soil. Before planting in difficult, shallow soils, build the soil by stockpiling layers of leaves and topsoil on the beds. The decomposing leaves will raise the soil level and increase the life expectancy of your bed.

Growing Tips
Magic lilies don't need a great deal of water. Water only during the bloom period and when there is a dry period in spring. Fertilize when the foliage appears, using a complete fertilizer such as 10-10-10, scattering it over the bed at a rate of 1 pound per 100 square feet. If using bulb-booster fertilizer, apply at a rate of $1/2$ cup per 10 square feet.

Care
Mark planting locations to avoid accidentally digging up or damaging bulbs. Prune back foliage after leaves yellow in late spring, and divide. Bulbs can be lifted and air-dried, and replanted in June. Lycoris doesn't like to be moved and can take a couple of years to bloom again. Remove flower stalks after blooms fade. There are no serious insect pests. In Zone 8 counties, red spider lily is the more dependable bloomer.

Companion Planting and Design
The strap-like leaves complement hostas, autumn ferns, and Japanese anemones. Plant in an entrance bed or by a terrace or patio. Naturalize along a woodland walk. Magic lilies are elegant, whether planted in groups or in ground covers. Bloom stems popping out of mum beds or low ground covers in summer is truly magical!

Our Personal Favorite
They are all so special, like the 'Peppermint' cultivar. Experiment with the Chinese introductions.

When, Where, and How to Plant

Plant bulbs between the first frost and Thanksgiving. Adequate root systems must develop before the ground freezes. Given sun and fertile, well drained soil, tulips are generally very easy to grow. Loose, well drained soil is more important for tulips than for most other bulbs—a complete new bulb must form for the plant to bloom again or perennialize. Plant tulips in raised beds or borders. Ideal soil pH is 5.4 to 7.0. Spade soil to a depth of 12 inches and add generous quantities of pine-bark soil conditioner. Use bulb-booster fertilizer at the recommended rate. Tulips can be planted in a trench in the border or in groups of 9 to 15 for the best effect. Plant the bulbs 4 to 6 inches deep and 5 inches apart. Water the bed and mulch well.

Growing Tips

Water beds during drought. Fertilize tulip beds twice each year, first in mid-September then again when the plants emerge in late winter. Use a bulb fertilizer such as 9-9-6 at a rate of $2^1/2$ pounds per 100 square feet of bed. For large bulb plantings, one application of bulb-booster in early fall will suffice. Remove weeds before they set seeds and multiply.

Care

Cut back foliage when it dies back and turns yellow. Bulbs can be divided at that time. Discard the weak ones and dry the rest in the sun for a week or so. Store bulbs in a cool basement until planting. Many gardeners have lost tulip bulbs to voles. Use snap traps, poisons, or sharp gravel in beds to control them.

Companion Planting and Design

Tulips show best when planted *en masse* using a single color and interplanted with pansies or violas. Fancy double-flowered hybrids are gorgeous in planters and used as cut flowers. Plant along a path or at the edge of a water garden.

Our Personal Favorites

'Apeldoorn' is a red Darwin hybrid that returns well. The double-flowered 'Angelique' is a real show-stopper.

In fifteenth-century Netherlands, when elitist Europeans lusted after exotic flowers, three tulip bulbs could be sold to pay for a house. Now sensational tulip bulbs are three-for-a-dollar. With hundreds of tulip varieties to choose from, the color opportunities are boundless. Varieties include peony-flowered, singles, fringed, parrot, and the diminutive species tulips that grow to only six inches tall. The biggest and showiest of all the tulips are the Darwin hybrids. It was long felt that it was just "too hot" in the South for tulips, but studies conducted at North Carolina State University led to the formulation of a special bulb fertilizer and a list of tulip cultivars that are dependable when planted in the Carolinas. However, mild winters can produce freaky-looking tulips that hold their blooms at ground level in a cup of leaves.

Bloom Period and Seasonal Color
Early to late spring in all colors.

Mature Height × Spread
6 to 24 in. × 4 to 8 in.

Flowering Vines *for the Carolinas*

The popularity of vines continues to grow as rapidly as the plants themselves. Gardeners are always looking for a quick fix when they need instant shade or want to hide an unsightly area. Vines fit the bill in both cases. Beautiful vines, like the spring-flowering clematis, are the pride of seasoned gardeners. Others, like the climbing hydrangea, provide a burst of color in the off-season when little else is in bloom.

The Two Sides of Vines

Being a Carolina resident may affect your opinion of vines. We are all too familiar with the poor examples around us—namely, kudzu and poison ivy. With these two out of mind, there are some fine native vines that can be found across the state. Carolina jessamine, the state flower of South Carolina, serves both as groundcover and an evergreen vine; its pure yellow flowers are a welcome sight in late winter and early spring.

Vines offer diverse visual qualities and are valued for the rich texture of their foliage. Some, like wisteria, perfume the evening air with delightful fragrances. Others, such as moonvine, evoke mystery and wonder as they open spontaneously in the evening. Cross vine and trumpet honeysuckle attract hummingbirds and provide nesting sites for songbirds. Though most woody vines are deciduous, a few old-fashioned evergreen favorites, like smilax and armand clematis, can be found in many landscapes.

Vines can soften the architecture of a home and cool a harsh leisure area by a patio. Vines are a must on a decorative arbor or trellis where they can add a vertical dimension as well as seasonal flowers. Lamp-posts and mailboxes can serve as supports for a host of showy vines. Even Master Gardeners have gotten hooked on tender vines because of their rampant growth and color. The tropical mandevilla vine is a favorite for trellises and mailboxes. Unfortunately, it is not hardy away from the coast, but when grown as an annual it flowers early and continuously.

Clematis and Roses

If You Give Them an Inch . . .

A vine has a mind of its own. One will refuse to climb a trellis in spite of much coaxing, while another will gallop up a tree trunk unaided. Every vine employs a unique mechanism for clinging; many have special plant tissues for this physical attachment. Clematis clings by way of leafy stems that twine around posts and arbors. Climbing hydrangeas and English ivy form "roots" on their branches that act like tiny suction cups, giving them an advantage on a brick or stone wall. A wisteria's twining stem growth ensures a tight hold on anything that crosses its path. Whether twining in a clockwise or counterclockwise direction, a vine has a "plan" to reach its destination and make its presence known.

Get to know a vine's requirements before planting one in the garden. It will save work in the long run. Vines are frequently planted in cramped spaces. Don't be shy about pruning them—they need some

handholding. They're like toddlers . . .
give them an inch and they will take a
mile. Much like shrubs, perennial flowering vines are best pruned immediately
after they finish blooming.

Versatile Vines

If commonplace ornamental vines do
not excite you, consider a tender annual
vine for the landscape. Annual vines grow
quickly and can add marvelous color
while inviting bees and butterflies to the
garden. If you want edible plants, kiwis
and muscadine grapes will be right at
home on a sturdy arbor in your garden.

Whether flowering or evergreen,
vines are versatile ornamental plants that
are still waiting to be discovered. They
can be planted in so many wonderful
locations. A vine may be just the thing
that your garden needs as "icing on
the cake."

Planting Directions for Vines

Woody or tropical vines are sold in one to
five-gallon containers. Loosen the roots of

Wisteria

the plant, especially if it is a potbound specimen. Shake at least half the soil off the roots and prune back
the longest roots to encourage faster establishment. Dig a planting hole as deep as the depth of the rootball and three times as wide. Mix a five-gallon bucket full of an organic soil conditioner, such as dried
cow manure, with the excavated soil. Add two cups of pelleted dolomitic limestone and a couple of
tablespoons of slow-release flower fertilizer, or use a phosphorus-rich organic fertilizer. Firm-in the roots
with the conditioned backfill soil, and water thoroughly. Put down a two-inch layer of compost or mulch
to enrich the soil. Water twice a week for the first month.

Annual vines such as morning glory or moonvine grow best if direct-seeded where the plants are to
remain. There is no advantage to starting with young plants; in fact, annual vine seedlings are difficult
to transplant. Soak seeds overnight in tepid water just before planting. In clay soils make low mounds
(hills) by mixing a five-gallon bucket of play sand and a bucket of dried cow manure with an equal
volume of clay. Add slow-release fertilizer and an organic fertilizer such as cottonseed meal per directions
on the packages. Skip the play sand in sandy soils, of course. Provide strings for the vines to run; they
will begin twining within a week of emergence. Annual vines will climb like homesick angels!

Carolina Jessamine

Gelsemium sempervirens

This native evergreen vine with bright yellow flowers is a great choice for a sunny spot. Though the flowers of Carolina jessamine are small, they appear in clusters, making a great show against the glossy foliage. The dark green leaves are lance-shaped and arranged opposite each other on rich brown stems. In the eastern Carolinas, Carolina jessamine also grows as a groundcover in woodlands where it can make its way up to the very top of understory trees. It is not overly invasive; it has a distinct fragrance and often flowers sporadically in the fall. Certain cultivars were selected for fall blooming. A real novelty is the double-flowered variety. This plant will thrive for many years in the right location. Don't confuse jessamine with jasmine; they are in no way related.

Bloom Period and Seasonal Color
In winter and spring, bright yellow flowers.

Mature Length
20 ft.

When, Where, and How to Plant

Carolina jessamine can be planted anytime from containers. If planting in fall, allow time for it to establish to avoid winter injury and burned foliage. Small transplants should be set in spring. Plant in sunny or shaded locations. It prefers moist, rich soil. This vine climbs high including, to the consternation of utility company workers, to the tops of power poles.

Growing Tips

Water deeply during dry summers. This vine is very drought-resistant once established. Fertilize with a high-phosphorus 15-30-15 fertilizer in September. Use water-soluble fertilizers monthly for rapid growth when establishing jessamine. **A word of caution:** All parts of the plant are poisonous to livestock, pets, and people.

Care

Carolina jessamine has no tendrils for clinging and must be tied to supports. Construct a trellis for this twining vine. Flowers come in spring on new growth, so early summer is the appropriate time to prune. Remove weak or dying twigs anytime. As the plant matures, lower branches will be shaded out and may die off; this is normal for vigorous vines on trellises. Overgrown specimens can be pruned severely in early March to invigorate the wood. Some root-pruning in early fall may help contain rampant growth. No serious pest problems are encountered.

Companion Planting and Design

Carolina jessamine cascading over a wall or fence makes an effective screen. Plant it on fences, arbors, or mailboxes, or next to the trunk of an established tree with open branching to admit light. The glossy vines look good all year. Jessamine makes a good groundcover if properly maintained, but the tangle of vines complicates leaf-raking.

Our Personal Favorites

'Pride of Augusta' is a prolific bloomer with double flowers. Swamp jessamine, *G. rankinii*, blooms in both fall and spring but is not fragrant.

Chinese Trumpetvine
Campsis grandiflora

When, Where, and How to Plant

Plant container-grown Chinese trumpetvine in early spring or fall. In the mountain region, plant after the last hard frost in spring. Sunny locations with well-drained soil are ideal. An arbor or west-facing fence is preferred. Chinese trumpetvines are grown in containers and are quite simple to plant. To establish a tree-form trumpetvine, set a 10-foot, 6 × 6 treated wood post $2^{1}/_{2}$ feet deep in the ground on a footing of ready-mix concrete. Fill in around it with tamped gravel. Plant the vine per directions (see introduction) and secure it to the post with plastic plant ties. Prune off side branches. When it reaches the top of the post, begin pruning off descending branches to make an umbrella-form canopy.

Growing Tips

Water deeply during dry summers; trumpetvines are drought-tolerant once established. Fertilize with a bloom-booster in late March. Too much nitrogen will mean more pruning and fewer flowers.

Care

The vine will need training; use masonry nails and sturdy wire on brick surfaces. Chinese trumpetvine flowers in the summer on new growth; delay pruning until early summer after flowering. When approaching maturity, the lower branches will be shaded out and may die off. Remove weak or dying twigs anytime. Prune overgrown specimens severely in early March to control their size and invigorate the wood. In the mountain region, this vine is not hardy above 3000 feet. Your plant may not bloom the first year or two until it matures.

Companion Planting and Design

Plant this deciduous vine as a summer screen or backdrop for a perennial border. Its main use is as an accent on a sturdy pergola or trellis.

Our Personal Favorites

'Morning Calm' is the Raulston Arboretum introduction bearing 3-inch orange-coral flowers with glossy foliage. 'Madame Galen', a hybrid trumpet creeper, is popular in Zone 8 gardens.

Chinese trumpetvine was the first vine selected for the North Carolina Association of Nurserymen Plant Introduction Program. It bears large, stunning, apricot to orange colored flowers. It is a strong grower, and is recommended for growing as a standard in tree form. It does not cling by aerial roots as does its weedy, overly-robust cousin, American trumpetvine. Chinese trumpetvine needs a substantial support to grow on; it is excellent on a garden arbor or similar structure but not on a house or outbuilding. When exposed to direct sunlight, this vine blooms heavily in early summer. Removal of seed heads will revitalize it and encourage even more flowering. This showy deciduous vine with its petunia-shaped blossoms and large compound leaves is appealing to gardeners and to hummingbirds.

Bloom Period and Seasonal Color
Spring and summer, orange to apricot blooms.

Mature Length
20 to 30 ft.

Clematis
Clematis spp.

There is a clematis for every garden. Select from types with cloudbursts of small fragrant flowers or huge blooms 6 inches in diameter. Deciduous clematis needs support for best display. Some species climb better than others, by means of leaf stems that wind around a trellis. The uncommon, spring-blooming C. armandii has long, leathery leaves that make it a marvelous evergreen vine for the arbor or a wall espalier. Its deep-green leaves and 2 inch, fragrant white flowers put on quite a show. Probably the most commonly grown clematis is Jackman, known for its pinwheel-shaped, violet-purple flowers. If pruned properly, the vines may have a second round of flowers in the fall. Another favorite is sweet autumn clematis, which perfumes the air with its sprays of sweet-smelling, lacy, white flowers in late summer.

Bloom Period and Seasonal Color
May, June, or August blooms in pure white and pink to rich red, mauve, and purple.

Mature Length
6 to 25 ft.

When, Where, and How to Plant
Both fall and spring plantings of container-grown clematis will work fine. The vines like their roots in the cool shade and their foliage in warm sunlight. This is a proven fact; just try planting clematis in full sun without shading its roots and you will get the point. Clematis likes moist, well-drained soil that is very fertile, and it will grow for decades in a good location. Follow the planting instructions in the chapter introduction to ensure quick establishment and long life for your clematis vine. Vigorous sweet autumn clematis can grow in virtually any location and does not benefit materially from special soil preparation.

Growing Tips
Keep the soil moist around your clematis during active growth and bloom periods. Add organic fertilizer in spring and summer, and lime periodically. Withhold fertilizer from October to February. Replenish mulch annually.

Care
Vines are easily trained to a trellis with bamboo stakes and plastic (not wire core) "twist-ties" or plastic tape. On a brick or rock wall, use masonry nails and run supporting wires over heavy picture-frame hooks. Prune to thin vines or to confine growth. Prune spring-flowering types immediately after flowering since their buds are formed in fall. Cut shoots back to two leaf buds. Late-summer bloomers can be pruned in early spring. Remove rangy twigs to keep the vine groomed, as older plants need thinning. The worst disease is a stem rot fungus that occurs in wet soils. Don't replant in the same spot; move to higher ground. Control aphids with horticultural oil.

Companion Planting and Design
Posts on decks serve as a trellis; other possible structures include wooden lattices, arbors, chain-link fences, mailboxes, and lampposts. Underplant trellised vines with shallow-rooted groundcovers, or shade the roots with a 6-inch mulch of pine straw.

Our Personal Favorite
'Nelly Moser' has huge 7-inch flowers with pale pink petals set off with red bars.

Climbing Hydrangea
Hydrangea anomala ssp. *petiolaris*

When, Where, and How to Plant

Plant climbing hydrangea from March until May or in late September. Climbing hydrangeas thrive in sun or shade but flower more consistently with a few hours of direct sunlight daily. An eastern or northern exposure is ideal. A hot, dry site will frustrate this vine—not to mention the impatient gardener! Amend gravelly soils with aged compost or peat moss. Train climbing hydrangeas up trees with an open framework of branches. Planting near a tree trunk requires frequent watering and feeding during establishment and periods of drought.

Growing Tips

Keep the soil moist the first year after planting because establishment may take some time. Mulch to conserve moisture and enrich soil. When planted in a sunny location by masonry, it needs water for several seasons or until it is well established. To encourage upward growth, secure vines to bamboo stakes with twist-ties. Or, construct a sturdy trellis to create a free-standing plant. For general care, irrigate your vine every ten days in dry periods, applying 1 inch of water (5 to 7 gallons). Apply a slow-release flower fertilizer (14-7-7 analysis) in spring or fall.

Care

Both drought and heat predispose the plant to spider mite infestations. Spray sharp blasts of water above and below leaves, apply insecticidal soap or a miticide, or use a pump sprayer that has never contained any herbicide. Prune immediately after bloom. Prune severely in late winter. Vines tolerate cooler, shaded locations in Zone 8 gardens.

Companion Planting and Design

Climbing hydrangeas appear most frequently in rustic settings cascading over a garden wall. Specimens can be trained to brick garden walls, provided they are planted on the shady (north) side. When erecting a trellis, use big timbers since the vines bulk up over time.

Our Personal Favorites

Climbing hydrangea and Japanese hydrangea-vine (*Schizophragma hydrangeoides*) are very attractive. You may have to turn to a native plant supplier to obtain *Decumaria barbara*.

In the South, climbing hydrangea is a "rare jewel" with four-season interest. There is no better clinging vine for softening a stark brick wall. This vine grows slowly in the early years, but once established, climbing hydrangea can grow 2 feet every year in the cooler western Carolina region. In warmer areas, the native Decumaria barbara, also called climbing hydrangea, grows better and is equally pretty. As summer approaches, magnificent white flower clusters appear. These flowers are similar to the lacecap hydrangeas except the 6 to 10-inch-diameter showy white blooms are mildly fragrant. In addition to the flower clusters, the stems of this ornamental delight for years to come—as fall arrives, the leaves drop and the handsome bronze exfoliating bark becomes visible.

Bloom Period and Seasonal Color
June and July white flat-topped blooms.

Mature Length
40 to 60 ft.

Cross Vine

Bignonia capreolata

The cross vine is a native of the Carolinas where it has evergreen to semi-evergreen foliage, depending on minimum winter temperatures. It is a twining plant common to warm, moist woodlands where it can climb to 50 feet. Cross vine gets its name from the leaves crossing over to latch onto things. The orange-red, 2-inch, trumpet-shaped flowers are fragrant and attractive to hummingbirds. Cross vine will bear a profusion of blooms, completely obscuring the foliage, when located in full sun. Most homeowners who seek cross vine desire fast growth and will be delighted by the plant's growth rate, especially if shade is wanted for your special garden arbor. It develops "hold-fast" anchors and is not recommended for running up walls of clapboard or shingled structures.

Bloom Period and Seasonal Color
In spring and early summer, orange-red blooms; in winter, leaves take on purplish color.

Mature Length
30 to 50 ft.

When, Where, and How to Plant

Plant cross vine in spring or fall. This vine tolerates a wide range of soil conditions from average dry clays to wet coastal soil. The best site has an organically rich, well-drained soil in a sunny location. The addition of a trellised cross vine enhances shade gardens, though you will have to settle for only a few flowers. It is important to follow the soil preparation instructions in the chapter introduction because cross vine is long-lived and needs your help to get off to a strong start.

Growing Tips

Keep the soil moist for the first season. During periods of drought, cross vine benefits from a deep irrigation every couple of weeks. Apply a general garden fertilizer like 10-10-10 in March during the second season and in the years to come. Spread $1/2$-cup of fertilizer in a circle beginning 2 feet out from the basal stem. Apply 3 inches of any organic mulch as hot weather approaches.

Care

Cross vine has "hold-fasts," little disks at the ends of tendrils and rootlets, that act as suction cups to help it cling to brick and stone walls. You will need to tie the vine to an arbor or support to prevent it from lying on the ground initially. When growing up a tree, cross vine clings tightly, giving a pleasant appearance. Prune this vigorous vine after it flowers and as often as is necessary to train it to a garden structure or support. It is pest free.

Companion Planting and Design

When in bloom, cross vine instantly attracts the attention of all who pass by your garden. Plant it for screening and shade. Place it on a fence or stone wall in the sun, or just let it sprawl over an old stump.

Our Personal Favorites

'Tangerine Beauty' is a superb North Carolina State University Selection bearing rich, ruby-tangerine flowers. 'Jekyll', a red cultivar, is especially vigorous in warm climes.

Five-Leaf Akebia

Akebia quinata

When, Where, and How to Plant

Plant akebias any time the ground can be worked. They are not at all fussy about soil type or location. Plant in full sun or partial shade. When growing for fruit, get a second plant to ensure pollination. Allow 15 feet between plantings, and provide a support for the vines. Most people prefer five-leaf akebia for its ornamental value and vigorous growth when planted on arbors and walls. If you espalier it, prune off all but the framework shoots and open up the foliage by judicious pruning.

Growing Tips

Mulch as summer approaches, and water during dry periods for the first season. It never hurts to sprinkle $^1/_2$ cup of pelletized limestone around hardy vines every three years. Fertilize your planting every spring with a slow-release plant food for a few years, and only as needed thereafter.

Care

Pruning should be done immediately after flowers drop. Fall pruning reduces the number of flowers, and thus fruit production, which may be unwanted. Prune to control rampant or errant growth. Remove dead and weak branches that have been shaded out over time. If you plant near a house, you will need to prune regularly to keep the growth off the roof and out of the gutters. Wear good-quality gloves when pruning vines in late summer since stinging caterpillars may hide on the undersides of foliage. Remedy aphid infestations with an application of horticultural oil or a sharp spray of water.

Companion Plantings and Design

Five-leaf akebia is a rapid grower covering arbors, fences, pergolas, or the side of an unsightly shed. To avoid messy fruit or stains, do not plant near a walk or patio. Crape myrtle, butterfly bush, and abelia are nice companion plants.

Our Personal Favorites

The unimproved species is the most readily available, but both the white-flowering 'Alba' and the slower-growing 'Variegata' selections are great finds.

If your garden has plenty of space, then five-leaf akebia is the plant to choose. Versatile and rugged, it works well as a groundcover or trellised specimen; it scales walls, provides shade, and has mildly fragrant flowers. The semi-evergreen, dark blue-green foliage offers multi-season interest in the landscape. The large, edible fruit can be a disadvantage for this rampant grower. Not all vines bear fruit, nor do fruiting vines produce every year. Landscape professionals are always searching for a vine that can tolerate poor soils and hot locations. Five-leaf akebia may be a viable solution for new home sites. These twining vines ask for so little—just a place to grow.

Other Common Name
Chocolate Vine

Bloom Period and Seasonal Color
In summer, small, dark purple flowers; airy blue-green foliage until frost.

Mature Length
20 to 40 ft.

Japanese Wisteria
Wisteria floribunda

Wisteria can be bittersweet. This deciduous vine is a rampant grower all across the Carolinas, and some rural folk would put wisteria and kudzu in the same category. But under strict management, Japanese wisteria can be a gem in the spring garden. It is best trained in tree form (see Chinese trumpetvine). It showcases attractive gray bark and abundant, grapelike racemes blooming with lilac-colored or white flowers. Flowers appear before the large compound leaves, and the display is spectacular. W. frutescens 'Alba', a later-blooming cultivar, is less susceptible to late-spring frosts. The Japanese wisteria flowers longer than its Chinese counterpart, W. sinensis. Investigate our native W. frutescens. It bears stubby clusters of lavender blooms after Japanese wisteria color is past, and its vines are much less robust.

Bloom Period and Seasonal Color
Spring blooms in white, lilac, red-violet, and purple.

Mature Length
20 to 30 ft.

When, Where, and How to Plant
Plant in late winter or fall. Suckers from the roots of established plants can be dug and moved when dormant. Wisterias are difficult to transplant during active growth periods. For the best flowers, plant in a sunny site. The plants grow well in filtered shade, provided you give careful supervision and pruning. Don't hesitate to lightly prune roots of container-grown plants; this prevents girdling and encourages root extension. Wisterias are not fussy about soil type—just provide light. If you already have an arbor or fence, you're ready to plant. A cedar or treated wood post circled with a welded-wire cage provides a cost-effective, durable support for this fast-growing vine.

Growing Tips
Water twice a week for the first two weeks, then every ten days for a month thereafter. Irrigate established plants during dry periods if growth is active. These vines are very drought-tolerant. Provide organic or slow-release fertilizer immediately following the bloom period in late spring for the first season or two. Over-fertilizing causes rangy growth and few flowers; in general, established wisterias do not need fertilizing.

Care
In late spring, prune back the twigs to 8-inch stubs. Continue with this practice throughout the year. By mid-August, cease pruning and fertilizing to preserve the flower buds. Remove the basal suckers from the tree forms in late summer to prevent regrowth; prune severely after the flowers fade. Wisterias are pest-free. Many self-sow, creating the chore of seedling removal that's best handled by hand; don't delay, remove them promptly.

Companion Planting and Design
Wisterias are wonderful when planted on pergolas, arbors, and gazebos but not on clapboard or shingled structures. They are grown on posts as standard or tree-form vines in small gardens. Many big porches in the South sport a well-groomed vine.

Our Personal Favorite
The native, *W. frutescens* 'Amethyst Falls', is not invasive and is a repeat-bloomer bearing small clusters.

Jasmine
Jasminum spp.

When, Where, and How to Plant

Set out container-grown jasmine or Confederate jasmine during the late spring or summer. Plant fragrant species where sweet smells will waft over leisure areas but not so close that it becomes cloying. Follow the planting instructions in the chapter introduction. While a flower-bedecked arbor is a show-stopper, the glossy, dark green foliage shows to good effect after the blooms have come and gone. Confederate jasmine survives winter better if it is grown as a groundcover, especially under high shade from evergreen trees.

Growing Tips

Jasmine requires little care other than feeding in spring and again in late summer. It is difficult to determine feeding rates on vines. The safest procedure is to water the soil deeply, wait a day, and drench the area around the plants with liquid fertilizer.

Care

You will lose some growth to freezing. When new growth starts in late spring, prune off dead stems. Lime your vines every other year, or yearly on sandy soils. Work 1 or 2 cups of pelletized dolomitic limestone into the soil around vines. At the same time, work 2 or 3 cups of organic fertilizer into the soil or drill it into a furrow encircling the plant 2 feet out from its base. Prune vines to keep them in bounds.

Companion Planting and Design

Prominent plants of angel's trumpet look good in front of jasmine on arbors. In Zone 8 gardens, try Confederate jasmine as groundcover with summer-blooming bulbs of the species *Lycoris radiata*. Train this vine to a trellis only in a protected spot in Piedmont gardens. To enjoy its fragrance, many gardeners locate a container plant in a greenhouse or sunroom.

Our Personal Favorites

The evergreen Confederate jasmine is a Tar Heel favorite. You may be able to find tender Arabian jasmine, *J. sambac,* perhaps the most fragrant of all. Its white flowers age to pink. Spanish jasmine *J. officinale grandiflorum* has larger flowers.

Confusion reigns in this large and diverse genus. Many jasmines are shrubby, and few are fragrant. True jasmine, the summer-blooming J. officinale, *is the most popular vining species with fragrant, white flowers; it lacks hardiness outside Zone 8. The second most popular is a different species, Confederate jasmine,* Trachelospermum jasminoides *(meaning jasmine-like). It has intensely fragrant white flowers and is hardy in protected areas in Zone 7. Gardeners often grow it as a groundcover. White-flowered star or downy jasmine will not survive Zone 7 winters without deep pine straw mulch. It has little fragrance and sets its blooms in many-flowered clusters. Plant labels are not always accurate. Your best bet for finding the right jasmine for your landscape is to check the actual plants for form and fragrance. Consult your nearest botanical garden for hardiness ratings.*

Other Common Name
Poet's Jasmine (*J. officinale*)

Bloom Period and Seasonal Color
Throughout summer, white flowers.

Mature Length
To 30 ft.

Moonvine

Ipomoea alba

Almost everyone is familiar with the morning glory vine. A lesser-known annual member of the family, moonvine, is just as intriguing. The major difference is that moonvine reserves its beautiful fragrant blooms for evening. It has saucer-sized white blooms that open each night. You can plan a "Moon Party" in this plant's honor, with the unfurling of its flowers as the grand finale. In a matter of a few minutes, the huge, fragrant blossoms unfurl from twisted buds. You can expect the nightly spectacle to occur in late evening but certainly before midnight. The lush summer foliage is a medium-green color with six- to eight-inch heart-shaped leaves. Plant this annual vine near a patio where you can appreciate its beauty; it requires a trellis or fence for support.

Other Common Name
Moonflower

Bloom Period and Seasonal Color
Summer into autumn, white evening blooms.

Mature Length
20-plus ft.

When, Where, and How to Plant
Sow seeds directly in the garden after danger of frost has passed. If you start 3 seeds per 1-gallon nursery pot indoors in late winter, you will have a longer bloom period when they're set outdoors. Nick seeds with a file or sandpaper for better germination or soak them overnight in water before planting. Moonvine grows best with at least a half-day of direct sun. This vine does not transplant well, so start the plant where it is to grow for the season.

Growing Tips
Water well during the first few weeks and in very dry periods. Apply a liquid plant fertilizer every two weeks. Be sure you use an analysis for flowering plants, such as a 15-30-15 or bloom-booster. In very poor soils, maintain a 3-inch layer of leaf compost around the base of the vine in a 2-foot circle.

Care
Provide support and training. Dig out the roots after a killing autumn frost. In coastal areas, moonvine is a tender perennial. In these regions, prune heavily in late winter to shape, and remove sun-scorched twigs. Save seed by collecting it after the first frost. Store the seed in the refrigerator in envelopes sealed in a canning jar. Sow them next spring, and share a few; they are expensive when purchased. Other than root rot if the soil is too wet, moonvine is disease free.

Companion Planting and Design
Plant anywhere you want a quick cover, such as on a chain-link fence, wire trellis, deck railing, or mailbox. Moonvines will not trail; it is their nature to climb by twining. Moonvine will perfume the night air. Many other annual vines can be successfully grown in the garden for quick effect, including hyacinth bean, Spanish flag, and scarlet cypress vine.

Our Personal Favorite
There are no specific cultivars, but you may see some variation in flower color.

Trumpet Honeysuckle
Lonicera sempervirens

When, Where, and How to Plant
Trumpet honeysuckle can be planted spring through fall as soil conditions permit. Set out divisions and rooted cuttings after danger of frost in early spring. Plant in sun or a slightly shaded area in well-drained soil. This plant grows rapidly, and you need to think big. There is no need to amend well-drained soil. Firm the backfill and water thoroughly. Add 2 inches of mulch. It is best to plant trumpet honeysuckle on a sturdy trellis, and it can also be espaliered on a wall.

Growing Tips
Use an open-ended hose to water; deep irrigation is needed twice a week. (Light frequent watering would be a waste of time.) Do this until the plant's roots are established, generally in three to four weeks, or when new growth begins. Fertilize in May, if needed, with a slow release 1-2-2 ratio fertilizer developed especially for flowering plants like roses.

Care
Prune to train trumpet honeysuckle during the first season or two, then prune to control its size after the summer blooming period. Avoid severe winter pruning or the next year's flower buds may be eliminated. There are no serious insect problems, though a few aphids may appear in spring. On occasion, powdery mildew may be observed where honeysuckle vines are planted in shade gardens. If you suspect a problem, contact your County Extension Service. Don't overfertilize, or you will have too few blooms and overabundant growth.

Companion Planting and Design
Be sure to plant where you can watch the hummingbirds work the reddish-pink flowers. Your vine can be trained to a lamppost, fence, or arbor. This honeysuckle can be grown in a sizable container backed up with a trellis.

Our Personal Favorite
'Leo' is a long-blooming variety with orange-red to red flowers. There are new hybrids appearing in the trade every year, crosses between native and exotic species.

For a native vine that is hardy and attractive to hummingbirds, try trumpet honeysuckle. Most Southerners are a hard sell for this ornamental vine since the invasive evergreen Japanese honeysuckle has naturalized and over-run fields and woodlands. Unlike its weedy Asian cousin, trumpet honeysuckle behaves. This semi-evergreen vine features clusters of trumpets or tubular flowers with unmistakable fragrance. Some vines produce 1/4 inch, bright-red berries in early autumn. In warmer parts of the Piedmont and near the coast, this honeysuckle may be evergreen. It is great for the gardener who has a large area to devote to a vine. New foliage is tinged with purple and changes to a bluish green as it matures. This plant is desirable for its long blooming period, ease of culture, and drawing power for hummingbirds.

Other Common Name
Coral Honeysuckle

Bloom Period and Seasonal Color
Summer-long blooms in creamy white, yellow, gold, and orange to pink or red.

Mature Length
20 to 40 ft.

Ground Covers *for the Carolinas*

At one time, only turfgrasses were used to prevent soil erosion and to provide green in the home landscape. In the New American Garden, ground covers can be used for these purposes. Often referred to as "living mulch," ground covers are what landscape designers use to carpet our outdoor rooms. A ground cover can be defined as any dense, spreading plant that covers the ground when planted *en masse*. It can transform a barren area into a blanket of lush foliage and, if you wish, flowers as well.

The Advantages of Ground Covers

Once established, ground covers choke out most unwanted weeds, reducing maintenance in the long run. Planted either in sun or shade, they will hide the ugly knees of some taller-growing plants. They are especially handsome when placed under small specimen trees or used to edge a flower border. Flowering ground covers, such as 'Purple Homestead' verbena, hardy iceplant, and dianthus are spectacular used in groupings for seasonal color. Ground covers are excellent plants to naturalize over bulb plantings, especially surprise or spider lilies. Local gardeners find it irresistible to plant flower beds without first edging the beds with monkey grass (clumping liriope).

Many gardeners love ground covers because of the savings in "sweat equity." More and more, gardeners want to reduce the time they spend mowing their lawns. (Not only do the fumes from mowing machines affect air quality, but the annoying racket also creates noise pollution in suburban neighborhoods.) Ground covers can solve landscape design problems. The right ground cover can grow better in shaded areas than lawn grass. They are ideal for steep slopes and rocky sites that make mowing hazardous and for open areas where exposed tree roots make mowing or gardening difficult. They can help define shrub beds and add variety to woodland gardens. As a supplement to turf areas, ground covers help blend and unite the yard into a harmonious picture.

Problems

Few insect pests affect shade ground covers, but several soil diseases can injure them. Chronic stem fungi, for example, causes circular dead patches in vinca and ajuga. Prune out wilted or browning foliage early in the season and replant the spots. The problems generally disappear as the season progresses and the ground cover continues to spread. Edging beds and weed control are important elements of grooming. In the early years, weed-preventer chemicals may prove useful.

How Much Is Too Much?

One of the questions that arises when buying ground covers is: How many do I purchase, and how much space do they require? Here is a handy guide to assist you in answering these questions.

Pachysandra

Space Covered by 100 Groundcover Plants

Planting Distance Apart (in inches)	Area Covered (in square feet)	Planting Distance Apart (in inches)	Area Covered (in square feet)
6	25	30	625
12	100	36	900
18	225	48	1,600
24	400	60	2,500

(Reprinted by permission from the *Tennessee Gardener's Guide: Third Edition.*)

A major advantage of ground covers is their increasing spread and thickness that becomes more attractive each year. Your task is to prepare the soil properly for a long-lived planting. It is important to have the soil tested a couple of months prior to the project and amend it appropriately. Some soil will not need special soil conditioners, but don't make the mistake of guessing.

Directions for Planting

- A month or two prior to planting, begin killing perennial grasses with a non-selective herbicide. Two or three applications may be needed to provide a clean area for planting.
- Except beneath the canopy of trees, work the planting area with a tiller or turn the soil by hand to a depth of eight inches.
- Incorporate lime and fertilizer per your soil test report, and on heavy clay or light sandy soils, a couple of inches of organic matter as well. In the absence of a soil test, use one pound of flower fertilizer per one hundred square feet and two pounds of pelletized dolomitic limestone.
- Rake out clods and rocks, then plant at the correct spacing.
- Beneath trees, spread three layers of newsprint. Lay down three to four inches of bark mulch from the trunk to the drip line. You will find that mulching prior to planting makes things go better.
- Dig planting holes of the same depth as the container and two to three times as wide.
- Loosen the roots, snip off long or girdling roots, set the plant in place, pull the soil around it, and firm it down lightly.
- Irrigate deeply and routinely during the first season and dig out opportunistic weeds.
- Ground covers are said to sleep the first year, creep the second, and leap the third. This adage is true for hardy perennials but not for the half-hardy and annual varieties.

A Few More Tips

When planting ground covers, choose the varieties that will flourish in your particular garden. Purchase vigorous plants and prepare the soil thoroughly. Once they have settled in, your patience will be rewarded with low-maintenance plantings. Remember to keep general yard maintenance in mind when selecting a ground cover. For example, a heavy growth of crisscrossed vines complicates raking.

Ajuga
Ajuga reptans

When spring bulbs are blooming, the deep blue flower spikes of the durable ground cover ajuga come shining through. The blooms are terrific—but it is ajuga's foliage that sets it apart year-round. Ajuga's oval rosettes and waxy, two- to four-inch leaves spread with a low growing habit that forms a thick mat. The leaves are burgundy in the cooler months, but in late summer and in shady locations they acquire a forest green color. Some recent cultivars offer tricolor foliage—purple, green, and cream. Ajuga spreads readily by stems that root on contact with the soil. It is so hardy that it sometimes escapes from a bed to a moist area or lawn. The unimproved species can become a nuisance, but named cultivars are usually well mannered.

Other Common Name
Bugleflower

Bloom Period and Seasonal Color
Blue flowers in spring; known for foliage.

Mature Height
2 to 5 in.

When, Where, and How to Plant
Ajuga plants are customarily sold in flats filled with small pots or 6-packs. When planted anytime from late summer to December, ajuga gives good results. Ajuga will grow well in a wide range of soils. To expand a planted area, dig and transplant crowns or runners in late winter or immediately after their flowering period. Unless they dry out, it is difficult to kill ajuga plants when planting. Water thoroughly after planting and keep the soil moist for the first month. Given plenty of water, ajuga will grow in full sun. Shady locations are best as you go toward the coastal plains.

Growing Tips
Use a garden hose with a water wand for gentle watering of individual plants in new plantings, but an oscillating sprinkler is more practical for large beds. Apply 1 inch of water per week if rainfall is short. Following spring bloom, apply a granular balanced fertilizer such as 10-10-10. Afterwards, promptly wash the fertilizer off the foliage, or time your application to precede rain.

Care
Once established, ajuga is practically invincible. Dig out dying plants if dead spots appear in spring. Ajuga is an aggressive ground cover that spreads relatively quickly. If ajuga runners invade flower beds or lawns, cut them back or dig out the crowns. Ajuga beds are occasionally injured by a soil-inhabiting fungus called rhizoctonia. Wilted leaves turn brown in circular patches; there is no good control for this short of removing infected plants. The bed usually fills in a month or so later.

Companion Planting and Design
Ajuga is stunning in rock gardens or when used to edge other perennials that lack interesting foliage or flowers. It grows well as a trailer in container gardens. Ajuga is especially adapted for under-planting beneath shade trees. This tenacious plant will last and last and provide beauty through all seasons.

Our Personal Favorites
'Burgundy Glow' is exceptionally colorful; 'Metallic Crispa' is exotic but well behaved.

Creeping Juniper

Juniperus horizontalis

When, Where, and How to Plant

Plant from late spring to early fall. Creeping junipers adapt to a variety of soils, from light sands to heavier clay soil. In their native habitats, creeping junipers grow best where exposed to full sun, so plant them in areas that receive eight hours of sunlight. 'Blue Rug' and other creeping junipers look best when planted in large beds rather than as individuals. Water well, scatter a granular weed-preventer, then mulch. On steep banks of poor soil, plant 'Sargents' juniper instead of 'Blue Rug'.

Growing Tips

Water your newly planted junipers for fifteen minutes twice each week for the first month, using a hose adjusted to a low flow. Water only during dry periods in summer for the first growing season. For better color and faster growth, fertilize with a slow-release product (for example, 12-6-6) in spring and early fall. You must not allow runner-forming grasses to get started among your creeping junipers.

Care

Prune creeping junipers only to contour the shape in early spring. Selectively remove individual shoots. Remove grassy weeds with herbicides; otherwise, hand weed. (One way to safely remove runner-forming grasses is to slip on a cotton glove over a rubber glove. Dip your gloved hand in an herbicide solution, grip the runner and slide it through your hand.) Common diseases and insects include juniper blight, branch dieback, and spider mites, each of which may become serious at times. Declining foliage color is a symptom. Creeping junipers tend to be most resistant to these problems when planted in full sun where there is good air circulation and excellent drainage.

Companion Planting and Design

The trailing habit of 'Blue Rug' makes it especially suitable for use on berms or just for its unique color when interspersed among broad-leaved evergreen shrubs. For edging borders, the dwarf Japanese garden juniper is a likely choice. 'Prince of Wales' has a similar growth habit but remains green year-round.

Our Personal Favorite

'Blue Rug'

From southern California to the coast of North Carolina, gardeners love 'Blue Rug' juniper, one of the woody evergreens we call "creeping junipers." This cultivar is arguably the finest prostrate juniper in its class. 'Blue Rug' juniper hugs the ground with intense blue-green foliage. It is a moderate grower, and it sporadically forms blue berries. When planted in full sun, it takes on a plum color during the winter months. When you plant it in the proper location, you can enjoy a soft-textured living carpet that is nearly weed free. Junipers can withstand hot, dry weather. If you plant creeping junipers in poorly drained soils, you can expect big problems. They can actually take a little shade better than they can tolerate wet feet.

Bloom Period and Seasonal Color

Evergreen blue-green foliage peaks in summer.

Mature Height

4 to 6 in.

Hardy Iceplant
Delosperma cooperi

With a name like hardy iceplant, you would think this ground cover would melt in our summer heat and flourish in the harsh winter weather of our mountains. The opposite is true. This wonderful plant is a member of a family of low-growing succulents native to the deserts of South Africa. Hardy iceplant is a semi-evergreen ground cover introduced to the Carolinas in the 1990s. The fleshy leaves of hardy iceplant, shaped like tiny sausages, are two to three inches long. The dense foliage grows quickly in a hot, sunny garden spot. The long creeping chains of its succulent stems lie flat on the ground and are clothed with daisy-like, cerise-pink flowers. No doubt the thickened leaves conserve the plant's moisture, allowing it to thrive in dry desert-like conditions.

Bloom Period and Seasonal Color
Summer blooms in yellow and hot pink; light green foliage year-round.

Mature Height
3 in.

When, Where, and How to Plant
Plant potted hardy iceplant during the warmer months. Divide plants for enlarging beds throughout the summer, even non-rooted 4-inch stem segments transplant with virtually 100 percent success. Plant in full sun in well-drained soil. The plants survive in poor soils, and they are pH-adaptable. New plants are somewhat fragile, so handle carefully. Needless to say, hardy iceplant is not one of the "Steppables" that can tolerate foot traffic. However, Toby reports that his plantings have taken a lot of abuse by his cats and always grow back.

Growing Tips
Irrigate new plantings lightly once a week. Keep in mind that this is a desert plant and too much water is detrimental. Don't water if the ground is moist to the touch. Just before new growth starts in the spring, feed hardy iceplant with a commercial shrub fertilizer. Hardy iceplant grows best in heavy clay Piedmont soil when 3 inches of play sand is spread to make a perfectly drained seedbed. Protect plants in cold western counties with pine straw mulch.

Care
Pruning is not needed, except following autumn frosts when the fleshy foliage "melts down." Hand shears and a rake will take care of cleanup. Remember, iceplant is not winter-hardy in the Mountain region, and it can look shabby from December to April. No pests attack it.

Companion Planting and Design
Use hardy iceplant as a low edging in front of beds of shrubs or other perennials. It offers a colorful cover on sloping ground and berms; use it in container plantings for its cascading habit. It can be tucked into crevices in stone walls or into open spots in rock gardens where a touch of color is needed.

Our Personal Favorites
The hot-pink *D. cooperi* species performs well in all gardens, including coastal gardens where it takes salt spray. 'Starburst' is another striking selection.

Hardy Verbena
Verbena × hybrida

When, Where, and How to Plant

Plant hybrid verbena from early spring through early fall. Clumps can be dug and separated, and cuttings root easily in summer in any type of soil. Prostrate growing branches that root while lying on the ground can also be transplanted. This verbena likes a warm, sunny location, especially in the western Carolinas. Space plants 5 to 6 feet apart. If purchased plants are potbound, force the roots apart before planting. A thorough watering after setting out plants is critical.

Growing Tips

After planting, water every third day for several weeks. Water once weekly during the dry periods of summer. Apply a granular garden fertilizer in the spring, and again in the summer if growth is slow. Wash it off the foliage right away. Do not overfertilize, or the plant will lose some color; fall feeding can make plants sensitive to cold. The success of these hardy verbenas can be attributed in part to their resistance to pests such as leafminers.

Care

In western counties, untouched cold-damaged foliage adds protection in winter. Mulch the beds with pine needles in December. Many plantings are lost when early cold sets in and the plants haven't hardened off properly. In other areas, moderate pruning and cleaning are acceptable in December when the plant is dormant. On the Coast, shear it at will in order to increase blooms. In western counties, take cuttings of this tender perennial in September and carry them over as potted plants. Mites and leafminers can appear; handpick affected leaves or use plant oil sprays.

Companion Planting and Design

Interplant in bulb beds, with daylilies, or with variegated foliage plants. You can get a "gardener's rush" when you see 'Homestead Purple' verbena teamed with the gold foliage of the mops cypress and lemon spirea. You will find it essential for container gardening and perennial borders.

Our Personal Favorites

'Homestead Purple' is hard to beat, though the new 'Taylortown Red' is quite cold hardy.

This semi-evergreen ground cover has risen to stardom in an incredibly short period of time since the introduction of 'Homestead Purple' cultivar by Dr. Allan Armitage of the University of Georgia. Dozens of new hybrid verbenas sporting a range of colors followed the path blazed by 'Homestead' (such as Verbena canadensis 'Rosea' shown above). Gardeners love the dependability of hybrid verbenas; they can be counted on to come back year after year and to cover difficult areas with a flowering carpet of deep green foliage. The richly colored blooms of 'Homestead' and its sister hybrids appear from early spring to fall at the tips of one- to two-foot stems. This plant serves as a half-hardy ground cover and is incredibly resistant to heat and humidity during the growing season.

Bloom Period and Seasonal Color

Deep purple, red, pink, lavender, and white blossoms depending on the cultivar.

Mature Height × Spread

8 in. × 24 to 36 in.

Ivy

Hedera helix and others

English ivy must hold the Southeast together! This ubiquitous ground cover is one of the most popular vining evergreen ground covers in the Carolinas. It has many uses and does well in heavy shade, although it will adapt to sunny conditions. When growing near trees it will take on a shrub-like form as it works its way up, attaching itself with root-like tendrils. In a moist location, English ivy can go forty or more feet up a tree and into the canopy and crown. The downside is that English ivy can jump the fence and become a terrible weed. It can cause trees to decline when it smothers their foliage. With over two hundred cultivars available, there are endless ivies including many that grow rather slowly and pose no ecological problems.

Bloom Period and Seasonal Color
Trellised English ivy will produce pale yellow flowers and berries in fall.

Mature Length
6 to 40 ft.

When, Where, and How to Plant
Plant English ivy anytime a shovel can be pushed in the ground. Tip cuttings are best planted in spring after the soil warms a bit, but root divisions can be planted in winter. Ivy can be planted in full sun, but to avoid foliage sunburn, plant in partial to full shade. Most any soil will grow ivy very well. Space rooted cuttings 6 to 12 inches apart and potted plants 24 to 36 inches apart. Water well.

Growing Tips
Keep the bed moist for three to five weeks after planting. Irrigate ivy beds during the first growing season throughout dry periods. Fertilize once in spring using a slow-release plant food or 10-10-10 fertilizer. Take a broom and sweep the fertilizer granules off the foliage to avoid beige burn spots.

Care
Don't plant ivy where you can't contain it. A potential problem with English ivy arises when it is trained onto the wall of a house. Wood rot and nesting birds are regular complaints. Vigorously growing ivy usually overcomes any pest problems; if there is a buildup of scale insects, you may want to control them chemically. Keep ivy away from the bases of young trees; the competition can stunt them. Prune ivy with shears as needed. In naturalized beds, either bushwhackers or push mowers can be used to invigorate overgrown matted ivy. Sunburned leaves can lead to secondary leafspot diseases.

Companion Planting and Design
Try using ivy in containers, or train it up a lamppost. Create a privacy screen by training ivy onto an ugly chain-link fence. Use the less aggressive varieties when planting as a ground cover. The small leaf selections are lovely choices.

Our Personal Favorites
'Needlepoint' has small leaves, and 'Gold Heart' is wonderfully variegated. Neither is reliably hardy in the Mountains, but on the plus side, neither will turn into a garden thug.

Liriope and Mondo Grass

Liriope and Ophiopogon sp.

When, Where, and How to Plant

Potted plants can be set out any time the ground is not frozen. Remove pulp, and plant seeds in early fall. Liriope and mondo grass will thrive in most soil conditions, but if planted in good topsoil, they will respond with dramatic results. Plant in sun or shade; in shade gardens, use either mondo grass or liriope as turfgrass. Score potbound rootballs with a knife. Space plants 15 inches apart. Water thoroughly to settle the soil. A liquid starter fertilizer can be used at planting time or one week later.

Growing Tips

Water young plants generously, especially during prolonged drought the first season. Fertilize in spring with a slow-release product. A supplemental summer feeding is also recommended. Keep crabgrass seeds from germinating in sunny beds by applying a granular weed preventer in March before mulching. Mulch to a depth of 1 to 2 inches.

Care

No pruning is required during the growing season. In late winter, before spring growth emerges, trim to within 3 inches of the ground to remove damaged foliage. In shade gardens, there is no need to shear back the plants. Sometimes rabbits will chew liriope or mondo grass down to the ground. Trap them or spray a repellent. Control unwanted grassy weeds by spraying the bed with a selective herbicidal "grass killer." Constantly wet soils can kill plants. If you notice scale insects or vole damage, consult your County Cooperative Extension Agent for advice.

Companion Planting and Design

'Big Blue' liriope is fabulous when underplanted *en masse* beneath river birches; it's a great shade plant where space is limited. The variegated form complements plantings of crimson pygmy barberries and crape myrtles. Dwarf mondo grass looks stylish in small, formal areas; plant in between stepping stones in a woodland setting. You will find it essential for container gardening and perennial borders.

Our Personal Favorites

'Variegata' is quite spectacular when in flower. 'Aztec Grass' lights up dark areas.

Liriope, also known affectionately as monkey grass, is extensively planted throughout the Tar Heel and Palmetto states. It is an evergreen, grasslike member of the lily family, and is popular for its ease in growing. In midsummer, spikes of violet blooms appear, followed by small berries that ripen to black. Mondo grass looks much like it but is better adapted for replacing grass under dense shade. A dwarf mondo grass is available; it forms perfect little buns of dark green. You don't need a "green thumb" to grow liriope or mondo grass, just a hatchet to divide their dense clumps of foliage. Use the creeping liriope, L. spicata, as a ground cover; it is especially suited to steep, sunny banks where it will tolerate deplorable conditions.

Bloom Period and Seasonal Color

Liriope: blue, white, or violet blooms in midsummer on solid green or variegated green-and-white foliage. Mondo grass: dark green or chocolate foliage and lavender blossom spikes.

Mature Height

12 to 18 in.

Pachysandra

Pachysandra terminalis

Pachysandra is an evergreen ground cover grown in shade gardens throughout the world. It has veined oval leaves, two to four inches in length, that grow in clusters at the top of upright stems. This plant may not be as exciting as many other ground covers since it doesn't produce showy blooms, but its redeeming quality is its aggressive growth in full-shade conditions. It grows by means of stolons (aboveground stems). Toby discovered quite by accident that this gem flourishes in the shade of dogwoods and oaks where his lawn had given up the ghost. The key is mulching then letting pachysandra do the rest. Jim is a fan of our underrated mountain native Pachysandra procumbens. It doesn't grow as fast as the Japanese type and has mottled leaves and small, fragrant pink flowers.

Other Common Names
Japanese Spurge, Allegheny Spurge

Bloom Period and Seasonal Color
Allegheny spurge develops a layered look when its year-round green foliage pushes up above the old foliage.

Mature Height
8 to 10 in.

When, Where, and How to Plant
For best results, set out potted pachysandra in spring or early fall. New plants can be started from divisions in spring; divide by cleaving clumps with two spades and prying them apart. Japanese spurge prefers full shade and moist, acidic soils. Allegheny spurge is more tolerant of limey soils. Ground covers are as close to being permanent plantings as anything, so a well-prepared bed makes good sense for large plantings. For the best growth, pachysandra needs moist soil with plenty of organic mulch. A mulch layer will encourage faster growth since the stolons don't have to fight their way into tight or compacted soils. For large projects, apply a pre-emergence grass preventer. Planting under trees may be a challenge, so put on your kneepads and dig wide, shallow planning holes. Water well for the first two months.

Growing Tips
Water as needed to maintain health in the drier years. Pachysandra should not need fertilizer the first year. If the color looks good in summer, do not fertilize at all. Every few years an application of slow-release fertilizer can be made in March; too much granular lawn or garden fertilizer can kill sections of the bed, so go easy! Scatter aged leaf compost over old beds.

Care
Pachysandra never needs pruning, though beds may be edged. Your County Cooperative Extension Agent can advise you if dead circular patches (*Volutella* fungus or tip blight) occur. Yellowing of plants in winter indicates sunburn. The biggest challenge is removing leaves from the beds in the fall. A leaf blower does wonders if you start early in autumn before rain packs down the leaves.

Companion Planting and Design
Pachysandra is suitable for large-scale planting projects or in small gardens for a lush look.

Our Personal Favorite
'Green Sheen' is a new variety with lustrous leaves. It adapts to partial sun. You may have to turn to a native plant supplier to get starts of Allegheny spurge, *P. procumbens.*

When, Where, and How to Plant

Set out potted plants in the spring or fall, or divide clumps in late winter and spring. Vinca prefers light shade and moist soil. In woodland gardens where the humus layer is deep with decaying leaves, this ground cover gallops across the forest and steep banks. Plant vinca with the top inch of the rootball above grade. Water the plants well and cover the surface roots with loamy topsoil or bark mulch. Apply a weed preventer in spring for large plantings. A water-soluble starter fertilizer can be applied when planting. You will need 100 clumps to cover a 10-foot by 10-foot area.

Growing Tips

Water as needed during the first two summers. Fertilize vinca only every other year, using a slow-release product. In older beds, maintain growth by mulching periodically with a fine layer of compost or bagged cow manure. Irrigate before and after fertilizing if dry products are used.

Care

Vinca is virtually maintenance free. Trim only if your personal taste dictates. If a stem blight disease strikes, prune out the plate-sized dead patches. Consult an expert about using a preventative fungicide in early spring, and repeat if necessary. To avoid fierce competition for water, don't plant vinca in an azalea bed or among newly planted trees unless those areas are irrigated well. Thin plants when the bed gets too crowded.

Companion Planting and Design

Plant vinca for its spring flowers that complement daffodil beds. Use it as an edging for shrubs or borders. Many of us have large shaded areas where it is difficult to grow anything; vinca will naturalize in these areas. Narrow-leaved vinca partners well with many foundation shrubs, but be sure you keep ground cover plantings from running amok.

Our Personal Favorites

'Bowles' is the standard in the trade; 'Illumination' and 'Wojo's Gem' have stunning gold variegation.

Whether you call it vinca or periwinkle, this spreading ground cover is popular anywhere there is a shaded garden. It sends out vine-like shoots that root readily, making the plant quite attractive to gardeners. Once established, this durable perennial will resist drought like a champ. The narrow-leaved, dark-green species of vinca plant has slender, one- to two-inch leaves that hold their outstanding color despite the cold of winter. In the spring, it delights the gardener with a wonderful show of nickel-sized blue flowers. What could be more peaceful than large shade trees surrounded by a forest-green ground cover dotted with soft blue flowers? Another vinca species, V. major, is not recommended because it grows rapidly and tends to escape and run wild in forest lands.

Other Common Names
Periwinkle, Myrtle (Neither is correct, though, because other species already have these common names.)

Bloom Period and Seasonal Color
Sky-blue flowers in early spring.

Mature Height × Spread
6 in. × 36 in.

Herbs *for the Carolinas*

Herbs have so many benefits and uses for daily living that they could be called God's gift to the earth. For centuries, humankind has grown and collected herbs for their medicinal, culinary, and scenting benefits, and the Bible makes frequent reference to herbal traditions. Some herbs make great landscape plants, and it is often difficult to differentiate between culinary plants or ornamentals. In modern times, there has been a resurgence of interest in using herbs for health, fragrance, and fine cuisine. These plants add a natural dimension to any garden and maybe even a "cure for what ails you."

Herb Garden with Yarrow, Allium, Thyme and Roses

Go Natural

As stewards of the Earth, we are concerned about the continual contamination of our water with harmful chemicals. In food production like herb growing, gardeners should consider using organic methods and products where possible. There are excellent organic fertilizers, botanicals, and biological controls for many problems. Herbs have few insect pests and there is little need for using pesticides. Some herbs even repel pests that may damage other plants in the garden. Beneficial insects increase in numbers as herbs are included in plantings; honeybees and tiny predatory wasps feed on their nectar. Soil management is important with most horticultural crops, including herbs. You will find that succulent herbs flourish in humus-rich soil while other herbs prefer plain mineral soil. But don't get your knickers in a knot trying to match soil conditions to specific herbs. Relax; an average garden soil moderately enriched with organic matter to improve drainage will do a fine job of supporting virtually all species of herbs.

How to Get Started

Begin your herb garden with the herbs you enjoy most. If you want fresh herbs for cooking, by all means plant them close to the kitchen door. A sizable container garden can produce up to a dozen kinds of herbs. Place it, or a small herb garden, only steps away from your kitchen and you will find yourself using more herbs to flavor salads and main courses and to garnish serving plates.

The biggest problem in growing herbs is coming up with enough ways to use them. There is always an overabundance—and the more they're harvested, the bigger the yield in the weeks to come.

Fortunately, these plants are easily preserved. Dry them in the dark, warm trunk of a car, hang them on coat hangers in a dark attic, or microwave on high power in 30-second bursts. You can even freeze fresh sprigs in ice-cube trays for use in cold beverages or cooking.

Plan your herb garden by grouping herbs according to light, irrigation, and soil requirements. Most prefer sun, but a few, like lemon balm, sweet woodruff, and orange bergamot mint, tolerate light shade. Be aware of the growth habits of your selections before you purchase them. Some herbs, like cilantro and anise, are thin and airy and are best used in groups for ornamental effect, while the mints are invasive and should be confined in containers. If you plant any of the culinary mints in garden soil, you will rue the day. French tarragon will behave itself and is happy growing alone.

Most herbs grow healthier and fuller if they are harvested frequently; shearing or pruning lightly is recommended whether you use the harvest or not. Up to three-quarters of the current season's growth can be harvested at one time. Flavor and oils are at their peak just before flowerbuds form. Harvest early in the morning before the sun becomes hot. Annual herbs can be harvested until frost. Stop cutting perennial types in late August to allow time for them to harden-off for winter. Keep flowers removed to increase leaf growth; some flowers are edible and decorative.

Using Herbs Safely

The uses for herbs are endless. Crafts and vinegars are popular gifts, and hot herbal teas made from leaves from your garden offer a winter treat. Herb butters, salsas, soups, salads, cheese, herbal baths, potpourris, and flavoring are the most common products resulting from home herb culture. Warning: Be careful

creating herbal medicines, as some herbs are toxic. This is best left to the pharmacist and medical experts! The mention of an herb's medicinal properties does not constitute a recommendation for use by either the authors or the publisher of this book.

Whether planted for their culinary or ornamental value, herbs make a worthy addition to Carolina gardens. They are surprisingly easy to grow and great to share.

Preparing Soil for Herbs

Jim operated an herb farm in South Carolina for several years, growing and shipping fresh herbs to fine restaurants. The soil on "Savory Farm" was typical red Piedmont clay. The farm grew great crops of herbs that were praised by chefs, but the clay required considerable modification. Based on that experience, here is how he would recommend you prepare an area of clay soil for growing herbs:

Perennials and Herbs

Catmint

- Take soil samples per the procedure recommended by County Cooperative Extension Service.
- Kill perennial grasses and weeds with Roundup®. Wait two weeks for vegetation to die.
- Rake off dead vegetation. Till or work the soil to spade depth. Remove trash and break up clods.
- Spread the recommended amounts of fertilizer and limestone. You can substitute organic nutrient sources such as cottonseed meal for mineral fertilizers.
- Spread a two-inch layer of aged pine bark soil conditioner.
- Mix it into the soil.
- Shovel the amended soil into raised beds or irregularly-shaped mounds, perhaps studded with boulders.
- Fill the excavated areas with pine or hardwood bark mulch. These will become walkways or aisles.
- Lay "leaky hose" (soaker hoses) on the raised areas so that each plant will be no more than one foot from the hose.
- Set out plants. Run the drip system for an hour every other day to start the new plants.

The steps would be the same with sandy soil until it comes to adding soil conditioner. No sand should be added, of course. Raised beds or mounds are not necessary, but they would help to display your herbs better, and the mulched aisles would keep your feet off the herbs and eliminate soil compaction.

Dealing with "Night-length-sensitive" Herbs

With the coming of summer, several herbs set flowers and seeds when nights grow shorter. Soon thereafter they die. It's a perfectly natural occurrence; they are annuals, after all. But you need green matter, not flowers, for flavoring foods. You can get around this by sowing seeds every two or three weeks and eating seedlings before they break into flower. Night-length-sensitive herbs include anise, chervil, corn salad, cilantro, cress, and dill.

Starting Herbs from Seeds

You can buy most herbs as grown plants. Should you wish to start from seeds, only the perennials require starting early indoors. See the Annuals introduction for directions on indoor seed starting. Some herbs germinate slowly, and some produce only one seedling for every three to four seeds. Typically, chives, oregano, parsley, rosemary, rue, sage, sweet marjoram, thyme, and a few other perennials are started indoors eight to ten weeks prior to the spring frost-free date. A few fast-sprouting herbs are usually direct-seeded in garden beds after frost danger is past and the soil is warm. These include dill, fennel, French sorrel, summer savory, and sweet basil. The mints, French tarragon, and named cultivars of oregano, rosemary and thyme are vegetatively propagated and should be purchased as plants to be true to type.

The Many Faces of Herbs

Most of us associate the word "herb" with cooking or potpourri, yet over twenty-five percent of our modern drugs contain plant extracts as active ingredients. Ethnobotanists continue to explore the far reaches of the earth to rescue genetic material found in endangered plants that may prove useful in offering cures for human diseases. Of course, much folklore goes with herb growing, and homespun remedies are a dime a dozen.

Many herbs are classified as herbaceous perennials, and their tops return each spring from crowns or rhizomes. Some, such as basil, must be planted annually, much like bedding plants. Rosemary, lavender, and hyssop are woody ornamentals that form small hardy shrubs. Drought tolerant lamb's-ear can perform as a ground cover or edging in sunny, dry beds. Combine herbs with perennials or ornamental grasses in the garden. When you stand back and look at your creation, you will wonder why it took you so long to consider the visual value of herb foliage or flowers.

Herbs are easy to grow in gardens and can serve many functions in landscape design. For example, wooly thyme makes a durable ground cover between steppingstones. Colorful sages are outstanding when used in drifts or for low edgings in perennial gardens. A rosemary topiary makes an eye-catching accent, and who wouldn't appreciate a rosemary bush in a planter? When space is limited to a small deck or patio, herbs can be very happy in container gardens and hanging baskets. Transplants and herb seeds are available at all garden shops, and do-it-yourself propagation kits make it easy to experiment with new varieties. The herbs profiled in the following chapter should be in every herb garden.

The flowers of perennials will complement the foliage of the herbs. The gray or silvery leaves of santolina, artemisia, and lavender may be exactly what your garden needs to bring it to life. Variegated cultivars of herbs are beautiful when used alone. What a delight to brush by the spicy foliage of an herb while working a bed in summer! With so few flower choices for cool weather gardening, parsley and chives are finding their way into pansy beds alongside flowering kale and red-leaved greens. The entire text of the *Carolinas Gardener's Guide* could have been dedicated to herbs, but with the start we are giving you, it won't be long before you could write a book on herbs yourself.

Oregano

Catnip
Nepeta cataria

There is considerable interest in this humble perennial herb for its medicinal properties. A tea or tisane made of dried catnip leaves can be used as a mild sedative and alleviates restlessness in children. (But does it work on teenagers?) Catnip produces two-inch-long, arrow-shaped leaves with toothed leaf margins. The plants grow like weeds, reaching three feet or more in height. Catnip can be a pretty (if somewhat coarse) plant with its crowded clusters of lavender or white flowers that attract bees. Grow enough to share with your cat, since the bruised foliage releases a scent that turns some but not all adult felines into playful kittens. Site your catnip plants carefully; cats can damage other plants during their rolling around when affected by catnip.

Bloom Period and Seasonal Color
Continuous white to lavender-blue spikes all summer long.

Mature Height × Spread
1 to 4 ft. × 1 to 1½ ft.

When, Where, and How to Plant
Plant containers of catnip in spring or summer in sun or partial shade. Seed can be sown in warm soil, or cuttings can be taken to propagate the plants in summer. This member of the mint family prefers well drained, sandy loam garden soil of pH 7 to 8. Most clay soils will need added limestone to sweeten the soil. Catnip transplants easily from pots after the soil has been loosened to an area twice the diameter of the container. Space plants 18 inches apart. Thin seedlings to 1 foot apart in the herb garden. Catnip self-sows freely but is easily identifiable; unwanted seedlings can be removed early. Water thoroughly at planting and twice weekly for two weeks. (Catnip is often confused with a related species, catmint. While catnip is grown principally to pamper one's pussycats, catmint serves as a beautiful, long-blooming ornamental.)

Growing Tips
Catnip is very easy to grow and can be killed with kindness. For an attractive ornamental, mulch and apply supplemental water during a drought. Water in very dry periods after catnip is established. A water-soluble flower fertilizer can be used twice a month until summer arrives.

Care
Shear plants back in late summer to produce new shoots and flowers. Remove faded blooms to groom the plants. Cut back to the ground after a freeze in fall. Harvest fresh leaves or dry them for teas. If you see mites, treat with insecticidal soap. New plants emerge in spring from central crown stems. Catnip does not transplant well from one place in the garden to another; start new plants from seed or cuttings every few years. This is the herb that repels bad bugs but attracts bees!

Companion Planting and Design
Tall, rugged catnip fits into informal borders with hardy herbs such as rosemary, purple sage, and golden oregano. The catmints are vegetatively propagated and more refined.

Our Personal Favorites
Catmint, *N.* × *faassennii* 'Six Hills Giant', thrives in Zone 6, and 'Dropmore' works for warmer gardens. A wonderful low-growing one is *N. nervosa*.

Chives
Allium schoenoprasum

When, Where, and How to Plant
Plant chive seeds or divisions in fall or early spring. Provide at least a half-day of sunlight and well-drained soil. This plant can tolerate a variety of soils and various moisture levels but performs best in moderately moist garden sites that are high in organic matter and have a 6.0 pH. Divisions work best if they have 6 or more shoots. Work the soil a bit and add an amendment such as leaf compost. Set divisions in holes twice the size of the rootball. Water well to settle the soil.

Growing Tips
Plants should dry slightly between waterings. The first year, water at least once every two weeks during spring and fall, more often during drought. Water outdoor container plants every third day. Chives do not need much fertilizer if they are planted in good soil. If you choose to feed, use a mild organic food like bloodmeal or cottonseed meal and limit to 2 feedings during the growing season. A water-soluble plant-starter fertilizer can be used every four weeks if you just want the foliage for cutting.

Care
After a freeze, remove dead growth and mark the location with a label. Remove faded flower heads promptly. Garlic chives is a different and larger species. It self-sows profusely and can be invasive if not deadheaded in summer after bloom. Divide clumps every three years. There are no pests that bother chives. In fact, chive flowers attract beneficial insects to the garden. Just prior to fall frost, dig and pot a clump of chives to grow on a sunny windowsill. It will extend the harvest season by a few weeks.

Companion Planting and Design
Chives complement the herb and perennial border by providing filler or edging plants. Flowers and leaves are edible. Plant alongside pansies, parsley, and small annuals. Garlic chives bear white blossoms in August.

Our Personal Favorite
Common chives make an uncommonly fine little ornamental for herb and flower gardens.

Garden chives grow in bunches like slender scallions. Flowering stems topped with ball-like pink blossoms shoot up in April and last for about a month. Chives endure for years but need dividing to continue flowering. They are a staple in flower, herb, or container gardens or planter boxes. In landscapes, chives are often set closely in rows as edging plants. In the kitchen, chives are chopped and scattered on baked potatoes or potato salad to add a faint taste of onion. Chives can be grown from very early direct seeding in the garden, but starting from potted plants or divisions is easier. The blooms can be eaten in salads or dried and enjoyed in everlasting arrangements. Chives are a different species from scallions or shallots.

Bloom Period and Seasonal Color
Pink or lavender globe-shaped blooms in summer.

Mature Height × Spread
12 in. × 8 to 12 in.

Cilantro (Coriander)

Coriandrum sativum

When you plant coriander seeds, cilantro comes up. Coriander is the name given the dried seeds—cilantro describes the green leaves. The surging interest in Mexican and Asian cuisine has focused interest on fresh cilantro. Unfortunately, it is a bit tricky to grow because lengthening days trigger it to develop flowers, set seeds, and die. Coriander can withstand light frosts, and in the Carolinas, it grows best when direct-seeded in early spring and again in late summer for a fall and winter crop. During summer months, sow seeds of coriander every three weeks; harvest the seedlings, roots and all; and use the entire plant in guacamole, salsa, soups, and cerviche. Cilantro looks a lot like plain leaved parsley but has a strong, distinctive flavor reminiscent of coriander seeds.

Other Common Name
Chinese Parsley

Bloom Period and Seasonal Color
Lacy, white flowered umbels in fall.

Mature Height × Spread
24 to 30 in. × 6 to 12 in.

When, Where, and How to Plant

Sow coriander seeds indoors or in the garden in February. Transplant seedlings outdoors in March. Wait until late August to sow your fall crop. When setting out started plants of cilantro, select large seedlings in 3-inch pots. Plant in loose garden soil, and water well every two days for the first ten days. Cilantro prefers a bright, sunny location and will grow in very dry to moist soils. Soil quality is not crucial, but a loose soil with a 6.5 pH makes it easier on both the gardener and the plant. Thin seedlings to 4 inches apart. When growing to produce coriander seeds, thin plants to 9 to 12 inches apart.

Growing Tips

With cilantro genetically programmed to go to seed quickly during summer, you need fertile soil and abundant water for fast growth. Cilantro prefers weekly watering, twice weekly in extreme heat. Fertilize with 20-20-20 water-soluble fertilizer every two weeks to encourage vigorous vegetative growth.

Care

Cilantro is practically maintenance free. In a dry site, mites may appear; wash them off with a sharp spray of water. Harvest cilantro as often as you need it. When cilantro is abundant, puree and freeze the surplus in ice cubes for near-fresh flavor. Coriander seeds can be gathered, toasted lightly, and stored in jars. If you are growing the plant for foliage, trim the lengthening seed stalks to delay seed production. If you want seeds, let the plants bloom.

Companion Planting and Design

Cilantro isn't pretty or enduring enough to rate as an ornamental and usually ends up being used to fill garden spots that are temporarily vacant. Beginners sometimes feel cheated when they bring home and set out a nice plant of cilantro only to see it quickly set flowers, go to seed, and die. That's just cilantro doing its thing; it does its job as an annual then checks out. Adios, amigo!

Our Personal Favorite

For early abundant foliage, 'Festive' is a winner.

Dill and Sweet Fennel

Anethum graveolens and *Foeniculum vulgare* var. *dulce*

When, Where, and How to Plant

See this chapter's introduction to help you prepare soil for superior herb crops. You can buy plants of dill, but they will quickly flower and go to seed. Dill grows rapidly from seeds sown in the garden two weeks before the last spring frost date If you sow seeds indoors, start four to six weeks ahead of the frost free date. Plants of sweet fennel are a better buy; however, seeds of sweet fennel can be sown anytime. Germinate dill or fennel seeds by planting them in shallow furrows and covering with 1/2 inch of play sand. Late summer is best for producing plants for transplanting during cool, moist fall weather. Be sure to plant enough for your needs and those of swallowtail butterflies that feed on the foliage of dill and fennel. Both dill and fennel grow wonderfully well in containers. In gardens, both species like well-drained soil and a pH level of 5.5 to 7.0. Raised beds with drip irrigation produce the best crops. Thin to one foot apart.

Growing Tips

Neither species needs mulching, but both like to be fertilized with cottonseed meal or bloodmeal. Water dill weekly during dry weather. Sweet fennel is less demanding of water.

Care

Drying the foliage of dill or fennel isn't worth the effort; instead, chop or puree and freeze it in ice cubes or in freezer bags.

Companion Planting and Design

Dill is too temporary and too lanky to use as an ornamental. But tall, erect, fernlike fennel can add height and grace to containers or borders for weeks on end, particularly the bronze variety. It combines well with tropical-looking copperleaf and the warm colors of variegated sun coleus. Sweet fennel can tolerate afternoon shade better than dill.

Our Personal Favorites

Dill varieties such as 'Bouquet' and the All-America Selections winner, 'Fernleaf,' are slower to flower and set seeds. Bronze fennel has a cachet in landscapes that the common green variety can't match.

These two herbs look a lot alike but are used in different ways. Dill is chopped and added to potato salad, sprinkled over green salads, or added to pickles. Anise-scented sweet fennel is popular for fish dishes and fruit compotes. Both have delicate flavors, thus chefs tend to use dill or fennel seeds rather than fresh foliage for flavoring cooked dishes. Both dill and fennel grow tall. Their ferny leaves give the plants a see-through appearance. Dill is a rather tender annual that grows best during short spring or fall days. During long summer days, you need to direct-seed dill every three weeks to keep a supply of fresh foliage coming. Fennel, a hardy, short-lived, ornamental perennial, will endure stresses and continue producing.

Bloom Period and Seasonal Color
Umbrella-like sprays of tiny yellow flowers in summer.

Mature Height × Spread
Dill, 2 to 3ft. × 1 to 2 ft.
Fennel, 3 to 5 ft. × 1 to 2 ft.

English Lavender

Lavandula angustifolia

Lavender has been called the "Queen of the Scented Garden" and has been a major player in the perfume and soap industry for decades. Horticulturists recognize this wonderful herb as a durable landscape ornamental. It has fine-textured foliage that can be a dull green or a pleasant silver-gray color and spikes of (what else) lavender-colored flowers. As with many herbs, it is pest free and ideal for a low-maintenance border. One of the better varieties, 'Lady', has attractive long lasting, lilac-colored flowers borne on ten-inch stalks that are great for drying. Lavender is a tough evergreen herb with a remarkable ability to withstand harsh winter exposure. Though rarely used in cooking, lavender is often dried for arrangements and potpourris. The silver-gray foliage spices up many a perennial border.

Bloom Period and Seasonal Color
Lavender, pink, or white summer flowers and gray-green to blue-gray foliage.

Mature Height × Spread
12 to 24 in. × 15 to 30 in.

When, Where, and How to Plant
Take full advantage of the first growing season and buy quart-sized containers of nursery-grown plants. Plant anytime the ground can be worked. Lavender thrives in full sun and likes alkaline soil. Incorporate limestone thoroughly into the planting bed at the rate of 1 pound per 10 square feet. Spread the roots horizontally to ensure that the plant is set high—or plant lavender in a raised bed, container, or berm. Improve poorly drained soil by mixing granite screenings or ground pine bark into it. No amendments or mulches are necessary when planting in sandy soils. Water twice weekly the first month, then only in dry weather as needed to promote healthy growth. English lavender can be grown from seed; 'Lady' will bloom ninety days after sowing. Cuttings can be taken in late spring, rooted, and set out in early fall.

Growing Tips
To succeed with lavender, select a well drained site or make it so. Over-watering can kill even the most robust lavender plants. Don't be afraid to move lavender if you discover a better location. It is incredibly resilient. Use a water-soluble bloom-booster fertilizer monthly.

Care
Shear lavender in early spring to clean up the plant. Trim off foliage burned from winter exposure by pruning the tips of stems by 2 to 3 inches. Research indicates that on clay soils the best mulch for lavender is a 1-inch layer of white sand that reflects light and heat. There are no special problems that require routine care. If you want to cut the spikes for drying, harvest when the flower buds are just beginning to open. The aromatic foliage is considered a natural repellent for a few common household pests.

Companion Planting and Design
Plant in drifts or edgings for the best floral impact. Compact lavenders, such as 'Hidcote' and 'Munstead', can line a walk or driveway. The handsome blue-gray foliage works well with wax leaf begonias and geraniums.

Our Personal Favorites
Try the taller, free-flowering 'du Provence', *L. intermedia*, or 'Grosso.' 'Lady' won an All-America Selections medal.

French Tarragon

Artemisia dracunculus var. *sativa*

When, Where, and How to Plant

Set out potted plants during cooler months, from October to May. Divide in spring, or take stem or root cuttings in fall or spring. Plant French tarragon in full sun or afternoon shade in rich, well drained soil. It does not take the heat well, so protection from the afternoon sun will increase its life expectancy. Space plants 2 feet apart because of the natural spreading growth habit. Tarragon is easy to transplant; simply spade a hole as deep as and twice as wide as the width of the rootball. Most herbs prefer limestone or wood ashes to sweeten the soil, so mix one of these into the soil as you plant. Water well with a water-soluble fertilizer solution such as 20-20-20. It prefers moist soil, so apply a mulch of aged manure or compost after planting. Water twice a week for the first month.

Growing Tips

Irrigate regularly in hot weather, especially in a full-sun location. Apply a 10-10-10 fertilizer in mid-spring. Fertile soil is important to French tarragon, so use an organic fertilizer during summer to avoid stressing the plants in hot weather.

Care

In the western Carolinas, French tarragon can freeze to the ground, but don't worry; it is quite winter-hardy. However, on new fall plantings, mulch with pine straw to prevent "heaving." Shear heavily in early spring to remove cold injury and to rejuvenate the plants. Divide crowns every three to four years to keep them growing vigorously. Tarragon does not suffer from pests but overwatering can cause root rot. In Zone 8 gardens, Mexican mint marigold, *Tagetes lucida*, may be used as a substitute for French tarragon, but professional chefs decry its lack of "bite." Harvest leaves any time, or entire plants in late summer.

Companion Planting and Design

Although no beauty queen, French tarragon grows well in containers and hanging baskets. Interplant with other herbs and annuals like nasturtium.

Our Personal Favorite

Any French tarragon is welcome in our gardens. There seems to be little difference in flavor regardless of where you buy the plants.

Genuine French tarragon must be grown from crown divisions or cuttings. It does not form seeds. "Russian" tarragon does set seeds but has little or no flavor. Anise-scented French tarragon is essential for sauce béarnaise, for tasty green beans, for flavoring fish, and for herbal oils and vinegars. It's not at all aggressive by nature, and its two-inch-long, narrow, grayish green leaves are reminiscent of dianthus foliage. It is a slow-growing perennial that spreads by underground rhizomes. Jim considered it the most difficult herb to grow on his Piedmont herb farm in South Carolina; it insisted on drying up during the summer, even with drip irrigation. However, a bit further north at Winston-Salem, Toby had no problem growing it. He reasons that the afternoon shade may have helped?

Bloom Period and Seasonal Color
French tarragon rarely flowers and is by no means ornamental

Mature Height × Spread
1¹/₂ to 2 ft. × 1 to 2 ft.

Lemon Balm
Melissa officinalis

Lemon balm is a lemon-scented member of the mint family, but unlike spearmint or peppermint, it doesn't produce rampant rhizomes that take over azalea beds and threaten flowers. Watch it, however, because plants can spread from abundant seed crops. Lemon balm is perennial across the Carolinas but may be short-lived in coastal heat. Small seedlings rapidly thicken into bushy plants. The lustrous leaves of lemon balm are two inches long, wrinkled, and oval shaped with scalloped edges. Its unremarkable whitish flowers come in short spikes. You will enjoy stroking its foliage for a whiff of its sharp lemon aroma. Fresh lemon-flavored sprigs are valued for their use teas and sauces as a garnish, to decorate drinks, and in aromatherapy to counter depression. Reputedly, it has antiviral properties.

Bloom Period and Seasonal Color
Tiny white blooms in midsummer.

Mature Height × Spread
2 ft. × 1 to 2 ft.

When, Where, and How to Plant
Lemon balm is easy to grow from seed sown in spring or early fall, but pot-grown plants and root divisions are faster and easier. Moist, fertile soil is best, but lemon balm will grow fairly well in poor, dry soil. It thrives in full sun or dappled shade, but plants grown in shade will be larger and more succulent than those grown in direct light. Scatter 5-10-10 fertilizer, 1 cup for a 25-square-foot garden space. Rake in the fertilizer. Set potted herbs in loose soil and water thoroughly twice weekly. Space plants 2 feet apart and divide them yearly to keep the clumps in bounds.

Growing Tips
Water seedlings daily or newly planted lemon balm plants twice a week until they are 6 to 10 inches tall. Later, irrigate when the top 2 inches of soil dries. Established plants of lemon balm are drought tolerant and need very little care. Apply water-soluble plant fertilizer every two weeks until summer heat arrives. Continue fertilizing at least monthly.

Care
Begin cutting sprigs anytime after the first month. Clumps may be sheared for vigorous growth. Pruning this way will keep the plant compact. It self-sows freely and may become a weed in mild regions. Remove and dispose of any terminal growth that appears to be flowering. Apply a 1- to 2-inch layer of organic mulch around the plant to control weeds and reduce the need for watering in dry periods. Clip back after frost and mulch in mountain counties. Pests are no problem. Use lemon balm fresh, frozen, or preserved in oil, wine, or vinegar.

Companion Planting and Design
Lemon balm is a stalwart citizen in herb gardens, always solid and substantial looking whether planted singly or in small drifts. But it is so determined to spread that many herb gardeners restrict it to containers.

Our Personal Favorite
The greenish-gold cultivar 'Aurea' makes a great pass-along plant.

Mint
Mentha spicata

When, Where, and How to Plant
Set out potted plants in early spring or fall; transplant divisions anytime. Use 5-gallon or larger containers for mint plants. Mints are seldom grown from seeds because seedlings can vary greatly in flavor and aroma. All mints can tolerate soil extremes from "bog-type" areas to dry clay soil. Not much preparation is necessary for planting this herb. The soil should be tilled or "turned over." Mix in pine-bark soil conditioner to loosen heavy soils. When setting out plants, make planting holes a little larger than the rootballs. Water twice weekly until plants are established.

Growing Tips
If not planted in a "bog-type" area, mints will need water 2 to 3 times a week. They can survive with less watering but will not thrive. Mints are not heavy feeders. You can use an organic food such as fish emulsion or a water-soluble fertilizer if you want to encourage more growth. Mints have no problem surviving—it is controlling them that is the challenge! They are the most athletic of the herbs; if they can't grow over or under or around a neighboring plant, they will grow right through it.

Care
Thin plants occasionally to prevent leaf diseases. Use a strong spray of water or botanical insecticide to remove aphids. Trim mints as needed for teas and culinary uses throughout the growing season. Just snip the stems with small secateurs or scissors, making a cut just above a leaf node. Cut back after a hard freeze and mulch lightly. Try chopping fresh sprigs to make "mint cubes" in refrigerator trays for use in summer beverages. Flowering spikes of mint make good garnishes for fancy meals.

Companion Planting and Design
Turning mints loose in flower beds and borders is not recommended. However, containers of mint can be set here and there among perennials.

My Personal Favorite
The showy 'Variegata' apple mint is pretty in color bowls and window boxes, or use the variegated pineapple mint.

Spearmint is one of the most popular culinary species within the great mint family, with peppermint a distant second. Garden centers and catalogs offer scores of fancifully named cultivars. Confine mints in pots. Anyone can succeed with these aromatic, flavorful plants, but any one of them could run wild in garden soil and become a troublesome weed. Mints love damp areas, but certain species can survive in dry spots as well. Given plenty of water, mints will thrive in full sun, but they do better in afternoon shade. Only a few cultivars, all with large leaves, can survive in full shade. The best cultivars of mints were originally bred for commercial production of mint oil, have intense flavors and aromas, and are vegetatively propagated.

Bloom Period and Seasonal Color
Tiny pink to purple summer blooms.

Mature Height × Spread
1 ft. × 2 ft. or more

Oregano
Origanum spp. and hybrids

Two major culinary types of oregano are "Italian" and "Greek." Italian oregano is preferred by most chefs. It has white flowers on erect plants and is not winter hardy in Zone 7. Greek oregano, on the other hand, has purple flowers on spreading plants and is quite hardy. Such named varieties should be propagated by cuttings or crown divisions to maintain their distinctive flavors and aromas. Many other species with different plant types and flavors are grown in southern Europe and the Middle East but are little known in the Carolinas. Culinary oregano is easy to grow and can be used in many cooked dishes. Fresh oregano is superior in flavor to the dried product. Dry the long-stemmed purple flowers of common or Greek oregano for winter arrangements.

Other Common Names
Wild or Pot Marjoram

Bloom Period and Seasonal Color
Purple or white flowers from June to September.

Mature Height × Spread
2 to 2^1/$_2$ ft. × 1 to 2 ft.

When, Where, and How to Plant
Plant potted oregano in spring and summer in full sun or afternoon shade. When setting out container-grown plants, remove a plant from the pot, loosen the roots a bit, and place the rootball at its original depth. Firm-in the backfill and water thoroughly. Transplant divisions anytime if you can water them frequently. The herb will grow in a wide range of soils with a pH of 4.5 to 8.5, but good drainage is important. The chapter introduction details how to prepare the well drained soil preferred by oregano. The only time oregano is started from seeds is when you are growing plants to produce flowers for cutting or drying. Direct-seed in prepared soil and cover with ^{1}/$_4$ inch of soil or play sand. Space plants or seedlings 1 to 2 feet apart. Apply a thin mulch; 1 inch is sufficient.

Growing Tips
Water weekly for the first month. Soil fertility and water needs are minimal, although some irrigation is recommended during a drought. Apply organic fertilizer in spring to invigorate established plantings.

Care
Start anew yearly with Italian oregano; it rarely winters over. Divide old plants of Greek oregano or replace with newer plants. Once plants are established, fresh sprigs can be harvested at will. Harvest before flowers appear. To enhance production of green shoots, shear off the flowers. When the plant matures, stems can be cut near the soil level, bundled, and hung up to dry in a dark, airy place. Store the dry leaves intact until shortly before use, then rub the leaves through a fine screen to ready them for seasoning cooked dishes.

Companion Planting and Design
Purple-flowered oregano makes a good trailer for planting with colorful annuals in container gardens. Oreganos make attractive fragrant borders in the garden. Try the highly ornamental (but not edible) 'Kent Beauty' oregano in containers and well-drained garden sites.

Our Personal Favorite
A beautiful golden oregano is 'Jim's Favorite', which will brighten up any garden. (No, it was not named after Jim Wilson.)

Parsley
Petroselinum crispum

When, Where, and How to Plant

Transplant potted plants from the nursery anytime during the growing season. Sow seed outdoors in late February, or start indoors in late winter. Plant parsley in full sun and in fertile, well drained soil. When starting it indoors for the spring garden, sow seed in sterile potting soil or vermiculite; it is slow to germinate and somewhat uncertain from seed. When setting out a potted plant, loosen the rootball carefully, and place it into a hole that's a little larger than the ball. Cover the roots with soil and water well. Use a water-soluble starter fertilizer once a week for the first month. Mulch lightly (if at all), as this plant has a thick, deeply growing taproot.

Growing Tips

When growing parsley in containers, allow soil to dry slightly between waterings. Parsley set in full sun in the garden should be watered well once a week during the growing season. In midseason, apply water-soluble organic or fish fertilizer; otherwise, no fertilizer is needed once parsley is established.

Care

No pruning is necessary other than the harvesting of fresh sprigs. Snip the outer stems with scissors, but don't cut the central bud. Handpick caterpillars if you don't want them to decimate the plant in a few short days. A spray of insecticidal soap will also control them, but you will need to soak and wash leaves carefully to avoid a soapy taste. Sudden withering and death of parsley plants may signal an outbreak of voles that eat off their roots. Remember, this herb will die naturally after it flowers. Cutting off the flowers will delay but not prevent flowering.

Companion Planting and Design

Mix parsley with annual flowers in patio pots and herb bowls for a unique combination. This mound-forming herb is a nice edging plant. Good companions are pansy, chives, and ornamental lettuce or kale.

Our Personal Favorites

'Green River' performs well, and it can take hot weather, as does 'Gigante', a flat-leaf variety.

This bright green, biennial herb comes in several varieties, some with curly leaves, some with flat or "plain" leaves. The flatleaf variety is favored by many chefs because it will retain its flavor longer in cooked dishes. Parsley is popular in Mediterranean cuisine and is used as a garnish to decorate dinner plates, salads, and cold meats. Parsley plants usually live through the winter then with lengthening days, shoot up flower stalks, set seeds, and die. But "it ain't necessarily so"...sometimes parsley acts like a perennial. It is very easy to grow from potted plants and forms dense, compact mounds of lobed leaves on branching stems. Parsley is a member of the same family as dill and fennel and, like them, attracts caterpillars of swallowtail butterflies.

Bloom Period and Seasonal Color

Greenish yellow blossoms in its second spring; green foliage year-round.

Mature Height × Spread

10 to 18 in. × 8 to 12 in.

Rosemary
Rosmarinus officinalis

In the Carolinas, we are able to grow rosemary to a great size. (Well, not in the mountains where it can be killed by severe winters, but over the balance of the two states.) What a treat to have big, evergreen rosemary shrubs ready year-round to contribute sprigs for seasoning meats, stews, soups, and chicken. And what a joy to be able to create rosemary topiaries such as Christmas trees and Valentine hearts. This ever-popular herb is at home in the perennial border or in a container garden. It is easy to grow, and its gray-green foliage gives it a carefree look. Its one-inch, needle-like leaves are intensely aromatic. The flavor of dried rosemary in meat or poultry dishes is distinctive and delectable, but wait until you have tried it fresh. Wow!

Bloom Period and Seasonal Color
Pale blue or pink flowers early to midsummer and sporadically through the winter.

Mature Height × Spread
2 to 4 ft. × 1 to 3 ft. or more

When, Where, and How to Plant
Plant container-grown rosemary from spring through fall. In the mountains, grow it in a container and bring it indoors for winter; a sunny window is adequate. Rosemary is a true sun-lover, though a semi-shaded location will suffice. It will thrive in fast-draining alkaline soil. Rosemary is *the* plant to grow in hot sites, as it stands up well in heat and drought. In containers, use a coarse soilless mix. In poor soils, amend the bed before planting; a soil pH of 7.0 is best. See the chapter introduction for advice on soil preparation. Rosemary should be planted shallowly, with its uppermost roots showing after planting. Use compost to cover the top inch of roots. Water thoroughly once a week during the next month. Leggy transplants can be sheared at planting and the trimmings used in the kitchen.

Growing Tips
Irrigate rosemary in containers or raised beds twice a week during hot weather. Don't over-water plants in clay soils. (Err on the dry side with most herbs.) Once plants are established, normally in ten weeks, dry weather is not a threat, but rosemary will use a lot of water in gravelly soils. Fertilize rosemary at least once during the year, in April or September, with a 10-10-10 garden fertilizer. Do not mulch deeply; mulch can hold too much moisture during winter.

Care
Prune rosemary in early spring and snip sprigs routinely. Train into a topiary using wire forms. It is not bothered by deer, drought, or pests. Harvest the leaves of rosemary anytime, although its fragrant oil is at its peak before the flowers open. Dry sprigs in a paper bag indoors.

Companion Planting and Design
Prostrate forms such as 'Renzels' are suitable for a ground cover. Rosemary is fantastic in rock gardens, cascading over walls, and in planters. Interplant with colorful perennials for an informal garden.

Our Personal Favorites
In large gardens, use 'Arp' for its wide spreading, shrubby form. 'Irene' has a pendulous habit. 'Tuscan Blue' is a beautiful, upright plant with leaves twice the width of standard cultivars.

When, Where, and How to Plant

Quart-sized plants can be planted successfully any-time the soil is warm. Seed can be direct-seeded in late spring. All varieties love to be planted in well drained, full-sun garden spots. Space 36 inches apart for air circulation except for edgings or knot gardens. If a plant is rootbound, use a trowel to loosen the roots so they can be spread out in a shallow hole. Unless the soil is very poor or sandy, organic amendments are not needed. It is impor-tant to lime the soil, since sages require an alkaline soil. Mix limestone into the soil at a rate of 5 pounds per 100 square feet. When transplanting sage, loosen the soil and set the top of the rootball even with or slightly above the surrounding soil. Water thoroughly after transplanting.

Growing Tips

Sage prefers to be left alone, though it is impor-tant to water weekly the first couple of months following planting. Sage loves dry soil, so don't over-water this plant in spring. Make a light application of 10-10-10 fertilizer in spring (1 pound per 100 square feet) to get your sage off to a good start.

Care

Divide every two to three years for sharing or enlarging the bed. Keep sage compact by pruning after flowering; use the prunings for cooking or in sage butter. Give sage plenty of room for necessary air circulation; this prevents foliar diseases in our humid summers. Avoid root and stem root dis-eases by planting in fast-draining soil. Nematodes can be a problem in dry, sandy soil.

Companion Planting and Design

Sages are drought tolerant and non-invasive. The variegated varieties work well with annuals or in container gardens. Groupings of sages are hand-some in perennial gardens. The round, grey foliage of 'Bergartten' sage arguably makes it the most beautiful cultivar. Golden sage is half-hardy in highland gardens.

Our Personal Favorites

Individual plants of culinary sage are attractive, but the variegated 'Tricolor' cultivar takes the prize, with golden sage a close second.

Sage offers so much more than pungent leaves to flavor turkey stuffing, cheese dishes, and teas. Certain cultivars rate highly as ornamentals, sporting beautifully varie-gated leaves of cream, light yellow, and burgundy. Few other evergreen herbs can survive subzero weather or extended drought. Narrow-leaved culinary sage is a com-pact plant, and its pebbly, grayish green leaves are soft to the touch. Spicy-scented sage has many culinary uses and a few practical medicinal uses from salve to laxative. Sage is heavily worked by bees, yet its flowers are often undervalued by humans. (Toby cuts the flower stems for arrangements.) The genus Salvia includes a wide array of showy ornamentals from the colorful annuals scarlet sage and blue salvia to the vigorous Mexican bush sage.

Bloom Period and Seasonal Color
Pink to blue spikes of spring flowers; gray or variegated foliage year-round.

Mature Height × Spread
20 in. × 18 to 30 in.

Sweet Basil
Ocimum basilicum

Common sweet basil, by far the most popular culinary herb, is a vigorous annual with bright green, wrinkled leaves. Fresh basil is wonderful in Italian dishes, pesto, soups, sauces, and more. Several varieties are available, including lemon, cinnamon, licorice, and purple. All the basils are easy to grow, and they grow rapidly. There has been much interest in basils for their ornamental uses in perennial and flower gardens. For example, 'Purple Ruffles' has a deep rich purple color and frilly foliage. 'Spicy Globe' is a wonderful border plant; its small compact growth habit makes it look a bit like a miniature boxwood. Basils can be enjoyed from May through October in gardens throughout the South. The genus name, Ocimum, is from a Greek word meaning "fragrant."

Bloom Period and Seasonal Color
Blue summer blooms; green or purple foliage.

Mature Height × Spread
Common sweet basil 3 to 5 ft. × 2 to 3 ft.
Dwarf basil 1 to 1$^1/_2$ ft. × 2 ft.

When, Where, and How to Plant
One to three plants will supply all the fresh basil needed by a small family, so most gardeners buy potted plants and set them out in sunny garden beds or containers. Yet basil grows well from seeds sown directly in the ground after the last killing frost. Plant seeds in shallow furrows, cover with play sand, and walk down the furrow to firm-in the seeds. When seedlings are 3 inches tall, thin to 15 to 18 inches apart. Site basil in well drained soils to avoid stem, crown, and root diseases. To prepare soil for planting basil, add limestone at the rate of 3 pounds per 100 square feet. Limestone will improve the growth of this herb. Toby liquid-feeds new plantings with fish emulsion for the first two weeks.

Growing Tips.
Basil needs plenty of water at the beginning of summer when plants are developing rapidly. Irrigate at least twice a week, more if the basil is in containers. Do not allow the soil to become dry. Water early in the day, and always keep the foliage dry to prevent leaf diseases. Drill a granular flower fertilizer around plants when they are knee high. Don't use lawn fertilizer; too much nitrogen adversely affects flavor.

Care
Snip off developing flowers weekly to stimulate new foliage. Pruning is a must to keep basil in bounds. Harvest just the tender tip growth: snip with scissors, and the plant will send out new growth at the cut points. Basils are frost-tender annuals; harvest the entire plant before the first killing frost. Freeze the tip growth and dry the older leaves.

Companion Planting and Design
In the Carolinas, sweet basil can grow quite large and is usually placed in the food garden. Use both the dwarf green and the deep-purple basil varieties when designing a knot garden or an herb container. For pesto, plant 'Genoa' or 'Sweet Danni'.

Our Personal Favorites
'African Blue' makes a gorgeous specimen plant and sometimes winters over in Zone 8.

Thyme

Thymus vulgaris

When, Where, and How to Plant

Thyme can be planted anytime from containers. Plant in well drained soil in a sunny location. In the mountain region, tuck thyme plants at the base of stones that retain heat. Review this chapter's introduction for advice on soil preparation and planting. Thyme prefers a loose soil with a near-neutral pH. In the absence of a soil test, add lime and a little phosphorus fertilizer at planting time. Mix the amendments to a depth of 4 inches. New plantings should be watered weekly for the first month. A thin mulch of leaf compost will be beneficial when planting during the summer months, but keep it off the crown of the plant. Seedlings can be produced indoors during the winter months for later transplanting.

Growing Tips

Thyme can tolerate dry soil, but irrigate your plantings during dry periods in the summer and fall to keep new growth coming. If the soil stays too moist, root rot may occur. Plantings in containers will require twice-weekly watering. Woolly thyme is often grown between stepping stones and will tolerate moderate foot traffic. Thymes thrive on neglect once the plants are established. For lush growth, apply an organic, nitrogen-rich fertilizer monthly.

Care

Keep thymes productive by shearing after bloom time. Harvest anytime for use in the kitchen; the best flavor is just before bloom time. Trim clumps to a 3-inch height before spring growth starts. Plants can be divided in fall or spring. Pests are no problem. An apiarist will want plants nearby, as they are a favorite of bees. Small patches of thyme can be grown as ground covers but must be weeded regularly.

Companion Planting and Design

There are two habits of growth—upright and spreading. English and French thyme form clumps; woolly, creeping, and caraway thyme lie flat and spread. Few plants can match hardy thyme for flowing among stones in rock-studded herb gardens.

Our Personal Favorites

Both Jim and Toby grow English thyme for cooking and the golden thyme 'Aurea' or silver thyme for show.

Thyme is one of the robust, full flavored, "savory herbs" that will hold its potency through extended cooking. Some species, such as mother of thyme (T. praecox), make temporary ground covers, while others are perfect for herb bowls. "English" thyme is vegetatively propagated and is preferred for cooking, but seed-grown "French" thyme is also powerful. Lemon thyme is preferred for seasoning light broths. Thymes have small, tender, aromatic leaves on wiry stems. The leaves are generally smooth, but some can be woolly or bordered with gold or silver. Terminal clusters of tiny white- to rose-colored flowers form in early summer. Many named cultivars are available, but read the label or catalog description carefully before you plant, as some of the decorative thymes are lacking in flavor.

Other Common Name
Common Thyme

Bloom Period and Seasonal Color
White to rose or purple summer flowers.

Mature Height × Spread
3 to 12 in. × 12 in. or more

Lawns *for the Carolinas*

Treat your lawn like a garden and you'll have great-looking turfgrass. Carolinians are blessed with a climate suitable for growing either cool-season or warm-season grasses. In the western region, we can have success with bluegrass, perennial ryegrass, and tall fescue. On the coast and south, St. Augustinegrass and carpetgrass are fine choices, depending on the location of your lawn. The Piedmont is the transition zone where you will find an almost endless number of turfgrass varieties and cool-season blends. The cardinal rule is don't mix cool-season and warm-season turfgrasses together, or your lawn will look like a spotted pup!

Where You Are and What You Need

Often the most important contributor to a high-quality lawn is the number of hours of direct sunlight your property receives in the summer. The warm-season turfgrasses win hands-down in the warmer Zone 8, and some Zone 7 gardens have bermudagrass or centipede lawns. Unfortunately, there's no way to have a green lawn twelve months of the year with this class of grasses unless you overseed with annual ryegrass in the fall—or paint the grass green! For this reason, most residents prefer to sow their lawns in tall fescue mixtures. These cool-season varieties tolerate partial shade and provide a lush green lawn during the time that our dogwoods and azaleas are at their peak of bloom. Again, turfgrass requires some sunlight to survive more than a year or two.

Follow the Program

North Carolina State and Clemson University agronomists have developed an establishment-and-maintenance program for every grass variety grown in the Carolinas. To have a beautiful lawn, it is important to follow the program. This means maintaining the proper mowing height for the variety, fertilizing on schedule, and irrigating during the growth cycle. As for the new lawn establishment, the key to a high-quality lawn is soil preparation. (This is a critical step whether you are seeding, sprigging,

Perennial Garden and Lawn

Centipedegrass
Eremochloa ophiuroides

When, Where, and How to Plant
March through early July is the planting season for centipedegrass in the Piedmont and Coastal regions. Centipedegrass won't grow in the cold mountains. It will take two or three years to establish from seed; a quicker method is to plant sod or plugs. Centipedegrass is a sun-loving turfgrass, but it will thrive in partially shaded lawns. Have the soil tested before establishing a centipedegrass lawn. Plant in soil with a pH of 5.0 to 5.5; a higher pH will cause it to be perpetually yellow due to an iron deficiency. Incorporate recommended amounts of fertilizer and limestone into the soil. You will have better establishment if you irrigate the lawn a few days before seeding to allow the soil to settle. Use a hand-cranked rotary seeder to sow. The seeding rate is $1/4$ to $1/2$ pound of seed per 1000 square feet of lawn. Apply clean straw mulch at a rate of 30 to 40 bales per acre. If plugging centipedegrass, for every 1000 square feet use 3 square yards of sod cut into 2-inch squares set on 12-inch centers. Water!

Growing Tips
Centipedegrass is slow to establish unless sod is used. Irrigate twice a week, more often for seedlings. Fertilize with $1/2$ pound of nitrogen per 1000 square feet in June (and again in August on the Coast). Avoid using any phosphorus after establishment. Overfertilized lawns, though dark green, are short-lived and might succumb to disease and winterkill. Save your money for other gardening activities.

Care
Use a reel-type mower at a mowing height of 1 inch to cut centipedegrass. It can tolerate drought by going semi-dormant. If thatch buildup becomes a problem, consider power raking or core aerification. Keep mower blades sharpened. Ground pearls and nematodes are serious pests in eastern counties. (Consult your County Cooperative Extension Agent.)

Our Personal Favorite
Generic seed is generally used. TifBlair®, a new cultivar, is available from commercial sod farms.

Centipedegrass is one of the most popular lawngrasses in the warm southeast. Its major strengths are low growth habit, tolerance of acidic soil and shade, and low fertilizer requirements. One major disadvantage is its susceptibility to winter injury when planted west of the Piedmont region. It is relatively easy to establish, and its seed, though expensive, is readily available in garden centers. Compared to hybrid bermudagrass, it grows slowly. It propagates by means of horizontal spreading stems. Centipedegrass does not produce a dense sod, but it makes a beautiful low-maintenance lawn where it can be planted. We would call it "an ideal grass for the couch potato."

Color and Texture
Gray-green color; fine-textured.

Recommended Mowing Height
1 in.

Kentucky Bluegrass
Poa pratensis

If you desire a grass that will stay green in the cooler months and a lawn that tolerates some shade, then choose Kentucky bluegrass. It is tolerant of medium-height mowing and makes a very attractive lawn. This is the turfgrass of choice in the mountain region and in the states north of us. Kentucky bluegrass is often mixed with perennial ryegrass or fine fescue in western Carolina counties to make a beautiful, durable lawn. This cool-season grass has a sod-forming growth habit, so when you purchase it as a mixture you will reap the benefits of improved color and disease resistance. In the Piedmont, it adds density to a tall fescue lawn, giving it the appearance of a thick, lush carpet.

Color and Texture
Rich green to blue-green color; fine-textured.

Recommended Mowing Height
2 to 2^1/$_2$ in.

When, Where, and How to Plant
In western counties, plant Kentucky bluegrass in early spring. In the Piedmont, plant in September. Bluegrass seed is very small and takes three weeks to germinate, so be patient. This grass species is most often used in mixtures. (Homeowners in the coastal region are advised to stick with a warm-season turfgrass.) Ideal soil pH is 6. Sow at 2 pounds per 1000 square feet. Broadcast a starter fertilizer to promote growth. Lightly apply straw at a rate equal to 1 bale per l000 square feet (40 bales per acre). To overseed an established lawn, broadcast 1 pound of seed per 1000 square feet. For example, mix 1 pound of Kentucky bluegrass with 5 pounds of tall fescue per 1000 square feet. Water heavily to establish.

Growing Tips
Water at a rate of l inch per week. Keep newly seeded lawns constantly moist until time to begin mowing. In February, apply a 10-10-10 fertilizer according to recommendations. In September and again in late November, apply a turf-grade fertilizer at the rate of 1 pound of nitrogen per 1000 square feet of lawn.

Care
Bluegrass requires less mowing than other turf-grasses. Maintain at 2 to 3 inches; this height will encourage deeper root growth and a healthier lawn. Watch for leaf spot, brown patch, Japanese beetle grubs, and sod webworms. If you notice an increase in mole activity or if the grass dies in spots, a soil insecticide can be applied. In April and November, apply a liquid broadleaf weedkiller to control unwanted weed growth, or a granular weed-and-feed product can be used in late fall. After application, always water-in any product containing a pesticide. Sweep up any granules that fall on hard surfaces, such as streets and walkways. (Let's protect groundwater and streams.)

Our Personal Favorite
'Georgetown' is superior for the mountain counties. Some cultivars are better for shade than others; check with your County Cooperative Extension Service or National Turfgrass Evaluation Program (www.ntep.org) for up-to-date cultivar information.

St. Augustinegrass
Stenotaphrum secundatum

When, Where, and How to Plant

Plant St. Augustinegrass when average daytime temperatures are above 60 degrees Fahrenheit. Small areas can be sodded until early July. This warm-season grass thrives in fertile, well-drained soil and part to full shade. It is not tolerant of heavy playground traffic, nor will it survive in the cold western regions. Begin with a soil test. Apply amendments as recommended. Using a rototiller, incorporate amendments into the top 6 to 8 inches of soil. (Toby prefers to hire a professional to do the initial soil preparation if it is a new lawn.) After leveling the yard with a rake or harrow, plug or sprig the lawn using plugs planted on 12-inch centers. Space and plant sprigs at the rate of $1^{1}/_{2}$ square yards of sod per 1000 square feet. Water thoroughly the first week after planting, applying $^{1}/_{2}$ inch of water every three days.

Growing Tips

Keep the soil slightly moist during the first summer to prevent drought stress. Proper irrigation will also prevent pest attacks. Fertilize in May, June, and August with $^{1}/_{2}$ pound of nitrogen per 1000 square feet using a 3-1-2 analysis turf-grade fertilizer.

Care

Maintain the mowing height at 2 to 3 inches. Dethatch when the thatch layer gets $^{3}/_{4}$ inch thick (check in late spring). St. Augustinegrass is sensitive to some post-emergence herbicides. Control summer weeds while they are small and when the grass is not drought stressed. Chinch bugs can kill this turfgrass. Check for these pests in sunny locations by pushing a coffee can into the ground and pouring a quart of soapy water on the turf. Treat if you see 20 chinch bugs per square foot. St. Augustinegrass encroaches on ornamental plantings, so be prepared to edge beds and do a little grunt work. Fortunately, this grass yields more easily than Bermudagrass.

Our Personal Favorites

The 'Raleigh' variety has the best cold tolerance. 'Floratam' is resistant to chinch bugs.

While zoysia grows at a snail's pace, St. Augustinegrass gallops like a thoroughbred when it is planted. This fast-growing turfgrass is in the same class as Bermudagrass; both flourish in the warm months and go dormant after the first frosts. Residents in the southeastern counties of North Carolina like this coarse, drought resistant, and shade tolerant grass. St. Augustinegrass has tropical origins and broad, rigid leaf blades. It spreads aggressively by means of stolons, making a dense, spongy sod and beautiful lawn. Anyone growing this grass knows that it will require edging periodically. It is best adapted to warm, humid areas without periods of cold weather. Beach-front property owners will appreciate its salt-tolerance and affinity for sandy soil.

Color and Texture
Pale to medium green color; very coarse texture.

Recommended Mowing Height
2 to 3 in.

Tall Fescue

Festuca arundinacea

Tall fescue is one of the Carolinas' most widely used turf-grasses. When compared with other bunch-type grasses, this cool-season grass has excellent heat and drought tolerance. It is often preferred over the warm-season grasses since it remains evergreen practically year-round. Though the standard is 'Kentucky 31', plant breeders have introduced new cultivars that are lower growing and darker green with narrower blades. These include 'Wolfpack', 'Rebel Sentry', and 'Jaguar 3'; all produce a dense, high-quality turf with better disease resistance. Studies support claims of improved brown patch disease resistance when a blend of several cultivars is used. We like the finer texture and color of these new turf-type tall fescue cultivars. You can have a lush, green lawn in sunny or filtered shade almost year round without a lot of fertilizer.

Color and Texture
Deep green color; medium to coarse texture.

Recommended Mowing Height
2 to 3 1/2 in.

When, Where, and How to Plant
The first step to a healthy tall fescue lawn is a soil test. Till and rake the soil, adding compost or soil conditioner. Lawns seeded in September have better summer survivability. Broadcast seed in dry or moist places at the rate of 6 pounds per 1000 square feet. Rake lightly to cover the seed. Spread fertilizer and straw. 'K-31', a pasture grass, requires full sun and high mowing for survival as yard grass. New cultivars, however, tolerate shade though they prefer open sunlight. Until germination occurs, you must irrigate—use a sprinkler daily.

Growing Tips
Once you begin mowing, water weekly or as needed; an irrigation system is preferable. Fescues survive dry summers by browning out; if you can not irrigate, water every two or three weeks to keep the roots alive. Fertilize twice in the fall (apply 1 pound of nitrogen per 1000 square feet in September and November) and at half that rate in mid-February.

Care
Mow when grass is 4 inches high, removing only 3/4 inch at each mowing. A thick turf properly mowed and fertilized is the best weed control. Don't scalp your lawn, and leave clippings if you mow regularly. Core aerify (known as "plugging") in fall for long-term maintenance and for reseeding. The rate for reseeding is 3 to 4 pounds of seed per 1000 square feet. Tall fescue is subject to brown patch disease in summer. In irrigated turf, consider using a fungicide at the onset of the disease. Otherwise, spend your hard-earned money on fall reseeding. Thatch only if you are preparing to reseed the lawn. Have your soil tested every three years just in case the pH falls below 6. Pelletized lime is wonderful for maintaining high-quality lawns.

Our Personal Favorite
A blend of tall fescue cultivars will provide a high-quality lawn. In shady lawns, purchase a mixture containing fine fescue. The NTEP (National Turfgrass Evaluation Program) offers a listing of the latest research findings for the South.

Zoysia

Zoysia japonica

When, Where, and How to Plant

Plant zoysia in spring and early summer—at least two weeks following spring "greenup." Don't fall prey to the slick zoysia ads. Professionals use sod, purchased by the pallet. Zoysia can be seeded, though the process is slow. It likes hot sites and full-sun exposures. It will tolerate partial shade, but grows slowly. The optimum soil pH is 6.0. Broadcast lawn-starter fertilizer and limestone; rototill the nutrients to a depth of 5 to 6 inches. This step is crucial for establishing a permanent lawn. Rake or harrow to leave the soil surface as smooth as possible. Sprig the lawn in May or June, using $1/4$ square yard of sprigs (1 to 2 bushels of stolons) for every 1000 square feet. Press the sprigs into the top $1/2$ of soil or cover with a $1/2$ of topsoil. When plugging, cut the sod into 2-by-2-inch or larger squares. Follow the same procedure as outlined above. Water daily for two weeks after planting.

Growing Tips

Maintain zoysia by keeping it well watered. Irrigate weekly, applying 1 inch of water during the first growing season. In succeeding years, prevent summer brownout by irrigating during drought. Fertilize zoysia twice a year with 12-4-8 or 10-10-10 analysis fertilizer, in May and July. Don't overseed these lawns with ryegrass in fall because it weakens zoysia.

Care

Mowing is very important. Mow before the grass gets 2 inches high, cutting to $1/2$ to 1 inch high. It helps if you own a reel-type mower since push-mowing a zoysia lawn is a strenuous activity for many senior adults. Zoysia will need dethatching routinely to prevent dieback. There are no serious pest problems. Edge your shrub beds to prevent encroachment. Use grass killers to take it out of ornamental plantings. Zoysia is low maintenance and can be used as a ground cover on sloping land.

Our Personal Favorites

'Emerald' is a fine-bladed cultivar that would make anyone proud. 'El Toro' is the fastest-spreading zoysia cultivar, covering a new lawn in one season.

Zoysia is so thick that weeds don't stand a chance! It becomes a lush green carpet under your feet in the hotter months. It is not invasive like bermudagrass; plant it in proximity to flower and shrub beds. However, zoysia is brown for as many months as it is green. Consequently, if you plant this grass in the Piedmont or western region of the Carolinas, you will probably get some disapproving looks each winter from neighbors who have lush, green, tall fescue lawns. This dormant period can also detract from the early-spring garden display. Zoysia grasses are drought tolerant and cold hardy throughout the state. Most cultivars are slow to establish, with the exception of 'El Toro', a rising star. Zoysia has tremendous utility and a pleasing feel on bare feet.

Color and Texture
Medium green; fine-textured.

Recommended Mowing Height
$3/4$ to 1 in.

Ornamental Grasses
for the Carolinas

Older gardeners remember when pampas grass was it. With a few exceptions, it was the only ornamental grass in the Carolinas. Then, plant explorers and landscape architects began to introduce and promote ornamental grasses for large commercial landscape installations. Adventurous home gardeners saw them and nagged garden centers to offer ornamental grasses. Now you see at least one plant of ornamental grass in almost every home garden.

Not everyone appreciates ornamental grasses, perhaps because they have spent hours pulling or digging unwanted grasses out of flowerbeds. And others prefer to populate landscapes with shrubs and perennial flowers rather than ornamental grasses. Yet ornamental grasses continue to gain popularity as more gardeners see their advantages in summer and winter landscapes and as they reach beyond the species that have become so popular as to be in danger of becoming landscape clichés.

Virtually all ornamental grasses are native to other countries. Ecologists call them "exotic" species. Along the way, a few bad visitors were brought in. They have bullied their way into wildlands and are pushing out native species that are ill-equipped to compete with these robust imports. For the most part, however, the ornamental grasses are not aggressive spreaders and represent little or no threat to the environment.

Landscape Advantages

Ornamental grasses come in many sizes, from small mounds of blue fescue to mighty clumps of pampas grass. All prefer full sun or afternoon shade. The size, texture, color, and flower heads of a given cultivar determine its best use in the landscape. For instance, many landscapes have sizable sunny areas where mowing is difficult, too expensive, or too time consuming. The gardener just wants to fill up the space with something that looks good, isn't expensive, and requires little maintenance. Among the many ornamental grasses, they can find species that will meet those requirements, with the exception of being low maintenance. Like any other landscape plant, the beautiful grasses require upkeep, and it is often in proportion to the size of the plant.

Towering Ornamental Grasses

Dense Ornamental Grasses at a
Woodland's Edge

Cultivar Versatility

The variegated cultivars of
ornamental grasses may carry cream
or white stripes the length of their
leaves (like hakone grass *Hakonachloa
macra* 'Aureola'), or with at least one
cultivar, porcupine grass, across
the leaves. All of these look especially
good against dark green backgrounds
such as those provided by coniferous
or broad-leaved evergreen shrubs.
And all look good as tall backgrounds
against which to display flowers or
flowering shrubs of significant size,
such as butterfly bush and rose of
Sharon. All are awesome when
backlighted by morning or evening
sun slanting low across the garden.

Certain ornamental grasses are an intense silvery blue color like lyme grass, or reddish purple like
annual fountain grass or the All-America Selections winner, 'Purple Majesty' millet. Some, like Japanese
blood grass, are dark red. Others, like inland sea oats and rattlesnake grass, are grown more for their novel
seeds than for their form or foliage.

Ornamental grasses change in size and appearance as they cycle through the seasons. Their presen-
tation varies from flowers and seedheads to blanched foliage caused by frost and winter rains. Many
gardeners don't trim back their clumps of ornamental grasses until spring, preferring to let them stand to
deliver strong architectural effect during the winter.

Disadvantages

Leaving large clumps of ornamental grass to fend for themselves leads to their eventual failure. Even near
the coast, clumps freeze back part-way, and all the way to the ground farther west. Emerging new blades
are partially obscured by the old, and the visual effect is messy. So cutting old clumps to the ground each
spring can be approached ritually or with trepidation, depending on your age and energy level. Even with
electric-powered hedge shears the job isn't easy, and you are left with large piles of hay. Fortunately,
ornamental grasses make good raw material for composting.

Certain ornamental grasses will reward you with far more seedlings than you desire. Common
maiden grass, *Miscanthus sinensis,* for example is spreading from its original planting sites along interstate
highways and invading adjacent farmlands. Inland sea oats drops so many seeds that the phrase, "like
hair on a dog's back," accurately describes the crop of volunteer seedlings. Near the coast, Japanese blood
grass, which spreads slowly by underground runners, can get out of control in moist, fertile soil. In city or

Shade Garden with Ornamental Grasses

suburban gardens these problems are manageable, but no potentially troublesome grasses should be planted in country gardens where they can jump the fence into wildlands.

The more responsible garden centers and mail-order suppliers of ornamental grasses are sensitive to environmental issues and present the advantages and disadvantages of ornamental grasses in their descriptions.

Grass Lookalikes

Virtually all ornamental grasses prefer sun and well drained soil. When it comes to shaded or wet sites, the sedges in the genus *Carex* really shine. Some of the forest understory types grow into perfect mounds of rather wide, grass-like foliage. Others that adapt to stream banks or the shallows of ponds grow knee to waist high. Out in the sun, the sweet flags, *Acorus*, are proving indispensable in moist soil areas. Mondo grass, despite its name, is not a grass, but no matter. It is found in almost every Carolina garden in either dwarf or standard height cultivars.

An Honest Confession Is Good for the Soul

It took Jim Wilson a long lifetime to come to terms with the ornamental grasses. Educated in agriculture, he was acutely aware that many grasses, though introduced to America with the best of intentions, have escaped to become pests. For years, he wouldn't allow even one ornamental grass in his garden. He watched the plantings of *Miscanthus sinensis* along Carolina interstates with a wary eye and muttered, "I told you so!" when clumps began showing up in adjacent farmland. Moving to Missouri in 2002 to share a large garden that kept many cultivars of ornamental grasses showed him the positive side of grasses and lookalikes, especially their astounding variety. One of his first chores in his new garden was to dig out some valuable ground cover plants that were infested with seedlings of sea oats. He potted up the ground covers, carefully pried out the sea oats to get their long roots as well, replanted the ground cover, and mulched it to discourage future sea oat volunteers. You can bet he was muttering, "I told you so," all through the process.

Soil Preparation

Most ornamental grasses will grow in unimproved soil. However, they will "take" more reliably, establish sooner, and produce better looking plants in improved soil. If you are among the fortunate few with clay loam soil, adding amendments will result in only marginal increases in performance. However, on red clay Piedmont soils, incorporating limestone and a two-inch layer of organic soil conditioner or aged pine bark will improve drainage, water intake, and microbiological activity in the soil. On sandy soil near the coast and on the old sand dunes running southwest from Pinehurst to Columbia and Aiken, generous amounts of limestone and moistened peat moss or leaf coompost worked into the soil will greatly improve its moisture retention. Aged pine bark generally works best on clay soils, peat moss on sand. Initially and thereafter, yearly applications of organic mulch will help maintain a healthy organic content in your soil.

Managing Ornamental Grass

Be prepared for a difficult job when it comes to dividing big, old clumps of ornamental grasses. You'll need a sharp hatchet or machete. When just getting a start, purchase vigorous plants and prepare the soil thoroughly as suggested above. It will take up to a year for these plants to get firmly established and two years for them to grow to significant size. Once they have settled in, your patience will be rewarded. Weeds and weedy grass will try to grow among clumps of ornamental grasses. Save yourself labor by applying an approved granular pre-emergence herbicide that keeps weed and grass seeds from germinating.

The Tip of the Iceberg

Descriptions of a few of the most popular ornamental grasses follow. Entire books are written on the subject. If you need to see the actual plants to visualize how they would look in your garden, visit your nearest botanical or estate garden. A visit to a well-stocked garden center will help, but their plants are young and can't give you more than a hint of how they will look when full grown.

Ornamental Grasses Add Texture and Depth

Blue Clump Fescue
Festuca ovina var. glauca

Densely tufted blue-gray blue clump fescue is one of the more diminutive ornamental grasses; it can also be considered a ground cover. It has wiry blades up to 10 inches tall that retain their intense color through the heat of summer. In early summer, blue clump fescue displays soft buff-colored flowers on fifteen-inch stalks. It forms clumps up to a foot in diameter, making it ideal for use as a border or as an edging plant. With close spacing, the icy-blue blades will grow together, forming a low mass that resembles puffy clouds. Blue clump fescue would be an interesting choice for a turfgrass-like edging alongside hardy perennials or as an accent by a water garden. Try plugging it into planting pockets among large boulders.

Bloom Period and Seasonal Color
Buff-colored flowers in early summer.

Mature Height × Spread
15 in. × 12 in.

When, Where, and How to Plant
Since blue clump fescue is sold in pots, it can be planted spring and fall as long as the soil is not too wet. Plant in full sun, or in afternoon shade if in hot, sandy soil. Avoid heavy, poorly-drained soil. Wet soils in summer or planting too deep will create problems with crown rot, a fatal condition. Dig a hole 3/4 as deep and twice as wide as the pot. Position blue clump fescue in the prepared hole. Backfill with a loosened or amended soil and firm it over the root system. Apply a shallow mulch to a depth of 1 inch. Water well to get this grass established.

Growing Tips
Water only when leaf tips begin to fade, and you will have a wonderful landscape plant. Use a trowel, spade, or bulb planter to check the soil moisture at the 3-inch depth during the summer months before watering. Once established, this grass tolerates drought. Fertilize in the spring with a slow-release product. Supplemental fall fertilization maintains the plant's health and encourages good root development. Establishment in summer plantings is poor due to this plant's dormancy in hot weather.

Care
This species needs very little pruning, but you should shear blue clump fescue in early spring to remove winter-damaged foliage. If scale insects are a problem, they can be taken care of with very little effort; just apply an oil spray or systemic insecticide as recommended. Broadcast a granular weed-preventer to established beds, or control weeds with mulch and handweeding.

Companion Planting and Design
Plant blue clump fescue in small groupings as a landscape accent or use it as an edging along a walk. Blue foliage ("glauca") makes a fine addition by water features and garden statuary. The blue color is more intense during the cool weather of spring and fall.

Our Personal Favorite
'Elijah Blue' is deep sea-blue with whitish flower stalks.

Feather Reed Grass
Calamagrostis × *acutiflora* 'Karl Foerster'

When, Where, and How to Plant

Feather reed grass, a cool-season grass, allows planting in early spring or fall. In the western Carolinas, this grass will remain green into early winter because of its tolerance for cold. Plant in sunny locations with good air movement, especially in hot eastern regions. 'Karl Foerster' grows best in well drained, fertile soil with sufficient moisture but adapts to heavier clay soils on drier sites. Set potted plants in beds fortified with organic matter. Prepare new beds by spading or rototilling clay soils and incorporating fine pine bark or compost. Firm-in the plants and water immediately; irrigate every three days for three weeks.

Growing Tips

Feather reed grass needs watering during the coolest months of spring and fall. It may go into a semidormant (but still attractive) state in midsummer due to the heat. Don't fertilize in summer. Apply a turf-grade fertilizer like 16-8-8 in March; $^1/_4$ cup per plant suffices for the spring season. Fertilize again after Labor Day.

Care

Heavy rain or wind causes stems to droop, but they return to vertical after the storm. Feather reed grass is free of serious diseases and insects, and it overwinters well in containers. In Zone 8, heat, humidity, and poor air circulation can aggravate fungal diseases. Korean feather reed grass, *C. brachytricha*, can tolerate hot summers in the eastern Carolinas.

Companion Planting and Design

Plant in groups for a striking vertical accent in the perennial garden or use as a specimen plant by a gate or water garden. For companions to feather reed grass, select perennials with large leaves or coarse texture. Some designers use it for a fast-growing screen and in large containers with trailing tricolor sweet potatoes.

Our Personal Favorite

'Karl Foerster' is one of the most dynamic of the ornamental grasses.

The first "Perennial Plant of the Year" award of the twenty-first century went to this ornamental grass. It is a shoulder high, erect, deep green grass with highly ornamental flowering plumes. Feather reed grass is one of the most versatile, attractive, low maintenance plants in its class. The deep green, shiny, narrow blades appear in early spring and hold their color until early winter. Loose feathery plumes called "inflorescences" pop out in hot weather, changing from a pinkish color to a golden-tan at maturity. 'Karl Foerster' forms a tidy, attractive clump. The growth habit is vertical with a tuft of foliage two to three feet tall and flower stems to five feet in height. Feather reed grass is called the "perpetual motion grass." The slightest breeze sets it in motion.

Bloom Period and Seasonal Color
Light-pink plumes appear by June, maturing to a tan color by winter.

Mature Height × Spread
4 to 5 ft. × 1$^1/_2$ ft.

Fountain Grass
Pennisetum setaceum

Fountain grass, a semi-hardy perennial, is immediately recognizable in landscapes or containers. It is by far the most popular and easiest ornamental grass to grow. The fountain grasses are well named, as their narrow leaves form graceful, arching fountains of foliage. Modern landscape designs use this fabulous grass in sweeping, undulating curves. Large containers show the fountain shape and tessellated plumes to good advantage. The purple variety with blond plumes, P. setaceum 'Rubrum', became an instant hit in the South following the 1996 Atlanta Olympic Games. P. orientale, 'Karley Rose', bears beautiful rose-tan plumes on dark green foliage. The newer dwarf selections look great as ground covers. The various species of fountain grass will overwinter in Zone 8 but further west are treated as annuals.

Bloom Period and Seasonal Color
Foxtail-like flower plumes in July; golden foliage in autumn.

Mature Height × Spread
2 to 6 ft. × 4 ft.

When, Where, and How to Plant
Fountain grass can be planted at any time spring through fall as long as the soil is not frozen or too wet. It prefers full sun for optimum growth, and average to good soil is suitable. Dig a hole as deep as the container and twice as wide for individual plantings. Rototill entire beds 10 inches deep for solid plantings. Space the fuller-figured varieties at least 5 feet apart, while the dwarfs can fill in with 2-foot spacings. Mix a starter fertilizer into the soil and backfill with the loosened soil. Water well at planting and a few weeks following. Apply a granular weed-preventer in group plantings for the first few seasons or be prepared to handweed later. Mulch to a depth of at least 2 inches.

Growing Tips
For vigorous growth, water fountain grasses occasionally; they flower more fully and for a longer period with adequate moisture. In spring, provide a slow-release nursery fertilizer or 10-10-10 fertilizer at $^1/_2$ cup per plant. To maintain plant health on sandy soils, summer feeding is recommended.

Care
Fountain grass is relatively trouble free. It requires no regular pruning during the growing season and is drought tolerant once established. In early spring or late fall, cut it back to 6 inches high if cold damage occurs. A couple of *Pennisetum* types, like *P. alopecuroides* 'Moudry', self-sow freely in the warmer zones; the black-seeded annual variety can become a weed problem even in Zone 7. Divide large clumps every five years to prevent centers from dying out in crowns.

Companion Planting and Design
Group plantings can have a breathtakingly beautiful effect when the wind swirls the foliage. Groups of fountain grass work quite well as an anchor for the ends of planting beds. Single plants can serve as focal points in beds of low-growing annuals.

Our Personal Favorites
Toby likes 'Hamelin', a 2-foot dwarf with rose-colored blooms, for edging shrub beds. Jim is still taken with purple fountain grass.

Maiden Grass
Miscanthus sinensis 'Gracillimus'

When, Where, and How to Plant

Maiden grass can be planted spring through fall as long as the soil is workable. Grow in sun, in any type of soil from wetlands to dry, rocky slopes. Dig a planting hole twice as wide as the rootball and of equal depth. Space plants 6 to 8 feet to allow for mature spread. Loosen the roots of potbound plants; make several vertical slits in the rootball and shake off soil into the planting hole. With group plantings, till the entire area instead of digging individual holes. Water well to settle the soil. Apply an approved weed-preventer in large beds before mulching. Mulch to a depth of 2 inches.

Growing tips

Water on a weekly basis until established. Afterward, water bimonthly if there is no rain. A little water during dry summers will win you a garden friend for life. Feed in spring with a slow-release turfgrass fertilizer. A supplemental summer feeding the first two years will help establish the new plant. (Note: Overly rich soil may cause stems to stretch and topple over.) Once established, clumps will not need fertilizing every year; they'll thrive on neglect.

Care

Remove suckers or daughter-shoots from the base of the grass in late spring for transplanting into new beds. Prune vigorous grasses using power hedge shears or handheld lopping shears. Cut back only during the early spring before new growth emerges. You may cut the grass as close as 6 to 8 inches to the ground. Thinning rejuvenates old plantings. Maiden grass resists diseases and insects.

Companion Planting and Design

The feathery plumes make photo ops when reflected in water gardens and pools. Group plantings can double as a summer privacy screen and a delightful backdrop for perennial borders. These plants are too massive to use as background for small annuals. Instead, pair them with Mexican bush salvia, 'Red Shield' hibiscus, mid-height sunflowers, or spiderflower.

Our Personal Favorites

'Cabaret' and 'Morning Light' are considered the best for color and texture.

Maiden grass, once plain green, has seen a transformation thanks to the breeding efforts of keen plantsmen. New introductions deliver improved forms, color, and dramatic plumes. The upright, arching leaves of this cultivar have a white midvein that is distinctly visible close up. It is completely hardy all across the Carolinas where it forms large clumps of finely textured silver-green blades. Maiden grass is most useful as a naturalizing grass where it can be used in groups for vertical accent and texture but also kept under control. Its substantial plants can substitute for shrubs. In autumn, the leaves are topped with large, fan-shaped, delicate, silver-white blooms. These flower heads are at first reddish, then silver. The autumn foliage turns vivid golden and looks good until beaten down by ice storms.

Other Common Names
Eulalia, Silver Grass

Bloom Period and Seasonal Color
Silver-white blooms in fall.

Mature Height × Spread
3 to 7 ft. × 3 to 5 ft.

Pampas Grass
Cortaderia selloana

Pampas grass is the grandfather of ornamental grasses. Summer foliage is light green, turning beige-tan in winter. In September, pampas grass develops its signature feature: two-feet-long, eight-inch-wide, feather-duster flower plumes suited for dried arrangements. They remain throughout the winter, providing visual relief to drab landscapes. The plumes display especially well in windy sites or coastal gardens where the tall fluffy heads are continuously on the move. In addition to its dominant presence in the landscape, this large, clump-forming grass offers low maintenance and high tolerance of drought conditions. Not every landscape is suitable for pampas grass because of its potential size and razor-sharp, arching leaf blades, but where it can be used it is a conversation piece in both fall and winter.

Bloom Period and Seasonal Color
Silvery-white flower heads from late summer into winter.

Mature Height × Spread
4 to 7 ft. × 5 to 10 ft.

When, Where, and How to Plant
Container-grown pampas grass may be planted during the spring through fall seasons. Plant in full sun in well-drained soil. Set the plant in a hole as deep and twice as wide as the container. Backfill with the original soil if it is loamy; mix bulb fertilizer and bagged cow manure or organic soil conditioner into heavy clay soil before backfilling. Water well to settle the soil around the roots. In large-group plantings, a weed-preventer may be practical. Consult with the County Cooperative Extension Service before applying herbicide around newly planted grasses. Mulch to a depth of 2 inches. Dig and divide clumps in mid-spring after leaf growth.

Growing Tips
Water thoroughly weekly for the first month. Drill or band a slow-release 2-1-1 ratio lawn fertilizer or similar organic fertilizer around plants when your pampas grass has greened up in mid-spring. Established plants require watering only during extended droughts.

Care
In the Piedmont and western regions of the Carolinas, delay pruning the spent foliage until the worst of the cold has passed, possibly into late March. Old leaves add winter protection. Cut back the entire plant (better wear gloves!) in late winter or early spring to a 6-inch height before any new growth begins. Note: pampas grass seeds produce both male and female plants. The female plants (unlike birds) have the large showy plumes. Purchase plants in the fall to get plants with the gaudy plumage. This species is pest- and disease-free.

Companion Planting and Design
Use pampas grass as a windscreen on the coast or as a background for a border of fall-blooming perennials. The fluffy plumage is wonderful against the red foliage of Japanese maples or alongside cannas. A pink-flowered variety would make a fine companion for large-frame perennials. If you see pampas grass with black or red plumes, suspect a Gamecock booster with paint spray cans.

Our Personal Favorite
The compact variety, 'Pumila', has gray-green leaves with white heads and fits small yards.

Purple Muhly Grass

Muhlenbergia filipes

When, Where, and How to Plant

To enjoy the purple fog the following summer, set out plants of muhly grass in the fall. Set out potted plants in full sun, in well drained soil. Muhly grass is particular about where it will spread and settle. It likes well-aerated, rather dry soil. Start with at least 12 plants set on 1-foot centers to create a drift that will stand out in a landscape. Place the drift on your property where you won't have to see the plain green plants during much of the year but where they'll get attention at bloom stage. Shake the roots before planting and loosen the root systems of potted plants. Set them at grade level.

Growing Tips

Water plants thoroughly immediately after setting them out and especially if you risk planting during warm weather. Water twice weekly for two weeks then decrease watering to bimonthly between rains. Fertilize with 10-10-10 or liquid feed in early summer. Be faithful in keeping your patch of muhly grass weed-free by using a granular pre-emergence herbicide or a scuffle hoe that doesn't dig deep into the soil.

Care

Let the seedheads stand until at least midwinter to drop seeds and thicken the stand. Muhly doesn't have to be mowed or cut with a string trimmer. If you don't mind a little natural messiness, the new shoots will come up through the old and hide them. Transplant volunteer seedlings to the perimeter of the patch to increase its size.

Companion Planting and Design

Muhly grass looks "born free" and out of place when prettied up with garden flowers or used as an edging. However, in drifts amongst other ornamental grasses, it's perfectly in place, as if it were there before you arrived and began rearranging things. Burgundy foliage and flowers blooming in September are fine companions in autumn.

Our Personal Favorite

Be sure you specify purple muhly grass. It is native across the Carolinas. Other species are native to entirely different ecosystems in Texas and the Southwest.

A native American species, purple muhly grass looks best in sizable drifts. Individual plants are green and rather ordinary and insubstantial looking for much of the year. But near the end of August, your drift of muhly grass will look as if a purple fog had settled on it. The flower heads are large and delicate, with the texture of spider webs, and spangled with dew each morning. Its autumn display is spectacular with fall blooming perennials. You won't need to be cautioned not to walk on or through a patch of muhly grass; common sense will direct you around it. If you think you've seen it somewhere else, wild stands of purple muhly grass grow in a few undisturbed grasslands across the Carolinas.

Other Common Name
Hairy Awn Muhly

Bloom Period and Seasonal Color
Frothy heads of purple flowers in late summer.

Mature Height × Spread
4 ft. × 2 ft.

Perennials *for the Carolinas*

A perennial, in the broadest horticultural definition, is any plant that lives three or more years. Although trees, shrubs, and vines are perennials, gardeners usually use the term to refer to herbaceous perennial flowers. In autumn, the soft tops of most perennials will die to the ground, while the root system persists through the winter. In spring the cycle begins anew, with growth from a crown or modified roots. Among the most rewarding traits of perennials is that they come up unprompted year after year to offer the garden masses of color in ever-changing patterns from April to November. They flower abundantly and multiply without being coaxed. Some will tolerate considerable neglect, and a few, like artemisia, prefer it that way. Perennial gardens are the rage all across the Carolinas.

Perennials are classified based on their hardiness. Hardy perennials will normally survive Carolina winters with little or no protection. Tender or half-hardy perennials will survive a mild winter in Zone 8 gardens but will need mulching in the mountain counties. Some, such as verbena and hardy iceplant, are usually grown as annuals in cold zones. Hardiness does not, however, refer to the ability to withstand heat and drought. Microclimates and soil drainage are factors in determining how long-lived a perennial will be at any particular site. Some peonies have been known to live for more than one hundred years.

How to Be Successful

The distinction between annuals and perennials is that annuals bloom continuously for many months, while many perennials bloom for only a few weeks each season. For this reason, it is important to consider what a plant will look like throughout the year. One of the basic goals of gardeners should be to obtain continuity of color by planting different varieties for bloom at different times. As one kind of perennial finishes, another begins to bloom. Perennials with colorful foliage, such as coralbells and purple heart, may be more valuable in the garden's design than those that only bloom and have foliage of marginal interest.

Site selection is very important to perennial gardens since these plants will be left in place for several years. Most thrive in full-sun conditions where the soil drains well. The showiest floral display is found in the sunniest beds. Soil pH requirements vary among perennials, but most prefer a pH between 5.5 and 6.5. A consistent, moderate level of soil moisture is important because most perennials are succulent and non-woody. While many will tolerate a wet location for a short period of time, most will be killed by extended periods of wet soil, especially during the winter. A two- to four-inch layer of fine pine-bark soil conditioner can be tilled into beds before planting to improve soil drainage and aeration. Sedum, salvia, and other semi-woody

Purple Coneflowers

perennials will benefit greatly from quick draining soils where coarse soil amendments are incorporated as needed.

Opportunities and Challenges

When growing perennial flowers, you are not limited to sunny borders, since many perennials flourish in the shade. Some of the best plants, such as lungwort, wild ginger, ferns, and hosta, can be used to create a showstopper garden where a majestic oak shadows the bed. Shaded sites can be problematic, however, in that tree roots forage into well prepared sites; and you will find it challenging to meet the water requirements of some perennials in shade gardens. Most woodland perennials will thrive in moist shade conditions, but there are precious few flowering plants that will survive in the dry soils found in some shady locations. The survival of many ephemeral wildflowers has to do with their ability to bloom in early spring when light and moisture are plentiful; after which they phase into dormancy during less favorable environmental periods. Many of our native woodland orchid species and trilliums flourish because of their resilience.

Another challenge with perennials is to keep some of them from overgrowing others in the same bed, becoming an unsightly jungle. Two examples of aggressive plants are obedient plant and pink showy primrose. (Ironically, the name of the former has nothing to with its land-grabbing proclivity.) Both native perennials will waste no time in dominating a border. Your success with perennials, as it is with so many other landscape ornamentals, has much to do with selecting the right plant for a particular site. Iris, for example, grows in a variety of soil types. Siberian iris is content in extraordinarily dry soil, while Japanese and Louisiana iris thrive in bog gardens. Planting in the right spot ensures that minimal care will be required to get the best results.

Perennial Maintenance

Whoever said that perennials were low-maintenance plants was either an exceptional garden designer or one who moved across town before the garden matured. Maintenance will be required for any species of perennial flower. Maintenance is an inescapable part of gardening.

Spacing plants so they produce a solid canopy and mulching are the best ways to minimize weed problems. Some plants will require staking, others deadheading to encourage repeat flowering. Gardens need water during dry periods and occasional fertilization for healthy foliage. While you can overdo it with fertilizer, you should not have problems if you amend beds based on a soil test report. Some gardeners fertilize every four to six weeks with a water-soluble bloom-booster fertilizer. An alternative is to use a slow-release product applied early at planting and again by midseason.

There has been much concern about the volume of water required to maintain horticultural plantings in the Carolinas. Many counties are experiencing water shortages and have set mandatory water restrictions to conserve this resource. In order to be good stewards, many gardeners in urban areas have elected to use perennials that are less dependent on supplemental irrigation. Since many perennials are water hogs, pay special attention to the ones that are drought-tolerant. County Cooperative Extension Service provides lists of these durable species. Many of these are found in the pages that follow.

While there is specific information about pests included in the "Care" section provided, consider these general comments apropos to perennial gardening. First, don't apply excess fertilizers to these plants as it is an open invitation to sucking insects, such as aphids or white flies. Insects feast on luscious new growth produced in abundance as a response to too much nitrogen. While beneficial insects found in flower gardens are usually sufficient to manage most pests, they need your help. Use a garden hose with forceful stream of water to dislodge insect pests. To eliminate infestations, reach for the non-toxic insecticides containing soaps and horticultural oils. To thwart diseases, irrigate early in the day to keep foliage dry at night, and mulch beds. It is important to consult a horticulturist when diseases appear and especially before purchasing a curative fungicide.

The Benefits of Planning

It is important to spend time planning a perennial garden, much as you would for a room addition. Traditionally, perennials are planted in large beds six to twelve feet wide and are best displayed against backgrounds such as evergreens, a stone wall, or a fence. Consider using a walk or edging material in the foreground to reduce maintenance. Place tall varieties in the back, graduating down to smaller plants toward the front. Use color in bold groups, not spotted here and there. Vertical interest can be achieved by incorporating ornamental grasses, accessories, and structures. While perennials are not generally associated with formal design, they are versatile and will provide enjoyment in myriad locations.

Creating Well-Drained Soil

Gardeners use this term to define drainage within the soil, not just water that runs off. Most perennials demand well drained soil, but most upland Carolina soils emphatically aren't. You can make them so. For preparing ground beds, use the same procedure as outlined in the "Annuals" chapter introduction. However, you will find that perennials are more often planted individually or in small groups, perhaps among established perennials or shrubs. This becomes a routine way to distribute the bounty that comes from dividing crowns of perennials, receiving plants from gardening, or moving plants for a better display.

"Spot" soil improvement, involving limited areas, is a good way to ensure that your new perennials will grow well and endure for years. Dig the soil to spade depth, break up clods, and add soil conditioners to loosen and aerate the soil. On Carolina clays, delay digging until the soil has

A Garden Full of Perennials

dried enough to crumble. Spread two inches of organic soil conditioner (see glossary) or PermaTill®, a heat-expanded slate product that looks like gray gravel. Also add 1-2-2 ratio garden fertilizer (also see glossary) at the rate of two pounds per one hundred square feet and pelletized dolomitic limestone at the rate of five pounds per one hundred square feet. If you have had your soil tested, use those recommendations instead. Thoroughly mix the additives into the soil.

On coastal sands and the rare sandy land that occurs elsewhere, add only the organic soil conditioner and cut the fertilizer and lime applications by half. Sandy soil has little capacity to store surplus amounts of mineral additives. It may sound implausible, but certain sandy soils drain slowly. If so, suspect a layer of compacted fine particles (called hardpan) some distance below the surface. Break it up by spading.

Berms

In clay soils, perennials grow better, live longer, and display beautifully when planted on "berms." Picture irregularly-shaped mounds of sandy loam topsoil in your yard, rising to a height of eighteen to twenty-four inches at the center, and sloping down to ground level around the perimeter. Now, surround that image with metal edging that protrudes high enough to trap mulch and keep it from washing into the lawn. Berms are expensive to install but are well worth their cost. However, if you practice pay-as-you-go gardening, you can expect as good results from less expensive raised beds created by adding soil conditioner and play sand or organic conditioners.

Planting Perennials

Perennials are almost always sold in larger containers than annuals because they are customarily grown from cuttings, divisions of crowns, tubers, or explants from micropropagation rather than from seeds. Read and save plant labels in a garden journal or record into a database. They will tell you which cultivars demand well drained soil and those that will thrive in wet, poorly aerated areas. (The latter includes obedient plant, Joe-pye weed, ironweed, turtlehead, cardinal flower, hardy hibiscus, and many others.)

Prepare soil as directed. Container-grown perennials can be planted at any time in the Carolinas, but fall through early spring is far and away the best time. In mountain areas, spring is the best planting time, after the soil has thawed. Cool soil, frequent showers, and decreased transpiration all encourage root development that prepares the plant to bloom the following year. Transplanting perennials from late spring through summer steadily decreases survivability due to increased water needs. You absolutely must water every two or three days between rains to keep up with the demands of a developing root system and burgeoning top growth and the loss of soil moisture taken up by roots and transpired through the foliage.

Dig planting holes the recommended distance apart, and have a hose equipped with a water wand or a five-gallon container of water when you're ready to plant.

Tap the plant out of the container. If only a few roots girdle the rootball or mat at the bottom, set the rootball in the planting hole with as little disturbance to it as possible. More often than not, perennial plants are potbound, with substantial root development girdling the sides of the rootball and matting at the bottom. Using hand shears, snip off the mat and cut major girdling roots. Then, bang the plant on a solid surface to knock off some of the rooting medium and to expose root tips. This seemingly rough treatment prepares the plant to send new developing roots into the surrounding soil.

Set the plant in the planting hole so that the top of the rootball is level with the surface of the surrounding soil or as much as $1/2$ inch above it. Pull the conditioned backfill around the rootball and firm it down lightly. Complete planting the other selections chosen for that spot and soak the area with water without delay.

Toby advocates adding a diluted, water-soluble organic fertilizer to this initial watering. Jim prefers to use only water at planting time and to drench the soil with liquid fertilizer two to three weeks later when the plants have begun to send out new feeder roots. This goes to show you that gardening is more art than science and that personal preference trumps written rules. Both approaches work well.

How to handle home-divided perennials is a different matter. When you dig clumps of perennials during fall or winter, wash the soil off the roots before surgery and cut, saw, or break the clumps into smaller, well-rooted parts. You can set out the divisions at the same time. Or if they are from choice, expensive plants or ones with sentimental value, you can pot the plants in potting soil, grow them for a few weeks, and set them in place with a well-developed root system. The former approach requires more frequent watering to guarantee that your new plants will "take." Both Jim and Toby have small "nurseries" at their homes where they can hold vegetative divisions while they are developing roots. Their holding areas are near water faucets and are protected from foraging by wildlife.

Watering

The difficulty of watering increases exponentially in proportion to the distance between plants and a water faucet. Most gardeners prefer to coil water hoses when they are not in use. But leaving them out, with a sprinkler attached, will simplify frequent watering of new plantings. Turn the pressure on just enough to water the planted area, set a timer for an hour, and turn it off. Do this every two or three days until you see new growth on your plants then reduce watering to weekly during dry spells. Thereafter, the frequency of watering depends to some extent on the species you plant. Most perennials will grow well within a wide range of frequency and duration of watering. A few kinds languish if not watered frequently and deeply, but some others will die with the same treatment. Research will help keep the species sorted by water requirements, but over the long haul, only experience will reduce your failure experience closer to zero.

Mulching

You will discover that you shouldn't mulch perennials as deeply as you do shrubs and trees. A depth of one to two inches is sufficient; if you apply it any deeper, the mulch will tend to drift into the crowns of perennials, which can lead to rotting of stems. In addition to the benefits common to mulching— suppression of weeds, conservation of moisture, and gradual conversion into humus—mulching around perennial plants also creates a seedbed where seeds dropped by perennials can sprout and grow into additional plants. (This can be a blessing or a curse, depending on the size of the seed crop and the difficulty of removing excessive seedlings.) Any of the many organic mulches, such as aged ground pine bark, hardwood bark, cottonboll compost, peanut or rice hulls, will work well. But across the Carolinas pine straw is preferred. It can be pulled in around perennials to a depth of four to six inches without causing stems to rot. It will soon pack down to an inch or two in depth and will begin slowly to decompose. Removal of pine straw is rarely necessary but easy to do.

Maintaining Fertile Soil

Most of the fertilizers mentioned in this book are not acceptable to organic gardeners. While both Toby and Jim applaud organic gardening, they recognize that in this busy world, mineral fertilizers are easier, faster, and more predictable than strictly organic nutrient sources. If applied wisely, mineral fertilizers need not damage the environment. Both Toby and Jim are pragmatic and realize that in the Southeast, creating enough homemade compost to maintain soil fertility is seldom possible without bringing in lots of organic matter from elsewhere. Organic matter decomposes rapidly during our many months of hot, rainy weather.

Highly disciplined organic gardeners insist that fertilizers made from byproducts from grain mills, abbatoirs, or fisheries be certifiably organic. That complicates matters because most grains and livestock are not grown "organically," and the packaged byproduct fertilizers such as cottonseed meal and soybean meal are impermissible. Fish byproducts are customarily juiced up with mineral additives to raise the nutrient content on the package label. Purists are trapped in a Catch-22 bind.

Toby and Jim take the middle route of using plenty of organic soil conditioners and mulches plus modest amounts of mineral fertilizers. Neither works at peak performance alone; they need each other to "feed the soil," which in turn feeds plants. The authors also believe in soil testing, in large part to regulate soil pH. Neither organic nor mineral fertilizers will release nutrients at optimum rates in the Carolinas' acid soils. Liming per soil tests every two or three years helps regulate nutrient release.

Included in the several categories of fertilizer are granular, "complete" garden or flower fertilizers, water-soluble crystalline fertilizers for liquid feeding, and controlled-release fertilizers. The most efficient is controlled or extended release fertilizer. It is also the most expensive. Next in efficiency is liquid feeding, but it, too, can be expensive if soils are drastically short on major nutrients. The least efficient but cheapest is granular garden fertilizer. You can improve its effect by "drilling" or "banding" it into furrows and covering the furrows with soil. Drilling decreases the amount of nitrogen lost to volatilization and traps the phosphate and potash so they don't wash away during heavy rains. Drilling the fertilizer into bands concentrates the fertilizer into a small area rather than mixing it with the soil. Digging fertilizer into the soil is better than scattering it over the surface, but it exposes fertilizer particles to fixation in insoluble forms.

If all this makes your head hurt, let's talk about some of the perennial flowers known to grow well in the Carolinas.

Perennials and Ornamental Grasses

Artemisia

Artemisia spp.

Dozens of artemisias, including some annuals, are available, but it is the robust ornamental perennials that are most garden worthy. While the flowers are not particularly attractive, the silver-gray foliage of artemisia is quite distinctive and delivers great value as an accent in the garden. The variation in texture among the artemisias is as vast as their variation in height. Plant this perennial herb in dry sites where many flowers shrivel. Gardeners in rural or suburban parts of the Carolinas often have problems with deer browsing their gardens. Artemisia is one perennial that deer seem to ignore while they forage through landscapes. The day or night luminescence of artemisia, its season-long foliage color, and its drought tolerance make this plant an irresistible choice for the garden.

Other Common Name
Wormwood

Bloom Period and Seasonal Color
Flowers are not showy, appearing in late summer on feathery gray foliage.

Mature Height × Spread
1/2 ft. to 4 ft. × 1 to 2 1/2 ft.

When, Where, and How to Plant
Plant artemisia after the soil has warmed in May and through early November. Plants are usually sold in 1-gallon pots. Do not plant in moist soils but in sunny, poor, dry sites. When planting in clay soils, incorporate a shovelful of granite screenings, aged pine bark, or Perma-Till® per plant for drainage purposes. All major cultivars are adapted to container gardening as well as ground beds. Spacing varies from 1 to 4 feet. Read plant labels carefully; some cultivars grow to impressive bushes while others lie flat on the ground and grow to only 2 feet across.

Growing Tips
Artemisia will grow in poor soils but develops better color with light fertilization. Feed when you cut plants back in the spring and again in late summer. Water established plants only when tip growth flags a bit but before plants begin to lose color.

Care
Some artemisias spread like wildfire, especially 'Silver King,' and 'Oriental Nights.' You may wish to grow them in containers. Others, such as the popular 'Powis Castle' spread slowly by roots but billow out to cover large areas. You will need to cut them back severely, preferably in early spring. Few pests bother strongly scented artemisia. Divide crowns in late summer and fall, or locate where branches have touched the ground and rooted. Cut fore and aft of the rooted area, dig up and pot the plant, and set it out when a full root system has formed. Flower arrangers who grow artemisias for drying often confine them in raised, framed-in beds.

Companion Planting and Design
The silver artemisias look great interspersed among other perennials and shrubs. The tiny 'Silver Mound,' while beautiful, may be too delicate for the coast and hot sandhills but flourishes in the mountains. Try pairing artemisias with plumbago, perennial salvias, and blue mist shrub.

Our Personal Favorites
'Powis Castle' is a winner. Southernwood, a shrubby, green artemisia, makes an attractive (if smelly) waist-high bush.

When, Where, and How to Plant

Plant in full sun or light afternoon shade at any time through early summer. Plants are usually offered in 6- to 8-inch pots during the spring season. A few garden centers grow them to first color stage and sell the plants for instant color in the fall. Set plants 2 to 3 feet apart. Most asters aren't well suited to container growing; they grow too large. Native aster species will grow in unimproved soil, but all will perform better with a little help from friends.

Growing Tips

Two drenches with water-soluble flower fertilizer thirty and sixty days after spring planting should prevent nutrient deficiencies. Fall-planted asters shouldn't be fed until the following spring, in order to avoid tenderizing the plants.

Care

In early spring, cut perennial asters back to 4 to 6 inches in height. In rich soil, when blooms begin to open, you may need to circle clumps with twine and pull the stems into a loose column to keep them from flopping.

Companion Planting and Design

Asters bloom so late that they have the show pretty much to themselves. For this reason, buy 3 of each cultivar and set them in groups. Single plants can be lost in the jumble of late summer foliage. In large gardens try Tatarian aster, *A. tataricus,* which can grow taller than head high. Its huge trusses of small, light blue flowers sustain Monarch butterflies on their way to Mexico for the winter.

Our Personal Favorites

Aromatic aster performs well all over the South, as far west as Texas. 'Purple Dome' is the first true dwarf form of New England aster; it never needs pinching or support. 'Fanny's Aster' is a real "looker," with spectacular powder-blue flowers on a compact 18-inch plant. Our native *Aster concolor,* Eastern silvery-aster, was designated Wildflower of the Year in 1996 by the North Carolina Botanical Garden and The Garden Club of North Carolina.

Experienced gardeners usually grow several species or hybrids of asters among their spring or summer-blooming perennials. For much of the growing season, perennial asters put their energy into developing rounded clumps of foliage. Then, when days begin to grow short, flower buds form and break into bloom. Unimproved species of asters tend to grow waist-high, but dwarf varieties are available for small gardens. A. frikartii, a hybrid, is perhaps the most popular of the asters, beloved for its 2½-inch blossoms in blue or violet shades. A tougher native, aromatic aster (A. oblongifolius) blooms later and has smaller but more numerous blooms in violet-blue shades. One that always attracts admiration is the pink 'Alma Potshke,' a hybrid between two native species, New England aster and New York aster.

Other Common Name
Perennial Aster

Bloom Period
Late summer to fall in shades of crimson, pink, lavender, violet-blue, and white.

Mature Height × Spread
Dwarf cultivars, 1 to 1½ ft. × 1½ ft.
Taller cultivars, 2 to 4 ft. × 2 to 3 ft.

Baptisia
Baptisia alba

You may find it hard to believe that the beautiful and showy baptisia is a wildflower. It grows along many rural Carolina roadsides where it is spared the ministrations of the DOT mowing teams. In early summer, tall, curving spikes of white, pea-like flowers are in bloom for two to three weeks. The flowers are followed by bladder-like seed pods. Its three-parted leaves usually keep their blue-green color long after the flowers have faded. Less common but equally beautiful is the violet-blue-flowered species, B. australis. No, it isn't native to Australia; the botanical name simply indicates it is from the South. Plant breeders have intensified the color of blue baptisia to such a degree that even the stems of these selections take on a deep purple tinge.

Other Common Names
Wild White Indigo, White Indigo

Bloom Period
Early summer; white or violet-blue, depending on species

Mature Height × Spread
2 to 3 ft. × 1 1/2 to 2 ft., depending on the age of the plant.

When, Where, and How to Plant
Set out plants in spring so they can become established before bloom. Handle carefully; new growth is brittle. Plant seeds in pots filled with potting soil and leave them outside to "stratify" the seeds with colder temperatures and hasten germination. Baptisia develops a deep root system to support heavy crops of spikes that are notoriously sensitive to being moved. Although baptisia tolerates afternoon shade, it grows best in full sun. Baptisia does not demand good soil, but it does seek out well-drained sites in the wild. You might have to wait two or three years for baptisia to bloom.

Growing Tips
After blooming is over, water the plants well then drench the soil around each plant with 1 gallon of water-soluble flower fertilizer dissolved per directions. During a very dry year, give them a good soaking when flower spikes begin to lengthen.

Care
Baptisias aren't accustomed to being fussed over. Being a deep-rooted legume, they don't need regular watering and benefit from being planted away from wimpy perennials that need an inch of water a week from rain or sprinklers. To maintain plant vigor, snip off spent spikes before they form seeds. If you wish to save seeds, harvest them early and let them dry in a paper bag. Mix and store the seeds with a handful of ground hot peppers to keep seed-eating insects away. Don't trim back the clumps until fall; the blue-green or purple-green foliage is handsome all summer. Baptisia blooms from persistant crowns and develops very rapidly.

Companion Planting and Design
The commanding spikes of baptisia combine well with the vigorous plants of 'Becky' Shasta daisy, artemisia 'Powis Castle', and salvia 'May Night'. The blues bloom later than the white species that gives a succession of color.

Our Personal Favorites
Jim admits a fondness for 'Purple Smoke,' one of the blue baptisias. Toby's favorite is the vigorous 'Carolina Moonlight' hybrid with soft yellow spikes.

Coneflower

Echinacea purpurea

When, Where, and How to Plant

Plant purple coneflower in full sun or dappled shade in spring and fall. Transplant volunteer seedlings after rain has soaked the soil. If buying native coneflowers, make sure they were not dug from wild populations but were grown from seeds. Seeds can be started in early spring or summer in nursery flats and transplanted when plants have 4 to 6 leaves. Direct-seeding also works, but survival will be low. Expect flowers the second year. Rich, sandy soils provide the best growth, but well-drained mineral and clay soils also produce fine plants. Dig planting holes twice as wide and of equal depth to the container. Plant in groups with individuals 12 to 18 inches apart. Consult the "Annuals" chapter introduction for soil preparation.

Growing Tips

During extreme drought, deeply water every two or three weeks to sustain blooming. Once established, coneflowers are very drought-tolerant and do not demand fertilization, but keep an eye on plants and if they develop poor foliage color, feed them. Thin layers of bark or leaf mulch aid in weed control and stabilization of soil moisture.

Care

Disease- and pest-resistant purple coneflower will rebloom if deadheaded. Remove dead stalks in fall and winter, and thin beds. Once established, it requires no extra care for survival. Japanese beetles may feed on the petals during bloom.

Companion Planting and Design

Dependable coneflowers are the backbone of wildflower areas or more formal borders. Because of their height, place plants toward the back of your perennial border. Plant in sizable drifts for best effect. Good companions are artemisia, bluebeard, aster, and butterfly bush. Expect goldfinches to appear when the seeds mature.

Our Personal Favorites

Award-winning 'Magnus' with its 5-inch flowers is hard to beat. 'Knee-High' will fit in among shorter flowers. To confound your expert gardening friends, plant *E. paradoxa* (yellow flowers!) or Wayside's unique double 'Razzmatazz'.

This wonderful perennial has daisy-like flowers, each with a prominent center cone or disc surrounded by a skirt of ray petals. An easy-to-grow native of North American prairies, purple coneflower has been accepted as a garden plant around the world. It produces long-lasting flowers from early summer through late fall; the strong-stemmed blooms make excellent cut flowers. A sturdy, rather coarse plant, purple coneflower has showy purplish-pink to almost-white flowers. The seed-bearing cones last for months until discovered by songbirds. Butterflies are attracted to the large flowers all summer long. Once established, purple coneflower seeds produce abundant volunteers. Echinacea laevigata, the smooth coneflower, is an endangered sister species native to the Piedmont. Other worthwhile hardy perennial coneflowers include yellow coneflower, Ratibida pinnata, and Mexican hat, R. columnifera.

Bloom Period and Seasonal Color

Summer blooms in purplish-pink, white or yellow ray petals with dark central cones.

Mature Height × Spread

2 to 5 ft. × 1 to 2 ft.

Coralbells
Heuchera sanguinea

Today's coralbells boast long-stemmed flowers, foliage in many colors, and tolerance of hot, humid weather. A parent of many improved hybrids is a Carolina native, H. americana. Coralbells is a low-growing perennial with maple-like, lustrous foliage that radiates from a rosette. Its beautiful foliage alone would be reason enough to grow this semi-evergreen perennial. Some of the showiest coralbells have plum-colored leaves glistening with a metallic sheen. Others display foliage patterns like stained glass windows. The airy flower spikes range in color from cherry to coral and can be as lovely as the distinctive foliage. In early summer, the sway of the 18-inch spikes will create movement in the garden as the delicate bell-shaped blooms toss about in the breeze. Surprisingly, hummingbirds are attracted to the tiny individual blossoms.

Other Common Name
Alumroot

Bloom Period and Seasonal Color
White, pink, and crimson flowers during summer months.

Mature Height × Spread
1 to 2 ft. × 1 1/2 to 2 ft.

When, Where, and How to Plant
Plant potted coralbells in spring or fall. Sow seed in early fall for spring seedlings. Seedlings can be divided in early summer and set 15 inches apart in beds. Coralbells prefer dappled light and are happiest in partial shade. To prevent problems, plant coralbells only in moist, fertile soil. Good drainage is essential. Plants grow well in acidic soils, so there is no need to add lime. When setting out potted plants, dig a hole three times the size of the rootball. In heavy clay soils, work leaf compost or granite screenings into the soil before you transplant. In wet sites, plant on slightly elevated berms. Water well to settle the soil. Mulching can enrich the soil and improve the survival of plants.

Growing Tips
Water deeply, twice weekly, until plants establish. When flowering begins, water weekly, particularly during dry periods. Mulching in summer is important, but keep mulches away from the fleshy crowns. Scrape back the mulch and apply slow-release fertilizer in spring. Replace the mulch as needed.

Care
Rake beds clean in spring to remove old debris. A heavy layer of leaves can suffocate plants. In autumn following a hard freeze, remove frozen foliage. Clumps of coralbells can get quite large over time. Divide every four or five years to invigorate the bed and increase your holdings. Slugs and snails can damage or destroy young plants; use a slug bait or saucers of beer for control.

Companion Planting and Design
This perennial is suitable for using along a walk or by a water garden. Collections of several varieties of coralbells plus related foamflowers and hybrid "heucherellas" look great when interspersed with *Lamium* 'White Nancy', ferns, and astilbes in shade gardens. The low growing, variegated, yellow and green *Vincas* make exotic foils for coralbells.

Our Personal Favorites
'Garnet' is one of the few that adapt well to hot sites, but 'Palace Purple' has it all—durability, lush burgundy foliage, and white flowers. The novelty 'Sunspot' is for the *Heuchera* connoisseur.

Daylily

Hemerocallis spp.

When, Where, and How to Plant

Plant in early spring or late fall. Daylilies prefer full sun. They tolerate part-shade conditions, but require six hours of direct sun for explosive blooming. Any good soil is appropriate if it is well drained. In heavy clay, loosen the soil with an organic soil conditioner. In good garden soil, plant with very little preparation other than a wide planting hole, 10 inches deep. Soak the crowns of bare-root plants for several hours. Make a cone of loose soil in the middle of the hole and spread the roots out as you do for roses. Work the soil in and around and between the roots. Firm the soil and water well. Space daylilies at least 1 foot apart or farther if you will not be dividing them.

Growing Tips

Irrigate during the flowering period. Fertilize in spring with a general flower fertilizer and again in late summer for fall blooms.

Care

Cut daylily stems for arrangements, but remember each morning to remove the spent blooms. They last for only a day. Daylilies are virtually pest free, durable and resilient, with daylily rust being their only disease problem. They divide easily, though it is best to retain two to three fan sections per clump when transplanting in late summer. Remove stalks completely once the blooms have wilted. Aphids may be a problem on the unopened flowers; blast them off with a sharp spray from a garden hose. Rake out frozen foliage in December. Mulching daylilies deeply can cause crown rot.

Companion Planting and Design

Daylilies perform admirably near tall pine trees. They are best used in mass groupings for a color accent and preferably with an evergreen background. Use near the entrance to the home or in foundation beds. Enjoy the blossoms of 'Stella de Oro' alongside sun coleus, purple heart, or 'Homestead Purple' verbena.

Our Personal Favorites

'Stella de Oro' is our favorite, with 'Happy Returns' a close second. In large-flowered types, look for a high bud count that will guarantee a long succession of blooms.

Most Southerners don't appreciate Hemerocallis *fully unless they've visited a daylily nursery in late spring. Impressive introductions include colorful miniatures, sturdy tetraploids, spider-shaped blooms, and repeat bloomers. Pink, plum, or scarlet colors? Sure, there's no need to settle for just yellow or orange. Most daylily cultivars have one primary bloom period. Enthusiasts plant cultivars that bloom one after the other. Some new introductions, however, break ranks. One continuous bloomer is 'Stella de Oro' daylily, an eighteen-inch beauty with yellow or yellow-orange flowers and a "Perennial Plant of the Year" status. It is a star performer in Carolina gardens with the longest bloom season of any daylily. If it slows down, shear off the top third of plants, feed and water, and the plants will rebloom in the fall.*

Bloom Period and Seasonal Color
A plethora of color from late spring to September, with cultivars blooming in succession.

Mature Height × Spread
1 to 4 ft. × 1 to 2^1/$_2$ ft.

Fern-Leaf Yarrow

Achillea filipendulina

This showy garden favorite is tough and reliable. It should be found in the garden of every floral designer since its dried flowers are truly "everlasting." Fern-leaf yarrow has basal leaves forming a rosette of gray, finely divided, aromatic fernlike foliage. This easy-to-grow perennial produces tall stems bearing the golden-yellow blooms often seen in cutting gardens. The three-inch flattened flower heads called corymbs are delightful, fresh or dried. Adaptable, resilient yarrow can rescue a barren area and cover it with bloom. It has been proven from the dry Southwest to the hard-baked clay soils of the Carolinas. Grandmother's garden may have included another species of yarrow as well, called milfoil, which comes in white, pink, cinnamon, and dark red shades. Milfoil is lower-growing and has lacy, see-through, green foliage.

Bloom Period and Seasonal Color
Yellow or gold summer color.

Mature Height × Spread
3 ft. × 1 to 2 ft.

When, Where, and How to Plant
Plant yarrow in spring or early fall from divisions and container-grown stock. Tip cuttings can also be rooted. Yarrow grows easily in average to poor soil. Given a full-sun location, fern-leaf yarrow will bloom in late spring throughout summer. Shade causes tall species to grow lanky and open. Give yarrow plenty of space (3 feet apart) to minimize mildew. If you have trouble with yarrow, it's most likely due to "wet-feet." Prepare the soil so it is loose and friable. Gravel or bark amendments can be added along with a 1/2-cup of superphosphate per plant. Break up the soil to a depth of 1 foot, and set your plant shallowly. In heavy soils, plant on berms to ensure excellent drainage. Fern-leaf yarrow can be damaged by a deep mulch.

Growing Tips
Water weekly the first month only. Supplemental watering can be beneficial, but keep the foliage dry. Fern-leaf yarrow survives drought and our hot summers better than most perennials. Feed with any liquid general garden fertilizer monthly if you wish to increase flower production.

Care
Once established, yarrow thrives on neglect. A systemic fungicide or application of baking soda with horticultural oil can help prevent mildew. Prune back the plant to encourage new foliage and repeat-blooming. To produce dried flowers, wrap bunches of long-stemmed flowers in paper and hang them upside down in a dry, dark area. Deadhead routinely. Divide the heavy clumps by digging them, washing the soil away with a water jet, and cutting them apart with a hatchet or sharp spade. After a hard freeze, remove the spoiled foliage. Termites may burrow into their woody stems in dry weather.

Companion Planting and Design
Interplant yarrow to set off the colors of dwarf purple salvias or red cosmos. Good companions are santolina, lavender, and ornamental grasses. Consider growing various species of *Achillea* to get the full range of colors for your garden.

Our Personal Favorites
'Coronation Gold' and 'Moonshine' have been given the highest accolades.

When, Where, and How to Plant

Hardy species of ferns can be planted practically all year when the soil can be worked, but "take" best in late winter, early spring, or fall. Once established, some ferns can tolerate up to four hours of direct sunlight. Plant them in moist sites, such as by a stream or leaking air-conditioner or next to a water garden. Prepare the soil by tilling in large volumes of sphagnum peat moss or aged leaf compost. The soil mix should be a minimum of 50 percent organic matter. Good soil drainage will ensure that oxygen reaches the fine, fibrous roots. Ferns adapt well in acidic or alkaline soils. Don't add garden fertilizer to the planting hole; ferns rarely need it. When planting, be careful not to break the tender fronds. Plant shallowly, water well, and apply mulch.

Growing Tips

Ferns are truly low-maintenance plants, amazingly resilient after they are established. Watering is essential during the first season but only in dry spells in the years that follow. Water three to four times per week after planting, especially during growth spurts. Organic mulch provides some nutrients for ferns as it decays, but applying a natural slow-release organic fertilizer every few years will keep them in tip-top condition. Spread mulch annually.

Care

Evergreen ferns require only an occasional light pruning to remove sunburned foliage or injury from weather, pets, and slugs. In late winter or spring, you can nip off discolored fronds. Hardy ferns are long-lived and moderately drought-resistant when mature.

Companion Planting and Design

Ferns provide summer and fall interest after the ephemeral spring wildflowers have finished their song and dance. Certain species like cinnamon fern and royal fern grow tall and command attention at quite a distance. Companions are cyclamen, hellebores, lungwort, hosta, and wild ginger.

Our Personal Favorites

An outstanding evergreen fern for landscaping is autumn fern (*Dryopteris erythrosora*). The deciduous Japanese silver-painted fern, *Athyrium nipponicum* 'Pictum' is elegant. Ferns with golden foliage are available.

For care-free shade gardening, investigate our native Carolina ferns. Christmas fern goes virtually unnoticed until fall leaf drop, then its deep green fronds show up against the tan of fallen leaves. Christmas ferns can frequently be found along streams and in damp woodlands. They are easy to transplant and will brighten up dark corners where almost nothing else will grow. Even less demanding is the small native ebony spleenwort fern often seen in dry sites. Holly ferns grow best near the coast. There, their leathery leaves are often seen in landscapes resembling woodlands. Japanese painted fern (pictured above) is one of the ornamentals recognized as a "Perennial Plant of the Year." Its broad, silvery fronds can light up moderately shaded beds. Ferns like a rich loamy soil and a constant supply of moisture.

Bloom Period and Seasonal Color
Evergreen with medium green to deep green or silver fronds replaced each spring.

Mature Height × Spread
2 to 2¹/₂ ft. × 2 ft.

Foxglove
Digitalis purpurea

Foxgloves provide a substitute for tall delphiniums, which are forbiddingly difficult for gardeners in the midsouth to grow, even in the cool mountains. When given plenty of organic matter in their root zones and grown in afternoon shade with abundant soil moisture, foxgloves can produce spikes that top forty-eight inches in height. The spikes are clothed with pendent bells that stay in color for nearly a month. Little children are fascinated by the story of how foxgloves got their name, from the bells that will just fit over Reynard's front paws. Foxgloves are often grown as biennials. Set into a deep organic mulch in late summer, the seedlings will grow through mild winters as hardy rosettes and shoot up flowering stalks early the following summer.

Other Common Name
Digitalis

Bloom Period and Seasonal Color
Early summer, in mostly purple, pink, and white. A yellow species is available.

Mature Height × Spread
2¹/₂ to 5 ft. × 2 to 2¹/₂ ft.

When, Where, and How to Plant
Foxgloves purchased in full bloom can have difficulty adjusting to garden conditions. Smaller green plants purchased in spring have time to set the expansive root system needed to power the development of tall spikes. If the planting site is beneath trees, don't dig the soil. Mow the grass short, lay down 3 to 5 layers of newsprint, and spread pine or hardwood bark mulch 4 to 5 inches deep over the area to be planted. Scrape the mulch aside to make planting holes and create an equal mixture of mulch and potting soil. Set the plants in place, 24 inches apart, and backfill around them with the mixture. Water daily for the first seven to ten days. The water will soak in slowly until the newspaper begins to degrade, so trickle it around plants.

Growing Tips
Beneath trees, drip irrigation through a soaker hose serpentized among your plants will give them the abundant moisture they need. Trees can suck up the soil moisture and nutrients needed by understory plants. Feed your foxgloves every seven to fourteen days with water-soluble flower food dissolved per directions.

Care
When spikes begin to form, buy 3-foot bamboo stakes and secure the spikes to them loosely with twine or florist's tape. If you fail to stake them, the first wind or rainstorm will flatten your crop. Keen gardeners mark plants with the colors they like and, when pods form, cut and store them in paper bags to catch the seeds, or take their chances on volunteers from the seed crop.

Companion Planting and Design
Ferns are natural companions for foxgloves. Both love shade and thrive on humus-rich soil and abundant moisture. However, use a different nutrient source and schedule for ferns; they resent overfertilization. For midsummer color, try the native "Indian Pink," *Spigelia marilandica*.

Our Personal Favorite
'Foxy', an All-America Award winner, will bloom in late summer from spring-planted seeds. It matures at 2 to 3 feet, a more manageable height than is seen in the towering giant varieties.

Gaura
Gaura lindheimer

When, Where, and How to Plant

Most garden centers offer plants in early bloom stage. When carefully transplanted, they adjust quickly. Hardened-off plants can be set out quite early but should be covered with a floating row cover if frost threatens. In clay soil, build up beds by mixing 3-inch layers of organic soil conditioner and play sand with the surface 6 inches of soil to create a fast-draining environment. Even better, order a cubic yard of sand and spread it 6 inches deep over clay soil. Plants that like dry soil will grow like never before. In pure sand or sandy soil, mix in 2 to 3 inches of moistened sphagnum peat moss. Set out gaura plants in full sun, 1 1/2 to 2 feet apart. Stir a tablespoon of controlled-release fertilizer into the backfill soil. Water plants every two or three days until new growth shows.

Growing Tips

Drill more controlled-release fertilizer around your guara plants in late summer. A layer of mulch is okay on sandy soil but tends to keep clay too moist. Despite guara's drought resistance, an occasional deep watering won't harm your plants. But you can kill gaura with kindness by overfeeding and over-watering.

Care

At season's end, if you want lots of seedlings for gifts to friends, scatter the plants over a prepared site or dry seeds in a paper bag and plant them in pots of seed starter mix, a formulation of fine particles of peat moss, vermiculite, and perlite. Or, when flowering spikes begin to look shabby, deadhead them to encourage new spikes if you wish to reduce the number of seedlings that will sprout from dropped seeds.

Companion Planting and Design

Plants that also like dry soil include Texas plume, Texas bluebells (*Eustoma grandiflora*), blazing star, creeping zinnia, portulaca, and purslane.

Our Personal Favorites

'Siskiyou Pink' has darker flowers than the wildling and matures at a shorter height. Its terminal growth is dark pink. Toby prefers the white variety, 'Whirling Butterflies'.

In the 1980s, Jim saw this wildflower blooming merrily along dry, sandy fencerows in East Texas wildlands and wondered why the green industry hadn't promoted it to gardeners. Well, it happened, and gaura (pronounced "gow-rah") moved into the mainstream of southern perennials. Designers like its wispy, see-through plants and the way the individual blossoms perched on thin, flexible stems flutter in the slightest breeze. The original species with pinky-white blossoms has morphed into shorter, more manageable selections with larger, deeper colored blossoms and foliage. You can grow gaura easily in well drained garden soil, but keep the sprinklers away from established plants. In Texas, it gets by with scattered showers, no fertilizer, and no pampering. Think of "benign neglect" as an appropriate program for growing gaura.

Bloom Period and Seasonal Color
Early summer through fall in white or pink.

Mature Height × Spread
2 to 4 ft. × 2 to 2 1/2 ft.

Hardy Hibiscus
Hibiscus moscheutos

These are not the tropical hibiscus that grace landscapes in Florida and along the Gulf Coast. Hardy hibiscus has its roots in the southeastern United States—literally. The native H. coccineus, a marsh plant called Texas star, is cherished for its large iridescent crimson blooms. Its cut-leaf foliage bears an unfortunate resemblance to "pot" plants, which has led to visits by law-enforcement officers. The sturdy perennial hibiscus H. moscheutos is also perfectly legal and a more adaptable hibiscus for perennial borders. While both species are workhorses, the latter has blooms up to ten inches across and is available in an assortment of colors. The native hibiscus species grow quite tall. Accordingly, plant breeders developed the waist-high 'Disco Belle' for small yards. Its flowers are larger than salad plates.

Other Common Name
Rose Mallow

Bloom Period and Seasonal Color
Summer blooms in pink, red, maroon, and white.

Mature Height × Spread
4 to 8 ft. × 3 to 6 ft.

When, Where, and How to Plant
Plant in early fall and spring when the soil is moist but not wet. Divide in early spring or in early fall. A sunny garden and moist, average soil will encourage rapid growth. In dry or rocky soil amend excavated backfill with several shovels of leaf compost or rotted manure. This perennial is native to wetlands, and a site by a seep, water garden, or exuberant fountain would be perfect. Set clumps at the depth they were originally growing, 4 to 5 feet apart. Spade a little 5-10-10 fertilizer or similar flower food into the planting area at the rate of 1 pound per 100 square feet. Hardy hibiscus appreciates mulch.

Growing Tips
In dry sites, keep the plant irrigated during the bloom season. Remove faded flowers to encourage more bud development. A light fertilization of water-soluble plant food when flowering begins should get it up and running.

Care
Hardy hibiscus is a low-maintenance plant with few pests. Japanese beetles and weevils nibble on the leaves or flowers, but they can be removed by hand or with insecticides. Spent flowers drop off neatly. Cut the plants to the ground after a hard freeze. In Zone 7 and west, delay pruning until winter, and follow with a deep mulching to protect the crowns. Hot afternoon sun can scorch leaf tips if the soil is too dry. When clumps grow too large, dig them, wash off the soil, and divide them with a hatchet.

Companion Planting and Design
Grow it in the background of a perennial border where its height is an advantage. Perennial hibiscus is right at home in a sunny corner near a faucet for frequent watering. Feature it with colorful annuals such as sun coleus and sweet potato vine.

Our Personal Favorites
The immense flowers of the 'Southern Belle' mix are traffic stoppers. She grows taller than her little sister, 'Dixie Belle', which is often grown as a hedge plant.

When, Where, and How to Plant

Lungwort can be planted in fall and late spring following bloom. Divide established plants in October. They tolerate deeper shade than do most other herbaceous perennials, partly because they make much of their growth before trees leaf out. They thrive in moist, rich soil with morning sun. Provided with the proper location, lungwort establishes quickly. It prefers cool, moist conditions. Amend poor garden soil with aged compost or sphagnum peat moss. Space your plants 18 inches apart. Score the rootball of potbound plants with a pocketknife or boxcutter. Spread out the roots and dig a shallow hole in the bed. Firm-in the soil around the roots and water well with a slow trickle from a garden hose.

Growing Tips

This plant likes moisture. Serpentize a "leaky hose" between woodland plants so that no plant is more than 9 inches from the hose and turn it on twice a week for an hour during spring and fall. Irrigation is critical for lungwort, particularly where hardwood trees spread their shallow feeder roots. Lungwort normally wilts a little in the heat of summer but over-watering at that time encourages root rot disease. Scatter an organic fertilizer such as cottonseed meal or a specialty slow-release flower fertilizer around your plants in early fall.

Care

Many lungwort cultivars are prone to powdery mildew during our humid summers. While unsightly, it seems to cause little problem with overall health or survival. Horticultural oils, systemic fungicides, or potassium bicarbonate applied at the first sign of the disease will keep the foliage clean. Divide lungworts as the weather cools, heading into fall, to give them time to establish a new root system to support early spring bloom.

Companion Planting and Design

Plant lungwort in the border or by a shaded water garden. It will will be right at home with other shade-loving plants such as cyclamen, hellebores, Virginia bluebells, and spring-flowering bulbs.

Our Personal Favorite

Dr. Allan Armitage gave his highest ranking to 'Little Blue' in the University of Georgia trial garden.

Nothing gets your attention in the early spring woodland garden like the lungworts. These durable early bloomers should be grown everywhere; perhaps their name holds them back. Named for the human organ that most resembles their foliage, this perennial quickly establishes to make a superb display. Lungworts grow from a basal rosette, usually no more than 10 inches tall, and flower around the first of March. The small, cup-shaped flowers, usually pink or cobalt blue, are spangled on short stalks that reach just above the spotted, silvery-green foliage. Lungworts retain their attractive foliage through most of the winter then shed their leaves just before the new season's growth cycle. In summer, their leaves look worn, but by that time the woodland ferns are taking over.

Bloom Period and Seasonal Color

Pink or blue flowers in very early spring, with foliage color continuing all season.

Mature Height × Spread

1/2 to 1 ft. × 1 to 2 ft.

Peony

Paeonia spp.

Peonies have long been a favorite of Piedmont and mountain gardeners. In coastal country, only a few herbaceous cultivars have the low threshold for winter chilling needed to induce bloom. There, tree peonies (they are actually more like shrubs) are better adapted. Peonies are the aristocrat of perennial flowers and one of the longest-lived. The large, showy, fragrant blossoms make fabulous cut flowers. Country churches have used them as altar flowers for decades, and back when it was permitted, families honored their departed with cut peonies in Mason jars. Flower forms include both single and double with new colors introduced every year. By selecting cultivars that flower in sequence, the color season can last for six weeks or more. The dark foliage adds substance to borders.

Bloom Period and Seasonal Color
May and June blooms in white, cream, yellow, pinks, and reds.

Mature Height × Spread
2 to 4 in. × 2 to 3 ft.

When, Where, and How to Plant
Plant in early to late fall and early spring, in full sun for herbaceous cultivars, in afternoon shade for tree peonies. Bare-root divisions should have 3 to 5 eyes (growth buds) to give your peony a strong start. Soak roots in tepid water overnight before planting. Peonies will grow best in a moist but well-drained clay loam. They are not as vigorous in strongly acidic soil. Add limestone at rates according to a soil test. Planting depth is critical. If planted too deeply, peonies will grow and spread but may never bloom. Space them 3 to 4 feet apart.

Growing Tips
Keep soil moist during the early months while the plants establish. Scatter 5-10-10 flower fertilizer around each plant after the bloom season and again after the foliage has died down. Don't mulch deeply over the crowns; a deep layer will insulate them from the cold necessary to induce flowering. Don't neglect weekly watering during the summer; that's when bloom buds are forming for next year.

Care
Peonies resent being moved once they are well established. They require up to five years to build the heavy crown needed to support an abundant crop of blossoms and should not be disturbed. Remove spent flower stems. Ants that congregate on flower buds are collecting minute drops of nectar and are harmless. Thrips, nearly invisible insects, cause flower bud deformity. Unopened buds can be caused by a lack of sufficient cold winter weather or by botrytis disease, the bane of the species.

Companion Planting and Design
Use single plants as specimens or in groups plugged into perennial borders. Shrub roses, bearded iris, and Siberian iris are good companions. You will need later-blooming perennials to fill the color gap left after peonies have faded.

Our Personal Favorites
For fragrance and exquisite form, try the pink variety 'President Taft'. The great old 'Festiva Maxima', white with red flecks, will bloom reliably in Zone 8.

When, Where, and How to Plant

Set out potted plants in full sun after frost danger is past. Space small-frame species 18 inches apart, but the big boys develop middle-age spread and need much wider spacing. Afternoon shade won't hurt unless it comes from surface-feeding trees. Not a lot of soil preparation is required: add lime and fertilizer per soil test directions and incorporate a 2-inch layer of organic soil conditioner. Spread out the roots and place the plants with the top of the rootball level with the surrounding soil or slightly higher. Backfill around the plants, then spread mulch, keeping it from contact with the stems. Have a sprinkling can of water handy and soak plants thoroughly. If you're transplanting, wait until fall to move plants so that they have as large a rootball as possible.

Growing Tips

Perennial salvia can get by with weekly deep watering during dry weather. A late-summer application of 1-2-2 ratio flower fertilizer will build strong roots and send the plants into winter with a good outlook for survival.

Care

Remove spent flower stems. Divide overly large plants in early fall. Leaf eating caterpillars may attack salvias. Grow a few plants of garlic chives or mountain mints in your garden to attract beneficial wasps and let them help take care of the woolly worms. Or, spray with *Bt*; it does a good job of keeping larvae in check.

Companion Planting and Design

The medium-height salvias are used for filling beds, but the tall, robust types are often employed like temporary shrubs and interspersed with pink or yellow annuals to bring out their splendid colors. Few quick-growing plants are taller than Mexican bush salvia. Hibiscus 'Red Shield' is one, and it looks elegant when grown in banks behind *S. leucantha*.

Our Personal Favorites

Well worth trying are Brazilian sage (*S. guaranitica*); *S. involucrata*; pitcher sage (*S. azurea grandiflora*); forsythia sage (*S. madrensis*); and the shrubby autumn sage (*S. greggii*).

A few knee-high perennial salvias such as the violet-blue 'May Night' (above) and S. farinacea, a sometimes perennial blue species, have long been known to gardeners. The shoulder-high Mexican bush salvia, S. leucantha, is beloved by all. But during recent years, thanks in part to North Carolina's Richard Dufresne, several tall blue, red, pink, and yellow salvia species have been introduced from their native Mexico and Central and South America. Some are winter-hardy in the Piedmont; others need to be heavily mulched with pine straw to make it through hard freezes, or they bloom very late. Collectively, the salvias offer great promise, but Carolina gardeners should consult their nearest botanical garden for advice on which species are adapted to their hardiness zone. All are easy to grow and undemanding.

Other Common Name
Hardy Salvia

Bloom Period and Seasonal Color
Mid to late summer, depending on the species, in red, blue, violet, pink, and yellow;

Mature Height × Spread
$1^1/_2$ to 5 ft. × $1^1/_2$ to $2^1/_2$ ft., depending on the species.

Phlox

Phlox paniculata

This old-fashioned, easy-to-grow perennial remains a garden standby. Wild stands of summer phlox along rocky roadsides in the Carolina mountains are especially picturesque. The wildlings provided genes to develop garden phlox, which is valued for its erect plants topped by spectacular sprays of flowers, its long bloom period in summer and fall, and the butterflies it draws. Because of our humid climate, volunteer seedlings and certain phlox cultivars can be disfigured by powdery mildew disease. Buy only the cultivars that are listed as resistant to mildew. Be merciless; pull out any mildew-infested artifacts from earlier gardens. Several other species of phlox are often found in Carolina gardens, most commonly the early-blooming creeping phlox and, in dappled shade in woodland glens, blue phlox or wild sweet William.

Other Common Names
Garden Phlox, Summer Phlox

Bloom Period and Seasonal Color
Summer blooms in purple, magenta, pink, and white.

Mature Height × Spread
2 to 3 ft. × 1 to 2 ft.

When, Where, and How to Plant

Plant or divide for transplanting in spring or fall. Phlox blooms best in full to partial sun. In shade, mildew problems are more numerous. Phlox grows quickly in hot weather and reaches full potential in moist, fertile soil. Spade a little compost or soil conditioner into the planting hole of a garden bed and set your plants at grade. Well-drained, fertile soils require no special soil preparation. Superphosphate works much better than bonemeal; organic gardeners may prefer to use unprocessed rock phosphate.

Growing Tips

Water weekly during the flowering season and when drought prevails. Irrigate in the early morning to avoid wetting the foliage, which leads to chronic leaf diseases. Phlox is not a heavy feeder. A little 5-10-10 or similar fertilizer applied twice during the growing season is sufficient. Apply a 2-inch layer of mulch in early summer.

Care

Thin new shoots in spring to five strong stems per crown. This allows air to circulate. Thinning discourages powdery mildew disease and favors stronger stems to withstand storms. Deadhead garden phlox after peak bloom to enjoy a second flush of flowers and to prevent a rash of unwanted seedlings. Divide summer phlox every two or three years to maintain vigor. Plant resistant varieties or spray with systemic fungicides. Organic gardeners use horticultural oil as a preventative, especially during hot, humid weather. Perennials, including phlox, are vulnerable to voles when planted in a woodland garden.

Companion Planting and Design

For the ambiance of an English cottage garden, try garden phlox as a background plant behind coralbells and purple coneflowers. Plant phlox against a picket fence or in front of an evergreen hedge to show off the brilliance of the flowers. In shady woodland gardens, *Phlox divaricata* is a great blue-colored companion that will enhance your spring daffodils and tulips.

Our Personal Favorites

'David' (white) and 'Laura' (purple) are mildew-resistant, while 'Nora Leigh' has striking variegated foliage.

Pinks

Dianthus sp.

When, Where, and How to Plant

Set out potted plants from fall through early spring in coastal areas, or during spring in the Piedmont and mountains. They are hardy, but hard freezes can kill newly planted pinks that haven't sent out a strong root system. Plant in full sun to afternoon shade. Dianthus plants are small and don't fare well in poor, dry soil. Work organic soil conditioner into your soil, be it coastal sand or upland clay, to improve drainage, aeration, and microbiological activity. In container gardens, pinks are a "natural" to follow spring-blooming bulbs. With such tiny plants, it is important to improve your soil and to prepare rootballs carefully prior to planting. Spread 2 inches of mulch before planting and set your plants through it. The mulch will discourage weed seeds from sprouting and encourage your pinks to spread.

Growing Tips

Spreading granular fertilizer over matted plants of pinks can be risky; instead, dilute water-soluble flower fertilizer per directions and drench the plants. Be sure to water well *before* applying fertilizer. Water weekly during dry weather, daily for plants in container gardens. Divide tightly matted plants every two or three years by snipping off short branches, stripping off the lower leaves, and sticking them in pots of potting soil. Kept moist, they will root in four to seven days.

Care

Pinks are nearly carefree. Deadhead spent blossoms and groom occasionally, and they will continue to perform for years. Near the coast, cottage pinks sometimes act like annuals and burn out after their peak bloom season. Be careful not to step on these tiny plants; they are slow to recover.

Companion Planting and Design

In containers, intersperse with thrift or sea pink (*Armeria maritima*), with dwarf mondo grass. To better enjoy the fragrance of scented cultivars, elevate containers on tables or benches or inverted pots. In gardens, pair with other fragrant kinds that bloom later: heliotrope; tall, evening-blooming nicotiana; and lavender, for example.

Our Personal Favorite

Little 'Firewitch' blooms intermittently during the summer.

The great carnation family includes several small-flowered perennial species and hybrids commonly called "pinks" in the South. One of the great performers is 'Bath's Pink' which forms short, blue-green mats of narrow, tightly spaced leaves. In early spring it sports 1/2-inch fragrant, pink blossoms with dark throats and will rebloom sporadically through the summer. A newer cultivar, 'Firewitch', has crimson blooms and slightly taller, blue green, bun-shaped plants. These two are valued for containers, raised planter boxes, and garden railway systems where the small plants can be better appreciated. For cutting, grow the taller, intensely fragrant, clove-scented cottage pinks. They offer a wide variety of blossom colors, some fringed, some zoned with contrasting colors, some single-flowered, some double, all fancy. True carnations require extended cool weather to bloom.

Other Common Names

Dianthus, Carnations

Bloom Period and Seasonal Color

Spring blooming in coastal areas and the Piedmont, with mountain-grown, summer-blooming carnations an exception; colors in the crimson-red, purple, pink, and white range with some bicolors.

Mature Height × Spread

Cheddar pinks, 9 to 12 in. × similar spread
Cottage pinks, 1 to 1 1/2 ft. × 12 in.
Staked carnations, 2 to 2 1/2 ft. × 1 ft.

Purple Heart
Tradescantia pallida

Southern gardeners love this endearing foliage plant. "Mail Carrier Plant" might have been a better name because come rain or shine it will deliver the goods. Its long, lax, brittle stems and fleshy leaves that remind you of dugout canoes flourish through extremes of heat and humidity yet can live through winter in Zone 7. Its small, purple-blue flowers in the leave axils redeem its plainness. Purple heart is an amusing plant, yet it is to be marveled at because of its courage and durability despite long periods of neglect. Purple heart is perfect for clothing steep slopes exposed to afternoon sun and where water has to come from rainfall, for windowboxes facing west or south, or for oft-neglected container gardens. Purple heart may be listed as Setcresea pallida.

Other Common Name
Setcresea

Bloom Period and Seasonal Color
Intriguing purple stems and latticed leaves by late summer/early fall.

Mature Height × Spread
8 to 10 in. × 16 to 22 in.

When, Where, and How to Plant
Wait until frost danger is past before planting. Give purple heart the most challenging, hottest, driest, most sun-drenched spot in your garden and it will be happy. It can withstand afternoon shade but doesn't require respite from the sun. Mix in 2 inches of organic soil conditioner before planting, not that purple heart needs it, but because organic matter makes it easier for water to soak into the soil. Potted plants or rooted segments from last year's crop should be set 18 inches apart. On slopes, set plants where they can trail down to cover exposed soil.

Growing Tips
Even with its desert-like endurance, purple heart appreciates an hour or so of water from a sprinker after a week of dry, hot weather. When drought-stricken, the leaves tend to fold up lengthwise to reduce their surface area. With a good watering, they will plump up and unfold. Two or three drenchings with water-soluble flower fertilizer during the growing season will help maximize foliage color and new growth.

Care
When you forget to water for weeks, purple heart can develop leaf scorch. Snip off and compost disfigured leaves. Spray with a repellent if deer sample your purple heart. Insect problems are few and far between; disease problems mostly come from summer root rot due to too much water from sprinkler systems set for the needs of lawn grass. Turn sprinklers away from your planting of purple heart. Top growth will die back during winter. Come spring, twist it off to allow new growth to emerge. Save the branches you shear off. Cut them into short segments, each including at least two joints, and stick them in potting soil to root.

Companion Planting and Design
Tall salvias such as Brazilian sage and 'Stella de Oro' daylily look good planted behind a bed of purple heart. Ornamental sweet potatoes, pink wave petunias, and fountain grass combine well with purple heart in containers.

Our Personal Favorite
Easy. There is only one variety in the species. You can't go wrong.

Russian Sage

Perovskia atriplicifolia

When, Where, and How to Plant

Garden centers usually sell Russian sage plants in 6-inch pots or 1-gallon containers, with spikes showing color. No special soil preparation is required except liming to bring the soil pH up to about 6.0. Lime doesn't move down readily in clay soils, so mix it thoroughly into the top 6 to 8 inches of soil. In sizable perennial borders or among shrubs, set plants in groups of 3, spaced 3 feet apart. A site receiving all-day sun is preferred. Loosen the roots on potbound plants and prune off any that have to be folded up to fit in the planting hole. Russian sage plants will stay with you for years; review the information on soil improvement and planting in the "Annuals" chapter introduction to ensure longevity.

Growing Tips

In September or October, dig a furrow around each plant about 2 feet out from the central stem. Trickle $1/2$ cup of granular 1-2-2 ratio fertilizer (example, 5-10-10 NPK analysis) in the furrow, and cover it with soil to increase its effectiveness. Farmers use the term "drilling" to describe covering fertilizer in furrows. Extended droughts can cause dieback in plants; prevent it by deep watering every two weeks.

Care

Flowering stems can be cut for bouquets. They may shed flowers, but the attractive leaves will still contribute to the arrangement. The outer stems of shrubby old plants may occasionally flop; just prune them off at the base. At the beginning of each season, trim back the stems to just above the lowest leaves. This will encourage new sprouts to form. Pruning off spent spikes can bring a second crop. Late in the season divide the crowns of plants.

Companion Planting and Design

You couldn't ask for a more versatile or longer blooming plant than Russian sage. Its silvery color displays well against a background of dwarf hollies, yaupon, or dwarf variegated nandina. Tall herbaceous plants such as hollyhock, cosmos, and Joseph's coat look good with it.

Our Personal Favorite

'Blue Spire' has deeper colored flowers than the usual lavender blue sorts.

One of the best "see-through" plants for perennial borders, Russian sage provides color all season long, either from its airy stems clothed with small, silver-white leaves or from its long, slender, lavender-blue flower spikes. Russian sage can withstand occasional periods of neglect and recover with a good watering. From a design standpoint, its erect plants, which reach up to four feet in height, make a strong statement in landscapes. Don't be misled by the name "sage." It may come from the superficial resemblance of the plant to native American sagebrush or its sage-like aroma. In well-drained soil, Russian sage plants can persist for years. Potted plants in nurseries are often sold without a cultivar name, which is regrettable because the various cultivars differ considerably in foliage and flower color.

Bloom Period and Seasonal Color

Peak bloom is from early summer through midsummer; tiny flowers range from soft lavender to a slightly darker blue-pink color.

Mature Height × Spread

3 to 4 ft. × 2 to 3 ft.

Sedum 'Autumn Joy'

Sedum × telephium 'Autumn Joy'

A garden favorite, sedum 'Autumn Joy' may be one of the first cultivars that gardeners think of when selecting perennials. Members of the genus Sedum are referred to as stonecrops because many of the cultivars are rock garden plants. Sedums like hot, sunny weather and don't mind thunderstorms. In early spring, established plants push fleshy, gray-green buds out of the soil. As the temperature rises, the powdery-blue leaves expand. By summer, the erect stems and leaves are topped by greenish flower buds. In mid- to late summer, the buds expand into three-inch flower heads that slowly transition to a reddish-to-brilliant-carmine color. The blooms fade to a coppery color then finally to rust by cooler weather. Butterflies flock to the broad, nectar-filled heads of flowers.

Other Common Name
Stonecrop

Bloom Period and Seasonal Color
Mid to late summer flower heads in reddish to brilliant carmine; attractive foliage earlier in the season.

Mature Height × Spread
1¹/₂ to 2 ft. × 1 to 1¹/₂ ft.

When, Where, and How to Plant
Buy plants in 6- to 8-inch pots and set them in the garden after danger of hard frost is past. The sunnier the site, the better this sedum flourishes. One of the "musts" for growing stonecrops is perfect drainage. Mix coarse gravel or rock screenings into the soil before planting to raise the soil level, or plant in containers. Sandy loam soils need no amendments. Avoid wet or shady sites. Dig a hole the same depth as the rootball and twice as wide. Work loosened soil in and around sedum's fleshy roots. Trim the longest roots back by one-third. Water to settle the soil around the rootball. Don't water again for two weeks unless you are planting sedums in dry midsummer weather.

Growing Tips
Irrigate the plants every two weeks in dry weather, but don't over-water. When 'Autumn Joy' has begun to push up in spring, scatter 5-10-10 fertilizer between the plants at the rate of 2 pounds per 100 square feet. This should take care of its nutritional needs for the growing season. Too much nitrogen can cause the flower heads to flop over in wet summers. If you mulch, do it sparingly—and keep the material a couple of inches away from the base of plants.

Care
These plants are drought tolerant and rugged. After frost, prune the woody stalks to the ground. Do not mulch for winter. The only serious pests are termites in dry weather. Control them with a soil drench of insecticide. An occasional rabbit, slug, or deer may nibble the tender spring buds or shoots. Repeated sprays of animal repellent should convince them to feed elsewhere. Divide clumps in fall or early spring.

Companion Planting and Design
Plant in groups in front of perennials and ornamental grasses. Plant some of the finer-textured spreading sedums at its base, such as 'Vera Jameson'.

Our Personal Favorites
The burgundy foliage of 'Matrona' is stunning with gray-colored perennials. 'Brilliant' has icy-pink flower heads that persist in spite of hot weather.

Threadleaf Coreopsis
Coreopsis verticillata

When, Where, and How to Plant

Plant potted threadleaf coreopsis in spring as the weather warms, or in fall. All coreopsis grow well in full sun. 'Moonbeam' lives longer and suffers less sunburn if it gets dappled shade in the afternoon. Prepare a bed where the soil drains well, or amend the soil with fine pine bark. Dig a hole larger than the rootball and plant at grade or slightly higher. Many container-grown perennials are potbound, so score rootballs with a knife to free up the roots. Firm-in the plants and water well. Irrigate twice a week for the first three weeks. Coreopsis can also be grown from spring sown seed.

Growing Tips

Water new plantings monthly during the first season. Thereafter, threadleaf coreopsis can handle a major drought, although any perennial will respond to irrigation during dry spells. A light application of fertilizer at planting and after the first flush of blooms is sufficient.

Care

Shear off spent blossoms to produce a second show of color. Removing spent flowers increases the plant's density and flower production but can be tedious. Yellow flowers appear all summer long with no pest problems serious enough to require spraying. Carolina gardeners can either allow coreopsis to do its thing naturally, or they can encourage late-season growth with a light shearing as the weather cools off in September. Don't be afraid to cut plants back halfway when blooming ceases in summer. Divide crowns in late summer and fall. Threadleaf coreopsis is virtually free of insect pests and diseases.

Companion Planting and Design

Yellow threadleaf coreopsis 'Moonbeam' is compact and makes a neat edging or an amenable neighbor for plumbago, blue sage, veronica, or verbena. 'Zagreb' is a look-alike with darker golden blossoms. They weave themselves between bulkier perennials. *C. rosea* 'Sweet Dreams' offers a new crimson-on-white look for container plantings. Also consider 'Crème Brûlée'.

Our Personal Favorite

'Zagreb' is a great warrior for landscape conditions. It is compact and has deep yellow flowers.

American native threadleaf coreopsis is the perennial of choice when you need to brighten up an entryway or to create a low-maintenance garden. This species produces abundant summer color with a profusion of single, daisy-like yellow flowers on mounded plants. The light green, airy foliage is drought resistant, and the compact plants insinuate their way between bulkier natives. Gardeners who have had great success with the lanceleaf varieties like 'Early Sunrise' will appreciate the threadleaf varieties because they don't fall over after a storm. 'Moonbeam' has light yellow daisy flowers underlain with green and is easily recognized in landscape beds. If low maintenance with consistent color is a priority, check out this versatile perennial. Try its sister cultivar, 'Zagreb', if you prefer a slightly deeper yellow color.

Other Common Name
Tickseed

Bloom Period and Seasonal Color
Yellow to golden yellow flowers from spring until October.

Mature Height × Spread
15 to 24 in. × equal spread

Roses *for the Carolinas*

Perhaps no flower in all the world is more popular than America's national flower, the rose. Its beautiful form, rich pleasing colors, delightful fragrances, and incredible versatility have made it a favorite of gardeners and flower lovers for generations. No wonder it is called the Queen of Flowers. The rose is a testament to human creativity. Once a wildflower, it has been cultivated and engineered to suit all types of gardens. There is a rose for every region of the Carolinas, a form for every location. Varieties are available for borders, for growing on arbors and trellises, and even miniatures for color beds. The unique tree roses grown as standards are ideal for container gardening, while the newer ground cover roses adapt well to small spaces. Of course, the hybrid teas are superb for cutting and are the rose of choice for millions of Americans.

Why We Grow Roses

Is there anyone who doesn't like roses? People have grown them for centuries and for many reasons. In times past, the rose was revered for its value as food and medicine. Its quaint herbal concoctions were believed to cure many ailments. Not until recently have we known that rose hips have as much Vitamin C as do citrus fruits. Their flavor is coveted in Middle Eastern and Indian cuisine. Rugosa rose provides both lovely flowers and large, red hips.

Today we grow roses mostly for their beauty in the garden. Another magical allure is the color combinations available. There is a rose that complements any color bed or accessory. Flowers like *R. mutabilis* frequently open with one color and fade to another hue; then there are the bicolors such as 'Double Delight' with blooms that are bordered or marbled with contrasting colors. In the past, people hesitated to grow roses because of widespread fungal diseases. However, with the latest landscape hybrids, such as 'Knockout'™, these problems are not as daunting. New introductions, especially among the shrub roses, allow success without heavy pesticide use. Gardeners are revisiting the heritage roses because of their hardiness, fragrance, and tolerance of neglect.

Roses and Perennials Along an Adobe House

First Things First

When researching roses, begin with the All-America Rose Selections (AARS). Winners of these awards will perform best and are most resistant to blackspot and mildew disease. Several websites carry the AARS list and a handbook that rates varieties. The greatest challenge will be settling on a few plants to avoid crowding your garden bed—a BIG no-no in rose culture.

Not too long ago we thought roses for cutting, like hybrid teas, were the only choice for gardeners. Nowadays, landscape roses are the best route for color and easy maintenance. In the spring of 2000, an international plantsman introduced the revolutionary Dream™ roses to American gardeners. Their large flowers resemble hybrid teas, but the plants have glossy foliage on compact shrubs. Colors range from pink and red to yellow and

Roses Arching Over Daylilies

orange, and bushes rebloom freely. They have been successfully grown in beds and in containers for patio gardening. Their long blooming season and no-nonsense pruning needs appeal to every homeowner. There are numerous roses entering the marketplace today with similar care-free characteristics. It is exciting to think that these will grow anywhere in the Carolinas—but for some gardeners, old garden roses and English roses will always take first prize.

What Do Roses Want?

A traditional garden of roses for cutting is like a marriage. The first heady rush of blooms in spring is wonderful. The flowers are perfect, the leaves deep green, and the fragrance divine. By June, the Japanese beetles arrive, and blackspot sets in. By August, the reality of growing cut roses in the South confronts you. It's like facing a sink full of dirty dishes after a romantic candlelit dinner. Like a good marriage, the benefits justify wading through the thick and thin.

What Do Roses Require?

Choose a site with good air circulation and six hours or more of daily sunshine. Morning sun is best for disease prevention. You had better do your homework in bed preparation, too. Follow the rule: "a 50-cent plant in a 5-dollar hole." Roses love water and need perfect drainage to flush surplus water away from their roots. Dig a deep bed in clay soils and consider installing a drainage system. Have the soil tested, and amend as needed. Organic amendments such as leaf compost or aged manure will improve soil condition. Most rosarians emphasize the importance of air circulation in growing roses. (In less-than-ideal circumstances, plant landscape shrub roses.)

Roses Cascading Over a Garden

Care for roses is equally important. They benefit from monthly fertilizing using either 10-10-10 or special rose fertilizers. Water-soluble fertilizers can be applied to supplement dry feeding, as can organic products ranging from alfalfa and cottonseed meal to Epsom salt and fish emulsion. You can overdo it with fertilizers. Be sure the bed is moist before feeding, and don't fertilize after mid-August so plants can harden-off before winter.

Successful gardeners recognize rose pests and diseases and treat them with the appropriate materials. Apply a variety of garden fungicides weekly to prevent chronic diseases such as canker, mildew, and black-spot. The County Cooperative Extension Service has current pesticide recommendations; these change occasionally. Some old pest-control recipes still circulate; they may or may not be effective in specific locales.

Pruning is an enigma for many people. How can you butcher a plant and expect more flowers and vigorous growth? You had better know up front that you prune climbing roses after they bloom and shrub-type roses (summer flowering) in early spring. To gain confidence, we suggest attending a rose-pruning clinic sponsored by a local rose society or Master Gardener program. Here are some general pruning tips that are worth noting.

- Use bypass-type hand shears. They cut cleanly. Anvil-type shears tend to crush stems.
- Pruning causes new growth, and pruning too early is risky. Should a late frost come after pruning, new growth won't survive. Wait until two weeks after your area's frost-free date to start pruning.
- Pruning and training are different. Pruning is a seasonal chore which increases the number and size of blooms. Training is the removal or shortening of errant shoots or sprouts originating from the rootstock.
- Prune to an "outside" bud, meaning cut one-half inch beyond a bud on the outside of the branch or cane. If you cut above an inside bud, the shoot that grows from it will congest the interior of the bush.
- In order to avoid transferring disease from one plant to another, hand shears (secateurs) should be cleaned in rubbing alcohol before moving on to another bush.
- The cut tips resulting from pruning should be painted with a dab of Elmer's glue or tar to prevent boring insects from entering the freshly cut surfaces.

- At times, you will need to use a pruning saw or loppers to remove woody old canes so that new canes can sprout from the crown. Prune flush with the crown to avoid leaving a stub. Be careful not to damage surrounding canes. Rejuvenating old rose plantings is prudent and should be done by early summer.

Buying at the Nursery

Increasingly, garden centers are selling containerized rose bushes in full bloom, which allows you to preview the color, blossom form, and fragrance of the various cultivars. Numbers are assigned to the bushes based on the number of buds that will develop into branches. The apparent weight or substance of the plant—whether it is heavy and stocky or light and spindly—also enters into the rating. Substantial, well-branched plants have low numbers.

The Old and the New

Mail-order specialists supply most of the newest roses by mail. Breeders announce them in their catalogs and, when demand has built up, sell to garden centers for resale to home gardeners. Traditionally, garden centers sell the bushes with tops waxed to decrease water loss and with the root system pruned and wrapped in a bag filled with peat moss or shavings to keep the roots from drying out. Buy No. 1 or No. 2 packaged rose bushes soon after they arrive at the garden center. Take them out of the package and soak them in tepid water overnight. Plant them in prepared soil after frost danger is past; their performance is similar to containerized bushes.

Jackson & Perkins' latest series, Generation Roses®, hails the advantages of "own-root" roses. Grafted (budded) roses have been the mainstay of the industry for decades, but there is now a rapid movement toward own-root rose production. Gardeners may appreciate the easy care of own-root roses since no graft union means no suckers to remove. Survival rates for roses go up when gardeners know how deeply a grafted plant should be planted.

Climbing Roses Adorning an Archway

Roses Scaling a Patio in a Bordering Bed

Choose Wisely to Avoid Diseases

Search for roses that have genetic resistance to blackspot and powdery mildew diseases. These plagues disfigure bushes and can weaken them to the point that they will gradually decline and die. The humid climate of the Carolinas, the rose grower's worst enemy, fosters serious foliar diseases. We must underscore the importance of good air circulation to ensure success with your roses. Plant pathologists periodically evaluate the cultivars for disease tolerance, and each class has something to offer. Experiment with these if your garden has less than ideal conditions for roses. And if your garden has shade, there are even some shady ladies for the choosing. Good choices include: Knock-Out™, 'Playboy', Carefree Wonder™, Mary Rose®, 'New Dawn', Ice Meidiland®, and 'Sea Foam' (just to name a few).

A new trend, started in the 1960s from an environmental awakening of sorts, gave rise to the first modern shrub roses, such as Carefree Beauty™. Years later, the immensely popular disease-tolerant Bonica™ rose followed from the successful breeding efforts of the Star Roses® project. These roses were an instant hit because they provided all-season color yet required little or no spraying. However, experienced Carolina rosarians have learned that regular spraying with a battery of chemical controls can reduce damage from foliar diseases in susceptible cultivars. Not everyone is willing to take on the work, expense, and environmental risk posed by chemical fungicides.

Finally, when buying rose bushes you need to understand what is meant by "miniature." Most miniature roses have considerably smaller frames and smaller blossoms than their standard prototypes. However, some have fairly large plants with miniature blossoms. So, check out the ultimate height listed on the label. Be aware, too, that most miniature roses are own-rooted, which means that they are grown from cuttings taken from stock plants of the cultivar. As such they can withstand colder weather than can grafted cultivars. The "union" or "bud union" where the rootstock meets the "scion" on grafted roses can fail due to extreme temperatures.

Planting Rose Bushes

- Soil preparation for roses is similar to that of shrubs (as directed in the "Shrubs" chapter introduction).
- First and foremost, have your soil tested, and amend as directed.
- Dig planting holes to the depth of the rootball or root system and twice as wide.
- For containerized roses, since extreme cold is rarely a consideration in the Carolinas, set the rootball so that its top is one inch above the surface of the surrounding soil.
- For bare-root roses, shake off the packing material, soak the roots overnight, and dig a planting hole to the depth of the root system. Amend soil with limestone, superphosphate, and soil conditioner as recommended by soil tests.
- Make a cone of amended soil in the bottom of the hole, and straddle it with the roots.
- The original soil line on the plant should be one inch above the surface of surrounding soil.
- Pull in amended soil around the roots, and firm it down with your hands; don't tamp it down.
- Spread two inches of mulch in a circle two feet in diameter.
- Settle the roses in place by trickling water over the dug area. For the next month, water twice weekly between rains.
- Wait two weeks, scatter granular rose fertilizer around the plant at the rate recommended on the package, and water it in. Fertilize monthly, but not past Labor Day, which encourages winter hardening.
- Note: The slight difference in planting depths evens out as the plants settle. Having the graft or bud union slightly above the soil reduces the incidence of suckers growing up from the rootstock and weakening the scion.

A Delightful Ornamental

With proper feeding and maintenance, many roses will bloom continuously for up to seven months in your Carolina garden. It is not unusual to find a rose bloom right up to Thanksgiving and beyond in coastal gardens. Most of them are spoiled by frosts in the foothills region by early November. They have served the gardener well by the time Old Man Winter arrives and have earned their rest. It would be difficult to find a more delightful ornamental than the rose.

Roses at a Garden Entrance

Climbing Rose
Rosa species and hybrids

Nothing is more picturesque than a gorgeous climbing rose. Traditionally, the large-flowered climbers are the most popular roses because of their longer flowering time. While no rose is a true climber (having no tendrils for attaching to a support), these plants do produce long canes that can be trained and tied to a fence or trellis. The climbing rose consists of a single group known as "ramblers." They bloom only once, in late spring to early summer, but their full-bloom display is well worth the wait. Climbers have mixed parentage and therefore vary in aroma, height, and color. Some can be pruned into cascading bushes or permitted to crawl on the ground. The fragrance is wonderful as it wafts across the landscape.

Bloom Period and Seasonal Color
Late spring to early summer blooms from white and yellow to pinks and reds.

Mature Length
To 20 ft.

When, Where, and How to Plant
Plant bare-root climbing roses February through April. Potted roses can be planted any time if proper watering practices are followed. Early fall planting is acceptable, though they must establish well before the ground freezes. Planting where the rose receives six hours of intense sun and air circulation is good. Support with fences, arbors, or trellises. Spade in plenty of compost, aged cow manure, or bark soil conditioner. Remove a container rose from its pot carefully. Keep the ball intact and place gently into a hole large enough to accommodate the roots. Plant a grafted rose with the bud union (the swollen bulge at the plant's base) just above the soil. Roses benefit from facilitated drainage with 1/4 of their planted rootballs above the soil. Backfill and firm the soil around the roots. Water thoroughly and mulch.

Growing Tips
Drip irrigation, rose food, and mulching keep roses looking good. These plants prefer at least 5 to 10 gallons of water per week with the moisture penetrating deep into the soil.

Care
Prune climbers in spring only to remove errant shoots. Prune hardest immediately after blooming to control growth or to invigorate older plants. Use carefully placed structures to support climbers' stiff canes. Spray dormant oil at least once during a winter warm spell and consult your local County Cooperative Extension Office for a spray schedule for the growing season. Well-established climbers are less dependent on water and pesticides than are other rose types. Apply fungicide if blackspot appears.

Companion Planting and Design
Use climbing roses to create a privacy screen or trellis on a bare wall (plant 2 feet from wall) or grow them for the shade they will cast on an arbor swing or gazebo. Opt for the fragrant varieties. The species 'Lady Banks' requires plenty of space but thrives on neglect even in coastal conditions.

Our Personal Favorites
'New Dawn', an everblooming hybrid, grows rapidly. Eden Climber™, ideal for small gardens, offers pastel blooms.

Floribunda Rose

Rosa hybrids

When, Where, and How to Plant

Plant in their dormant stage; this is particularly true of the mail-order plants shipped bare root. Container-grown roses can be planted successfully throughout the growing season and can grow in large containers. Roses need at least six hours of intense sunshine to thrive, preferring full sun all day long. They also require organically enriched soil with excellent drainage. Dig a hole 12 inches deep and 18 inches wide. Blend plenty of organic matter into the backfill soil and adjust the pH to 6.0 by liming. Spread the roots of bare-root roses over a soil mound. When planting a container rose, keep the rootball intact and place gently into the hole. Plant grafted roses with the bud union just above the soil. Backfill the hole, firmly pack the soil until level with the ground, water-in, and mulch.

Growing Tips

The more often you water, the better your roses will perform. Apply 1 to 2 inches of water per week, giving a good soaking rather than light sprinklings. Roses need moisture to penetrate 18 inches deep. Keep foliage dry when watering and try to water in the morning. Roses love to be fed monthly. Use organic amendments such as composted manures or compost, or fertilize using commercial rose food. You can root many roses by taking cuttings from new growth in summer.

Care

Thin floribundas in midsummer to encourage more blooming. Prune lightly in late fall after a killing frost. Final pruning is done as the buds swell going into spring. A regular fungicide spray to control mildew and blackspot is a must for floribundas; combining two different fungicides in the sprayer gives better results.

Companion Planting and Design

Use *en masse* in borders or as an edging along the front property lines. Monochromatic plantings create quite a show. Enjoy the new floribundas by a patio for their fragrance.

Our Personal Favorites

'Europeana' has lustrous foliage and rich red blooms. Nearly thornless 'Iceberg' will light up any garden.

During the early twentieth century, this class of roses originated from a cross between the hybrid tea and polyantha types. Floribunda roses have smaller flowers than do the hybrid teas, but they produce more flowers on each stem. Their name means "abundantly flowering." Floribundas are low growing, densely branched bushes that are quite adaptable to many landscape uses. Their buds and blossoms lack the grace of hybrid teas, but this is a consideration in rose shows, not in landscapes. They have fewer disease problems than hybrid teas, in our opinion. Floribundas bloom and rest, and by planting more than one cultivar, you can enjoy color through the season. They provide cut flowers for bouquets and can be planted among small shrubs.

Bloom Period and Seasonal Color
White to deep-crimson blooms in late spring and summer.

Mature Height × Spread
2 to 5 ft. × 2 to 4 ft.

Hybrid Tea Rose
Rosa hybrids

The aristocratic hybrid tea roses are known for their elegant buds and heavenly scent. The long stems and beautiful blooms make this the queen of flowers, perfect for cutting single buds or collecting for a bouquet. The number of colors and variegations is truly endless, and the fragrances can range from sweet and fruity to bold and spicy. Hybrid tea roses are grown more widely in southern rose gardens than all other roses combined. They are called "everblooming" roses by some rosarians. Most of the flowers are double with long, pointed buds. Hybrid teas are winter hardy over most of the Carolinas. Start at the American Rose Society's Handbook for Selecting Roses when choosing the best varieties for your hardiness zone. Also consider the recommendations of the Carolina Rose Society.

Bloom Period and Seasonal Color
A rainbow of colors from May until November.

Mature Height × Spread
6 ft. × 4 ft.

When, Where, and How to Plant
Plant bare-root roses while they are dormant. Container-grown roses in full bloom can be planted successfully through June if watered regularly. To thrive, roses require at least six hours of intense sunshine, good air circulation, organically enriched soil, and excellent drainage. Work the soil to a depth of 16 inches, incorporating plenty of bark soil conditioner. Dig a hole large enough to accommodate roots, allowing at least 3 feet between bushes. Keep the rootball of container roses intact. Plant grafted roses with the bud union 1 inch above the soil. Backfill the hole, firm-in the soil, water-in well, and layer 2 inches of pine bark (or similar) mulch.

Growing Tips
As a rule, roses need water regularly. Hybrid roses require 5 to 10 gallons of water per week. Water in the morning and keep the foliage dry. Rosarians prefer drip irrigation or soaker hoses for rose culture. Roses are heavy feeders, so fertilize monthly using organic products such as composted manures or rose food.

Care
Hybrid teas need the most maintenance of all. Cut them to waist high after the first hard frost in autumn. In early spring, prune to 15 to 18 inches. Remove the oldest and weakest canes, leaving 3 to 5 strong ones. For arrangement cutting, remove flower stems at the leaf node containing 5 to 7 leaflets. The remaining bud will produce another strong flower stalk. To harden off for winter in the western Carolinas, stop fertilizing and quit cutting the flowers by late August. Follow a rigid spray schedule to manage diseases, Japanese beetles, spider mites, and thrips.

Companion Planting and Design
A cutting garden of mixed cultivars will bring fragrance and beauty indoors. Or use a hybrid tea rose to accent a gazebo, patio, or barren lamppost.

Our Personal Favorites
'Double Delight' is fragrant and hardy; Elle™ is shell pink with glossy, disease-tolerant foliage.

Landscape Rose
Rosa hybrids

When, Where, and How to Plant
Plant during their dormant stage, although you can successfully plant them throughout the growing season. Shrub roses are vigorous and need space in a wide open, sunny location. Dig a 12 inch hole large enough to accommodate the roots, and blend in plenty of pine-bark conditioner. When planting a container rose, keep the rootball intact but free up circling roots if pot-bound. Plant grafted roses with the bud union just above the soil level. Backfill the hole and firm-in the soil until level with the ground. Water-in well and mulch with pine needle or bark mulch.

Growing Tips
Shrub roses will survive with once-a-week watering when they are established, but water more often the first month following planting. When watering, keep the foliage dry. Try to water in the morning. Shrub roses are not immune to pests but can recover lost foliage after receiving fertilizer.

Care
Prune in late winter, leaving enough cane so you can prune off cold damage later in the spring. These roses require the least amount of care in the "family," but watch for powdery mildew and blackspot disease. If these occur, spray with a fungicide and remove all infected foliage. Fertilize in the spring after the final pruning and feed only enough thereafter to keep the foliage healthy.

Companion Planting and Design
Plant in groups or use for mass plantings. They will "stop traffic" when placed in front of a picket fence or gate. Landscape roses are suitable for forming dense barriers and great hedges. The stiff branches and spines on *Rugosa* will keep passersby from snitching blossoms. Look at your local garden center for the new landscape roses designed for enjoyment at home.

Our Personal Favorites
Rosa × 'Knock Out'™ has bright cherry or pink blooms on 3-feet-tall plants; pink 'Bonica' is compact and free-flowering; 'Abraham Darby'®, a David Austin rose, has fragrance and old garden charm. 'DayDream'™ is perfect for small gardens or perennial borders.

Landscape roses often fulfill a gardener's desire to enjoy the beauty and fragrance of roses without employing a crew of landscape horticulturists. Easy-care shrub roses like rugosas, Meidiland, Knock-Out™, and Dreamland are a sure bet for superb hedges and informal plantings. They make great barrier plantings or no-shear shrub borders. Rugosa is the name of a species of rose as well as a rose classification. Rugosas, commonly called Japanese roses, are large plants with stiff, spiny canes. They are well suited for coastal planting since they are salt-tolerant and can hold down sandy slopes, preventing soil erosion. Two other likely candidates for hedge plantings are 'Carefree Beauty'™ and 'Simplicity' roses. These grow to four feet high, are very disease-resistant, and yield rather large, open pink flowers.

Other Common Names
Hedge Rose, Shrub Rose

Bloom Period and Seasonal Color
Spring or summer blooms in white, pink, and red.

Mature Height × Spread
4 ft. × 4 ft.

Miniature Rose
Rosa hybrids

Miniature roses are true dwarf members of the rose family and can easily be grown with a minimum of care and space. More of these little jewels deserve to be planted in the Carolinas. Since they are not grafted and grow on their own rootstock, they handle our unpredictable winters like little troopers, peeking their small heads out as spring arrives. They are available in a vast selection of colors and cultivars. Like an intricate tapestry, they will lend a captivating element to any garden area. They are generally much hardier than other roses and usually do not require winter protection in our area. Light mulching will give some winter protection as well as help conserve moisture during the summer.

Bloom Period and Seasonal Color
A myriad of colors from spring to fall.

Mature Height × Spread
15 to 30 in. × 12 to 25 in.

When, Where, and How to Plant
It's best to plant when dormant, though they can be planted in spring and early fall. They require at least six hours of intense sunlight and organically enriched soil with excellent drainage. Blend plenty of organic matter and soil conditioner into the existing soil. Dig a hole large enough to accommodate the roots. When planting a container rose, keep the rootball intact and place gently into the hole. Backfill the hole and firm the soil until level with the ground. Water-in well and mulch. When planting in a container, be sure it has good drainage and rich but porous potting soil. Move the container to shelter during severe winters. Miniatures can be grown indoors on a sunny windowsill or under fluorescent lights, but they do need more light than the average houseplant.

Growing Tips
Water weekly using a drip watering system to keep the foliage dry. Rosarians agree that all roses need regular fertilization. Use a specialty rose fertilizer or various organic products. Some of these contain systemic insecticides. Maintain a 2-inch layer of mulch.

Care
Prune miniatures in late March. Cut canes back to active new growth and remove any winter-damaged canes to maintain an appealing and healthy appearance. Miniature roses are propagated on their root systems, so they can endure difficult weather. These roses are also prone to blackspot and spider mites. Use a preventative pest control program. Protect greenhouse-grown roses purchased in early spring from frost by placing them in a sheltered location or holding them in a sunroom.

Companion Planting and Design
Miniature roses are great to plant in a perennial border or shrub bed. Though the flowers are small, arrangements of miniatures are attractive. This class of roses is suitable for container gardening when combined with million bells.

Our Personal Favorites
'Rise n' Shine', a vibrant yellow, makes a bold statement; 'Pride'n' Joy and 'Starina®' offer color in orange blends.

out and loosen the roots. Prune off long or girdling roots or, using hand shears or a sharp knife, cut any roots that are circling the rootball. If balled and burlapped, set the rootball in the hole and loosen the twine around the top.

- On small container-grown shrubs you can "butterfly" the rootball by using both hands to split open the bottom half of the rootball. This will encourage new roots to form.
- Bang the rootball on the ground a couple of times to dislodge some of the soil around the roots. This will also encourage feeder roots to penetrate the backfill.
- Turn the shrub so that the best side is out, not facing the house.
- Shovel the conditioned soil or unamended good topsoil into the hole in layers. Tamp or firm in each layer using your foot or the shovel handle, but don't over do it—roots need air.
- The top of the rootball should stand at least 1 to 2 inches above the surrounding soil. Form a low basin with the remaining backfill to catch water.
- Water each shrub with a five-gallon bucketful. If the water runs off, let the shrub soak for a while then continue watering around the rootball. Water trickled from a hose works best.
- Support tall, slender shrubs by tying them loosely between two stakes using degradable twine or flexible plastic tape. Loose tying allows the shrub to flex but not break in the wind, which strengthens the central stem.
- Spread mulch 3 inches deep to the outermost branches. Spreading three layers of newspaper before you mulch will diminish later problems with weeds and grass sprouting through the mulch. (Wet the newspaper immediately after setting in place.)

Special Planting Instructions for Rhododendrons, Azaleas, and Pieris

More ericaceous (acid-loving) shrubs are killed by too much water than by drought. In the wild, these plants grow in deep, well-drained organic "duff" in high shade. They send roots down into mineral soil to sustain them during dry weather.

Jim and Toby advise planting these special shrubs with half of the rootball above ground. Here's how:

- Spade or till the soil in the planting area. Don't walk on it prior to planting.
- Regardless of what you have learned previously, scatter a half cup pelletized limestone and one-half cup of controlled-release fertilizer over the area where the shrub will be planted. (Most Carolina soils have been depleted of calcium and magnesium by farming, and the rise in pH won't be significant.)
- Slide the shrub out of the container and loosen the roots. Bang the rootball on the ground a couple of times to shake off some soil particles.
- Pull circling roots loose from the rootball. If a pad of rootlets has formed on the bottom of the rootball, slice it off. Cut off long, stringy roots.

- Borrow five gallons of soil from elsewhere in your garden and dump it to the side of the planting site, or buy a bag of topsoil. Crumble the borrowed soil and mix it with an equal volume of organic soil conditioner or leaf compost. Avoid dried cow manure as it is alkaline in reaction.
- Turn the plant best side forward and set it in a shallow hole where it is to grow.
- Pull the conditioned soil around the rootball and taper it down to the original soil level. The plant may seem "high and dry," but it will love the good drainage and aeration.
- Shovel any remaining conditioned soil into a shallow basin to catch water.
- Mulch as directed for other shrubs. Do not use peat moss as a mulch; it repels water. Keep bark mulch away from the crown of plants. It is okay to tuck pinestraw beneath branches to conserve water and keep down weeds.
- Give each plant at least five gallons of water trickled from a hose.

Watering

Watering plants is a "seat of the pants" operation. There are no set rules. Amount and frequency depend on the soil and the weather. Drip irrigation allows you to conserve water while watering deeply for better root development. Without exception, fall is the best time for planting in coastal areas and the Piedmont . . . spring in the mountains. Fall planting, when the weather is usually cooler and rainier, will let you get by with little or no watering after the plant has settled in. But when planting during warm months, listen to your common sense. It will tell you that these plants, shocked by transplanting, will need frequent watering for their first month in their new location. If there is no rain, give each plant about five gallons of water every three days, preferably by trickling a hose. Carolina clay soils are notorious for shedding water, and Carolina sands are notorious for not retaining enough moisture to keep plants alive. However,

if you condition your soil with organic matter and mulch around your shrubs, water will soak into clay soils and stay with sandy soils. After the first month, you can decrease to weekly watering during dry spells. At the beginning of the second season, your shrubs will have "established" by sending many feeder roots into the soil surrounding the rootball.

If you notice new tip growth beginning to "flag" or droop, your plants are probably trying to tell you that they need water. Check them at 7:00 or 8:00 p.m. when water stress has decreased, and if the twigs have not plumped up, give them water regardless of what the schedule says.

Fertilizing

The controlled-release fertilizers (CRF) simplify feeding new or established shrubs. When you mix them into the backfill, they will feed plants for three to eight months, depending on the thickness of the plastic coating on the beads of fertilizer. When you feed established shrubs with

Azaleas

them, you should rake back the mulch, scatter the recommended amount, and replace the mulch. One cup of 18-6-12 or 14-14-14 analysis per shrub should be sufficient for all-season nutrition. However, if the foliage color pales, liquid feed in late summer.

CRF needs to be surrounded by moist soil or organic matter to release nutrients at the optimum rate. Simply scattering CRF around shrubs doesn't work as well. The wetting and drying slows nutrient release to a fraction of its programmed rate. Granular lawn or garden fertilizers are a different matter. They are "hotter" than CRF and more likely to "burn" plant roots by releasing excessive amounts of ammonia and mineral salts. They are not designed to be dissolved in water for liquid feeding. You need to take care not to get any hot fertilizer on the leaves of shrubs. If you do, wash it off right away. Shrubs take up more nutrients from the soil extending out from their drip lines, where feeder roots are most active. Measure the recommended amount of granular fertilizer and scatter it over the mulch beyond the drip line. Water it in promptly to kick off the movement of nutrients into the soil. For established shrubs, apply one-half cup of granular garden fertilizer per shrub in early spring, again after they bloom, and yet again in late summer, but not in the fall which could tenderize plants.

Soluble crystalline fertilizers are yet another matter. When you drench the soil around plants with them or apply them to the foliage, it is called "liquid feeding." They work well, but they don't stay in the soil as long as granular fertilizers and not nearly as long as CRF. It is risky to liquid feed plants shocked by transplanting. Wait a week or two, then begin liquid feeding each time you water. The usual dilution rate for crystalline fertilizers is one teaspoon per gallon of water, so if you pour five gallons of fertilizer solution around plants, you will have given them only five teaspoons of plant food. This is one reason why you need to liquid feed at the least every two weeks.

Last but not least are the organic fertilizers made from grain, seed, or fish byproducts. Cottonseed meal is an old-fashioned but still very effective fertilizer. It is sold by itself or mixed with other organic nutrient sources. It is especially desirable on coastal sands where nutrients are leached out by rain and irrigation. Fish emulsion is used for liquid feeding and will often produce good results where water-soluble mineral fertilizers are doing only a passable job.

Liming

Virtually all soils in the Carolinas are acidic due to many years of depletion of calcium and magnesium by farmers, livestock growers, the timber industry, and to leaching by our abundant rainfall. Soil tests by laboratories are the only way to determine accurately how much limestone is needed to neutralize the acidity in your soil. Clay soils need comparatively large amounts of lime to bring their pH into the 5.5 to 6.0 range preferred by most plants and to restore calcium and magnesium to desired levels. Sandy soils respond to smaller amounts of limestone but lose it faster to leaching.

Pelletized dolomitic limestone is the preferred instrument for pH change. It is easier and neater to spread than powdered lime and contains both calcium and magnesium.

Generally, ten pounds of pelletized dolomitic limestone per one hundred square feet is sufficient for clay soils, and five pounds per one hundred square feet for sandy soils. You need to reapply lime every two to three years on clay soils and every one to two years on sandy soils.

Limestone always works better when mixed with the soil. Calcium, in particular, tends to stay where you put it and is slow to move down into the root zone. Therefore, when liming established shrubs, pull back mulch, spread the lime, and restore the mulch. Tunneling by earthworms will gradually move the calcium and magnesium into deeper layers.

Arborvitae
Thuja occidentalis

Choosing a privacy screen is frequently a matter of neces-sity with suburban home buyers. The two likely options are a traditional wooden fence or a continuous row of ley-land cypress. Redtip photinias were once an option, but rampant disease problems are pushing them out of the picture. Too many folks choose leyland cypress. As lovely as cypress trees are, their towering height and pest sus-ceptibility give reason for looking at other evergreens. There are numerous Thuja cultivars appropriate for screening. High on the list should be Emerald arborvitae, 'Smaragd', and 'Holstrup', moderate-growing narrowleaf conifers well-suited to urban lots for privacy hedges or specimen use. These dense upright shrubs of unique emerald color stand like sentinels but are not overpower-ing when planted for a vertical accent.

Other Common Name
American Arborvitae

Bloom Period and Seasonal Color
Soft, emerald-green foliage year-round.

Mature Height × Spread
10 to 15 ft. × 3 to 4 ft.

When, Where, and How to Plant
Plant balled-and-burlapped plants or container-grown emerald arborvitae in fall or early spring. Site the evergreen in full sun to partial shade; strong sun is best. It can survive in a wide range of soils, including moist or dry clay. It is wise to have the soil tested prior to installing an expen-sive privacy hedge. Apply nutrients accordingly. The best pH for *Thuja* is 5.5 to 6.5. See page 176 for planting instructions. Space your plantings 3 to 4 feet apart. Loosen the roots in container plants, but handle balled-and-burlapped shrubs with care so as not to break the rootball. Water well after planting.

Growing Tips
Water twice during the first week, then weekly in dry periods. Though these plants don't wilt, a little water during a drought is worth the effort in the early years. Evergreens do not need annual fertil-ization. An occasional fertilizer application keeps the color sharp. Mulch with 3 to 4 inches of pine or hardwood mulch in sandy soils.

Care
One-gallon pots of arborvitae can grow 6 feet high in five years with no maintenance. You should not concern yourself with topping or shearing these since they rarely break in ice storms or stretch too high. Keep an eye out for bagworms and mites. They don't infest all arborvitae but can seriously weaken those they choose. Toby says that deer have shown no interest in his arborvitae, though they roam freely close by.

Companion Planting and Design
Emerald arborvitae is awesome when used with an underplanting of Japanese garden juniper or Carissa holly. Use it freely for screening and at the back of perennial borders. Another tall, fast-grow-ing selection is a western hybrid, *T. plicata* 'Green Giant', which is receiving a lot of press as a replace-ment for leyland cypress.

Our Personal Favorites
In small gardens, 'Golden Globe' arborvitae will glow in a sunny location. 'Degroot's Spire' is a nar-row plant for small spaces.

Aucuba
Aucuba japonica

When, Where, and How to Plant

Plant from spring through fall, but before the ground gets cold in winter. Transplant established shrubs in early spring; avoid planting when the soil is too wet. Leaves can burn in locations that receive full sun, so it's best to plant in shade gardens where the soil drains well. Aucuba thrives in medium- to high-moisture situations and actually prefers our heavy clay soils. Use native soil for backfill. Amend sandy loam soils with organic materials such as sphagnum peat moss. Add 3 to 4 inches of mulch, then water well. Turn to page 176 for more planting advice.

Growing Tips

Water new aucuba plantings for ten minutes every third day for two to three weeks until the shrub's roots are established. Deep watering is preferred over light watering. When in doubt, check soil wetness with a trowel before watering. Water during drought! Aucuba does not need much fertilizer if it is kept mulched. For older shrubs, apply a slow-release nursery fertilizer every other spring at a rate of $^1/_2$ cup per 10 square feet, under the canopy of the shrub and a little beyond.

Care

Prune in spring to shape, and remove winter-damaged stems. Aucuba's problems are usually limited to wind-damaged leaves and sunscald. Blackened foliage may be a sign of cold injury or of a soil nematode problem. Check with a County Cooperative Extension Agent for a nematode assay. Aucuba roots easily if cuttings are stuck in a pot of moist sand.

Companion Planting and Design

Use aucuba in shady corners or in planters by a patio. Grow it as a courtyard planting or privacy hedge in full shade, or as background for shade-loving perennials. A single plant will thrive in a 10-gallon container. This is a great shade-tolerant plant that produces beautifully colored foliage for fresh arrangements.

Our Personal Favorite

To brighten a dark corner, look for 'Picturata'.

Aucuba looks as if it belongs in Florida gardens among tropical foliage plants. But when it comes to choosing a hardy woody plant for shade, this shrub is always at the top of the list. Its long, lustrous, leathery leaves provide the coarse texture needed by shade gardens. Attractive red fruit on the female of the species is usually obscured by its thick, heavy foliage. Aucuba cultivars vary from solid green to the old-fashioned spotted variety, 'Gold Dust'. Aucuba actually suffers when placed in a hot, sunny location but endures for years in protected, shady areas in the Carolinas. Most homes have at least one corner on the north or east side that never gets direct sunlight yet needs a plant to dress it up. Aucuba is the perfect candidate.

Bloom Period and Seasonal Color

Purple spring flowers are not showy; red berries in winter on female plants.

Mature Height × Spread

6 to 10 ft. × 4 to 6 ft.

Azalea

Rhododendron × hybridum

Admired the world over, azaleas epitomize spring in the Carolinas. April in the Piedmont is an awesome sight, with landscapes that are a riot of color from the various hybrid azaleas, dogwoods, and spring-flowering bulbs. Carolina gardeners are hooked on the dwarf evergreen azalea varieties that mature to two to six feet in height. These members of the heath and rhododendron family are the most popular and are readily available at garden shops. The Kurumes are the "dime-store" variety that include the pink 'Coral Bells', 'Hershey Red', and the white cultivar 'Snow'. They are floriferous and durable in spite of the poor planting sites they are frequently destined to endure. Another group of hybrid azaleas is the Gumpo or Satsukis, a good choice for sunny locations in entrance gardens.

Bloom Period and Seasonal Color
Early spring blooms in white, red, and pinks.

Mature Height × Spread
4 to 6 ft. × 6 ft.
3 ft. × 5 ft. (gumpos)

When, Where, and How to Plant
Plant hybrid azaleas anytime in spring or fall. Toby prefers to plant them before flowering or wait until October when the weather moderates. They do best in dappled shade, protected from the afternoon sun. Hybrid azaleas thrive if they are "planted high" in a bed of loose organic soil; Gumpos will do fine in full sun in irrigated, mulched beds. Azaleas are a species of rhododendron with similar cultural requirements including moist, rich, well drained soil. Prepare planting beds by mixing in 4 inches of leaf compost or peat moss. Loosen and cut the rootball by cutting from the bottom about halfway. Butterfly the rootball, and place the plant on the prepared soil. Position the roots higher than the surrounding ground. Do not fertilize. Cover the roots, water thoroughly, then mulch well.

Growing Tips
Water hybrid azaleas well during the early years. Irrigate new plantings three times the first week, twice the second, and weekly as needed thereafter. Fertilize in spring after blooming, if needed. Established beds may need a little limestone even though these are acid-loving shrubs.

Care
Prune immediately after flowering; shear as needed to eliminate rangy shoots. Be prepared for an attack by lace bugs in hot locations. The translucent, 1/4-inch bugs appear on the undersides of the leaves. Spray to prevent injury; two insecticide applications are needed, one in April and another in September. Yellow foliage may indicate a need for nitrogen, magnesium, or chelated iron. Root knot nematodes or root rot fungus can stunt and kill azaleas. Gumpos are more disease resistant, but their flowers are short lived. Invigorate old plantings by transplanting or by reworking the soil.

Companion Planting and Design
Azaleas can be used as specimens, though they're usually planted in groups. They are best displayed with small trees like dogwood, Japanese cherry, and redbud. Encore™ azaleas promise two seasons of color and are gaining in popularity in Zone 8 and 9 gardens.

Our Personal Favorites
Two favorites are 'Sunglow' and 'Hershey Red'.

Barberry

Berberis thunbergii var. *atropurpurea*

When, Where, and How to Plant

'Crimson Pygmy' and other barberries are available exclusively as container-grown plants, so plant anytime the soil is workable. For the best growth and color intensity, plant this variety in full sun. Other cultivars can handle part sun. 'Crimson Pygmy' adapts to most soil types and growing conditions, though it will not tolerate soggy soils. Loosen roots of container-grown plants. It is better to plant high rather than have barberry rootballs sink deep into the soil. Space these 3 to 5 feet apart. Firm soil around the sides of the rootball, water thoroughly and spread mulch. See the chapter introduction to read more planting tips.

Growing Tips

Water newly planted shrubs directly for ten minutes every third day for two weeks, then irrigate weekly during summer until the shrub's roots are established. Deep watering is preferred over frequent light watering. Fertilize barberries in early fall every other year. Use a slow-release fertilizer at the rate of 1/2 cup per 10 square feet, and broadcast at the drip line of the shrub and a little beyond.

Care

Prune anytime, but only to shape plants. Heavy pruning on old plantings is best done in late winter before new growth starts. Barberries can be cut back to 10 inches to rejuvenate mature shrubs. 'Crimson Pygmy' and other barberries have no serious disease or insect pests. Wet soils, however, will predispose this shrub to root rot disease. When established, they thrive despite drought, urban pollution, and bone-dry soils.

Companion Planting and Design

Barberries provide a wonderful color contrast to the background of the overall landscape. 'Crimson Pygmy' can be used as a specimen in a small garden or as a low border in groupings. It will stand out visually in front of lighter-colored foliage, such as variegated ligustrum. The gold leaf 'Aurea' has many possibilities for design.

Our Personal Favorites

'Crimson Pygmy' is a standard in the trade. The newer 'Concorde' may rival them all.

As one landscape professional put it, "For the color you get and its nice contrast with other landscape plants, 'Crimson Pygmy' barberry is hard to pass over." He's right—this is a fine deciduous shrub. It has a dense mounding habit and stiff, spiny branches. Japanese barberries have distinctive red-purple foliage all summer long which changes to deep amber when cooler weather arrives. The colorful summer foliage makes these shrubs very popular when used in plantings with gold-variegated shrubs and small flower plantings. Barberry 'Rosy Glow' has pinkish-burgundy tricolor foliage and is great for a hedge or large border planting with low growing evergreens. A most unusual cousin, B. gladwynensis 'William Penn', has a beautiful compact form with arching branches. A Word of Caution: Barberries can jump the fence; don't plant them near wild lands.

Other Common Name

Japanese Barberry

Bloom Period and Seasonal Color

Small, bright yellow flowers in spring; red, purplish, or bluish-black fruit in summer.

Mature Height × Spread

2 ft. × 3 ft.

Boxwood

Buxus sempervirens

"American" boxwood is the aristocrat among shrubs, maturing to eighteen feet in height. When used as an evergreen screen, it creates a look of distinction and historical significance. Boxwoods are associated with great estates. They have been used in landscapes from the traditional English gardens to plantation estates. You will find grand old boxwoods all across the Carolinas, from the Biltmore House in Asheville to Old Salem's colonial gardens to Middleton Place near Charleston. The somewhat hardier, low-growing "English" Boxwood, 'Suffruticosa', is sought after for foundation plantings of homes with colonial architecture. The plants are quite expensive and slow growing, but they make excellent low maintenance shrubs. At high elevations, common boxwoods are not reliably hardy. Look-alike Korean boxwood makes a good hardy substitute for a low evergreen hedge.

Bloom Period and Seasonal Color
Tan-colored spring blooms are not showy; grown for evergreen foliage.

Mature Height × Spread
American 10 to 18 ft. × 8 to 14 ft.
Suffruticosa 3 to 4 ft × 4 ft.

When, Where, and How to Plant
American boxwood can be dug and transplanted or set out as container-grown plants year-round. Plant in full sun to part shade in well drained soil. Though many are planted in full shade, shade makes boxwood grow thin and open in its form. Avoid sites that stay wet constantly, such as near a downspout. Water well, then water every three days for the first couple of weeks. Always plant "high" in clay soils. Spread mulch to retard weeds and retain moisture. Refer to the chapter introduction for some helpful planting hints.

Growing Tips
Water routinely the first summer, applying water approximately one minute for each inch of diameter of the rootball. No supplementary fertilizer is needed the first year. In the springs that follow, use slow-release nursery fertilizer at the recommended rate. Some gardeners prefer to use a fertilizer mixture of one-half 10-10-10 fertilizer and one-half cottonseed meal. Spread 1 cup of this mixture around the drip line.

Care
Shear boxwoods lightly each June after the new growth is fully mature. Cut back overgrown boxwoods severely over a period of two years. Begin in February and remove the top third. Cut hard again the next winter, shaping plants as you reduce their size. Off-color foliage is symptomatic of nematodes or leafminers. Leafminers are the worst pests. Treat with an insecticide, such as malathion, as new growth emerges in spring.

Companion Planting and Design
Shape boxwoods as topiary or grow them as specimen shrubs. Use them to anchor the ends of beds, creating a regal appearance. Boxwoods may be planted as hedges, accent shrubs in foundations, or limbed up to tree forms. "English" boxwood is much sought after for landscaping foundations. Though it looks regal, try to avoid overloading your landscape with too many.

Our Personal Favorites
For a cone-shaped specimen, use 'Pyramidalis'. For a foundation plant or to edge walks, try 'Green Velvet', a compact, 3-foot hybrid.

Butterfly Bush
Buddleia davidii

When, Where, and How to Plant

Plant spring through fall. Butterfly bush performs best in full sun. Although it is satisfactory in partial shade, it stretches excessively and the thin-stemmed flowers will be weighed down by rain. Butterfly bush thrives in well-drained soil of a neutral pH. When transplanting, don't hesitate to prune extremely long roots. Root-pruning forces production of new feeder roots at the points where the roots are cut. Firm the backfill soil around the roots, and water as you backfill the planting hole. Mulch with bark or pine straw.

Growing Tips

In dry locations, supplemental watering will ensure rapid growth. Be prepared to irrigate during the first season of growth. Butterfly bush is basically a low maintenance plant that seems to bloom better in a soil that is not too rich. Fertilize in spring with a 10-10-10 analysis when growth starts. Another application following a summer shearing should suffice.

Care

The plant should be pruned to 12 to 20 inches from the ground in late winter. This induces strong new canes that produce a fuller shrub and plenty of large blooms. No further care is needed other than removing spent flowers and twiggy shoots occasionally. No major insects or diseases are known. Toby reports having to move and transplant a butterfly bush that he had planted only a few months earlier. To his amazement, the pieces of roots remaining in the ground eventually produced three small bushes at the first location. One secret to growing butterfly bushes is to prune early spring and midsummer.

Companion Planting and Design

Use near an outdoor sitting area where the butterflies can be observed and the scent of the blooms can be enjoyed. Plant alongside asclepias, asters, and Joe-Pye weed for a season of entertainment. Place a shallow watering dish containing moist sand close by for thirsty butterflies.

Our Personal Favorites

The flower colors of 'Black Knight' and 'Attraction' are an amazing horticultural accomplishment. A new blue, 'Nanho Blue' takes the ribbon.

This deciduous flowering shrub is highly attractive to butterflies and bees by day and moths by night. Long spires of blooms, up to a foot long and mildly fragrant, are what really attract attention. The spires are formed of clusters of tiny flowers that are borne on the ends of the long stems of new growth. They are 2 to 3 inches wide and resemble lilac flowers. Though the flowers of most butterfly bushes are lavender-blue with an orange eye, butterfly bush colors range from white to magenta to yellow and deep purple. This colorful display continues all summer and into the fall provided old blooms are periodically removed. Butterfly bush dons airy, gray-green foliage and narrow leaves up to eight inches long. It's a must for the wildlife garden.

Other Common Name
Summer Lilac

Bloom Period and Seasonal Color
White, purple, magenta, or lavender-blue summer blooms.

Mature Height × Spread
5 to 15 ft. × 5 to 8 ft.

Camellia

Camellia sasanqua

Camellias have been grown in China since the ninth century, but American home gardeners didn't catch camellia fever until the 1920s. C. japonica *caused much of the excitement, but in the upper Carolinas,* C. sasanqua *is more durable in the landscape. It is vigorous, flowering consistently without the devastating loss of blossoms from March freezes suffered by* C. japonica *in the Piedmont and westward. Sasanquas adorn many parks and college campuses, where it forms massive hedges. You will see this flowering evergreen espaliered on a wall or, when overgrown and cramped next to a foundation, limbed up to create a small tree. Delightful single and double blossoms can be enjoyed during fall and winter months. The South Carolina Botanical Garden boasts an incredible selection of over 360 cultivars.*

Other Common Name
Sasanqua

Bloom Period and Seasonal Color
Winter blooms in white, red, and pink.

Mature Height × Spread
6 to 15 ft. × 5 to 10 ft.

When, Where, and How to Plant
Plant sasanquas from March through October to establish roots during warm weather. Avoid planting when soil is frozen or too wet to work. They tolerate most well-drained soils. This species is more sun-tolerant than the japonicas, but it prefers afternoon shade or high shade all day. Expect winter sunscald on leaves if you plant camellias on a sunny, windswept site. A new sasanqua taller than 3 feet should be tied securely to a single stake. Mulch to protect the roots.

Growing Tips
Water sasanquas regularly the first summer and fall. They are drought tolerant when mature but will respond to irrigation during dry periods when they are flowering. Fertilize with a specialty camellia fertilizer in spring. Apply compost, aged manure, or cottonseed meal for fall fertilization during early September.

Care
Don't shear sasanquas unless they are used as a formal hedge. They need plenty of head room and should be allowed to grow open and full. The best time to prune is immediately after flowering; remove rangy shoots with hand shears. Prune out blighted shoots that die quickly. Keep an eye open for scale insects and spray any with horticultural oil. If voles are a problem in your area, bait mouse traps with slices of apple or peanut butter. Voles (not moles) can damage or kill camellias by eating their roots. The dense root mass of these shallow-rooted shrubs makes it impossible to grow perennials beneath them. Note: *C. japonica* will thrive in the Piedmont, but flowers and buds are subject to cold snaps; cover with bed sheets on frosty nights.

Companion Planting and Design
Sasanquas are appropriate for hedges along the property line or for training on a trellis. Use the dwarf cultivars when planting in close quarters. Sasanquas can be used with low spreading shrubs, such as Japanese plum yew, bluebeard, and loropetalum.

Our Personal Favorites
Favorites in bloom sequence are 'Dawn', 'Yuletide', and 'Setsugekka'. 'Survivor' is a good Zone 7 variety.

Cherry Laurel
Prunus laurocerasus

When, Where, and How to Plant

Cherry laurel is available mostly as container-grown plants. Plant anytime in spring and fall. In the western Carolinas, give them a month to establish before cold weather sets in. Plant in full sun or filtered shade. Cherry laurel grows best in well drained soil of moderate fertility. An acidic soil with a pH of 5.5 is ideal. Moist soils will be tolerated if the drainage is quick. See page 176 for planting instructions. Mulch after planting. Mulching will conserve moisture, control weeds, and decay to provide a richer soil.

Growing Tips

Water deeply with a soaker hose during summer dry spells. Use a hand spade or a pipe probe to determine the depth of soil wetness. Avoid over-fertilizing, but each spring, just before new growth starts, feed with a commercial shrub fertilizer with an analysis approximately 12-6-6.

Care

In clay soils, be careful not to over-water cherry laurels since they are susceptible to root rot diseases. (Landscapers report fewer problems with 'Zabeliana'.) Light pruning is preferred; severe renovation pruning should be done about one month before new growth starts in the spring. Prune again in July for size control. Winter leaf scorch causes foliage to shed. The plants are susceptible to wood borers, leaf spots, and scale insects. An insecticide spray for borers in June is beneficial and reduces scale infestations; spring fungicide applications can prevent leaf spots.

Companion Planting and Design

'Otto Luyken' cherry laurels are best used in groups in the foundation or border. 'Schip' (*Schiptaensis*) and 'Zabel' (*Zabeliana*) laurels are popular for low screening. They get much too large for entrance beds. Use them as a backdrop for perennials.

Our Personal Favorite

Though it grows a bit tall for small yards, you will enjoy the fragrant springtime flowers of 'Zabeliana'.

This species includes some of the finest broadleaf evergreens for Carolina landscapes. Its cultivars have rich, lustrous foliage and may be planted as large privacy hedges or as dense, spreading, foundation shrubs. The oldest variety, 'English laurel', is a massive evergreen shrub commonly found in large estate gardens. Hedges of English laurel grow to 15 feet high and 10 feet wide. The cherry laurels include some highly desirable landscape shrubs, particularly the compact 'Otto Luyken', which makes a fine foundation planting or low border. The cherry laurels are moderately fast growing shrubs and have a horizontal branching habit. They will grow to eight feet with a spread slightly larger. They take well to shearing and thrive in full sun to partial shade. This is a terrific evergreen plant.

Bloom Period and Seasonal Color
Small white flowers in spring.

Mature Height × Spread
4 to 8 ft. × 4 to 8 ft.

Cleyera

Ternstroemia gymnanthera

Lustrous foliage in late spring is but one of the many attributes ascribed to cleyera. This camellia cousin is another choice for shaded landscapes, though it lacks the showy flowers associated with the family. Taxonomists have played tricks on us by reclassifying this plant and using a botanical name that only a Latin scholar would love. Carolina gardeners still affectionately refer to this evergreen as cleyera. It is difficult to find a better screening plant where the soils are moist and deep. The shrub grows moderately fast and is pest free. Some large specimens can be found across the region in various light conditions from full sun to part shade. Cleyera's dark green foliage and globular seedpods on mature specimens are other identifiable characteristics.

Other Common Name
Japanese Cleyera

Bloom Period and Seasonal Color
Inconspicuous spring flower; some cultivars with bronze colored growth.

Mature Height × Spread
10 ft. × 6 ft.

When, Where, and How to Plant
Plant anytime the soil is workable during fall, winter, or spring. Cleyera's thick, waxy leaves hold up well in the planting process with little noticeable wilting until the soil is very dry. The plant will remain densely branched if planted in a sunny location. Purchase quality container-grown shrubs pruned properly for fullness of form. Thin, weak plants tend to become lanky, especially in shade conditions. Prepare a planting hole that is twice the diameter of the rootball or wider. Add soil conditioner to sandy soils. Refer to the chapter introduction for more planting advice. Water thoroughly after planting and weekly for the first month or so.

Growing Tips
Cleyera can survive moist clay soil provided it drains well. Mulch with several inches organic material and water thoroughly during the first two summers; afterward, it is considered drought tolerant. Apply a nursery grade fertilizer every few years to keep cleyera vigorous.

Care
This plant resists pests as well as drought. It tends to produce long, wispy growth where it gets too little sun, requiring routine pruning in the growing season. Prune as needed year-round to maintain its symmetrical plant form. This plant is practically pest free and lives for decades once planted in the landscape. Once it's established, there is little to the care of cleyera other than mulching as needed.

Companion Planting and Design
This plant is much too tall to use in a foundation planting, but it can make a very dense privacy screen (possibly another alternative to leyland cypress). The glossy green foliage is pleasant to the eye when used as a specimen shrub. Cleyera provides a wonderful background for perennial flower gardens and beds of azaleas, kerria, spirea and other similar deciduous, spring flowering shrubs.

Our Personal Favorite
The species is a fine shrub; however, the new bronze leaf cleyera cultivar 'Grewald' and the compact form 'Grevan' (Jade Tiara®) look promising.

Curlyleaf Privet

Ligustrum japonicum 'Recurvifolium'

When, Where, and How to Plant

Container-grown curlyleaf privet can be transplanted anytime the ground is not frozen, though fall or spring is considered best. It is pH adaptable and performs well in sun or shade. It will grow well in moist soils and will survive in dry soils if watered well during establishment. In exposed locations in the western region and foothills, it is subject to sunburn and moderate defoliation in the winter, but it rebounds in the spring like a trooper. You can read more about planting curlyleaf privet on page 176 in the chapter introduction.

Growing Tips

Water weekly for the first month after planting. Later, water only when the soil is dry to the touch, but water deeply when irrigating. Once established, it is drought tolerant. To hold the plant in check, do not overfertilize. Use a slow-release fertilizer in spring to improve the color of the foliage.

Care

Very little pruning is needed, though crowded branches can be removed for grooming. Shear to shape as it matures and for height control. Curlyleaf privet tolerates heavy pruning in late winter. It can be sheared following flushes of growth during summer months. Overgrown curlyleaf privet can be limbed up to create interesting multi-trunked specimens. Curlyleaf privet has no serious diseases or insect problems. Brown leaf spots may occur in spring from sunscald in winter; remove affected leaves.

Companion Planting and Design

Curlyleaf privet is a good specimen plant, or it can be used as an accent in the foundation or to frame a corner. The taller waxleaf privet is comparatively inexpensive for screening purposes where large quantities are needed. It can also be trained as topiary and grown in large containers.

Our Personal Favorite

'Nobilis' has superior upright form and cold hardiness.

This shrub is a handsome choice for gardens in the Piedmont and low country. Curlyleaf privet is one of the best-behaved ligustrums. Its dark-green leaves with wavy margins give it a distinctive appearance. Dense, slow growth and low maintenance appeal to busy baby-boomers. Few evergreen shrubs tolerate such a wide range of planting conditions from full sun to shade and from dry to moist soil types. Waxleaf ligustrum (L. lucidum) is another favorite evergreen found in Zone 8 gardens. It is a larger, fast growing evergreen for the landscape that can be used as a privacy screen. There are some undesirable species of Ligustrum, including the Chinese privet (L. sinensae). These robust, small-leaved deciduous shrubs have escaped cultivation and become field and forest weeds, giving the whole family a bad reputation.

Other Common Name
Curlyleaf Ligustrum

Bloom Period and Seasonal Color
White to yellow blooms in late spring.

Mature Height × Spread
8 ft. or more × 3 to 6 ft.

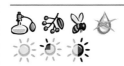

Deciduous Azalea
Rhododendron spp.

While most rhododendrons are evergreens, our native azaleas are deciduous. What they lack in foliar character they more than compensate for with color and durability. Deciduous azaleas flourish throughout the forested coast, thriving everywhere from upland slopes to river bottoms. Cold-hardy pinkshell azalea (R. vaseyi) occurs naturally at elevations above 3000 feet. Unlike other deciduous azaleas, its blooms are unscented. What it lacks in fragrance, it compensates with clear apple-blossom-pink petals. Locals refer to our varied woodland species such as pinxterbloom (R. periclymenoides) or Piedmont azalea (R. canescens) as "wild honeysuckle." The flame azaleas (R. calendulaceum) and heat tolerant Exbury cultivars provide vibrant flower trusses and excitement to any spring garden. It is nonsense to say that an azalea must be evergreen to make a statement in the garden.

Bloom Period and Seasonal Color
Deep pink to white blooms in early spring.

Mature Height × Spread
5 to 8 ft. × 3 to 5 ft.

When, Where, and How to Plant
Plant deciduous azaleas anytime from spring through fall. Set out seedlings and small container-grown plants in spring. Do not dig native azaleas from the wild—there is a law against this!. Site azaleas in morning sun or filtered shade, in well drained, moist, humusy soil (pH should be 5.0 to 5.5). Plant native azaleas in raised beds that have been amended with compost. Elevating the beds ensures good water drainage. Holes dug in poorly drained soils will only fill with water and hold excess moisture, regardless of the size of the hole. Thoroughly loosen the roots of plants grown in pots. For raised beds, mix equal parts soil, compost, and pine-bark soil conditioner. Settle in the rootball by watering well. Complete the job by adding 2 to 3 inches of mulch. Avoid fertilizing at planting. See the introduction to this chapter for detailed planting directions

Growing Tips
Water deciduous azaleas every three days for the first two to three weeks. Then water weekly as needed until established. Feed azaleas immediately after blooming ceases, then again six to eight weeks later.

Care
Pruning is rarely needed. If necessary, prune after flowering (during spring), trimming out branches to maintain a natural appearance. The plants may also be trimmed to keep a desired height. Powdery mildew is not a problem, but treat for lace bugs if this ornamental is planted in a sunny location. Irrigate in the dry summer months and maintain an organic mulch layer to encourage root development.

Companion Planting and Design
Plant deciduous azaleas in front of evergreen borders to make a show as they bloom before the foliage appears. Plant pinkshell azalea alongside early-flowering ornamentals in woodland shade gardens. Exbury hybrids tolerate the warmer locations found in sunny gardens.

Our Personal Favorites
In the Piedmont region, pinxterbloom azaleas (*R. periclymenoides*) are found growing in the wild. The native Piedmont azalea (*R. canescens*) thrives in warmer zones.

Dwarf Burning Bush
Euonymus alatus 'Compactus'

When, Where, and How to Plant

Plant from containers anytime the ground is not frozen. Dwarf burning bush grows well in sun or shade in ordinary garden soil, although it will not have brilliant fall color without at least a half-day of direct sun. Once established, it tolerates a wide range of moisture conditions from near-wet to bone-dry. In a hedge planting, space burning bushes 3 feet apart for a dense screen. For advice on planting, see page 176 in the chapter introduction. Note: Some states and organizations recommend against planting burning bush because birds eat the abundant berries and deposit them in wild areas, where they may become invasive.

Growing Tips

Water the plants deeply for the first six to eight weeks following planting. After that, water every ten to fourteen days. Maintain a mulch of compost, bark, or pinestraw. In early fall, apply a slow-release fertilizer with an analysis such as 12-6-6 at the rate of $1/2$ cup per 10 square feet; broadcast at the drip line area.

Care

Late winter is the best time for heavy pruning of overgrown bushes. It is best to do some heavy thinning the first year then take shrubs down to knee-high the next winter. Weevils may take bites out of the leaves, but scale insects cause more serious injury. Treat with a fall application of dormant oil and a June insecticide application. Too much shade reduces vivid fall coloration.

Companion Planting and Design

For a great fall display, use in mass groupings with Heritage river birch and garden mums. Hide the ugly feet and bare legs of these shrubs with santolina or junipers. Ornamental grasses are a good companion for a dazzling autumn display.

Our Personal Favorite

What would autumn be like without 'Compactus' burning bush?

Whether you call it burning bush or winged euonymus, this excellent landscape plant steals the show in fall. As the frosty days of autumn arrive, this unassuming shrub turns blaming crimson, snatching the attention from other ornamentals, plain or flamboyant. Burning bush is a deciduous shrub with two-inch, medium green leaves on horizontal branches. The individual stems have corky projections, or wings, that add interest in the winter garden. When the leaves drop, tiny orange berries are seen clinging to the bare branches. As the shrub matures, its vase shape takes on a fuller, rounded form with a pleasing texture. Dwarf burning bush makes a wonderful screen or accent specimen in summer. The dwarf variety 'Compactus' will grow slowly to 6 feet.

Other Common Name
Winged Euonymus

Bloom Period and Seasonal Color
Brilliant red foliage in fall.

Mature Height × Spread
6 to 10 ft. × 6 ft.

Dwarf Japanese Holly
Ilex crenata

Most of the shrubs selected by contractors for new home sites are likely an assortment of Japanese hollies. This holly adapts well to a wide range of environmental conditions. There are scores of cultivars from which to choose, and new ones appear every year. Dark green foliage and a moderate growth rate make them a choice shrub for home landscapes. 'Compacta' is a viable substitute for boxwoods, and in most cases people won't know the difference without a second look. The flowers of Japanese hollies are rather uninteresting, as are the black berries that follow. The dwarf mounding forms such as 'Helleri', 'Hoogendorn', and 'Soft Touch' are the most popular with gardeners. They produce symmetrical new growth, and they generally require very little attention.

Bloom Period and Seasonal Color
Evergreen foliage with few flowers or berries.

Mature Height × Spread
2 to 8 ft. × 2 to 8 ft.

When, Where, and How to Plant
Healthy Japanese hollies purchased in containers can be planted throughout the growing season. Allow enough time for their roots to establish several weeks before the ground freezes. Plant in sunny to partly sunny locations; in full shade the shrubs thin out and get leggy. Avoid planting in wet soil conditions. They grow successfully in moist, well drained soil. Thoroughly loosen the roots of plants grown in pots. Prepare a wide, shallow hole $3/4$ as deep and three times as wide as the rootball. Make a mix of $1/3$ organic humus or soil conditioner to native soil. Pack firmly around the sides of the rootball. Water slowly, applying a 5-gallon bucketful to settle the plant. Add 1 to 3 inches of mulch, staying clear of the crown.

Growing Tips
Irrigate in the early years during the dry periods of August into fall. Always water the plants in dry weather, as they appreciate moisture. A combination of landscape fabric and mulch can help eliminate drought stress. Fertilize with low rates of a slow-release product in fall or spring. Once the plants are established, use a slow-release or organic product for year-round green color.

Care
Shear in late winter or early summer to maintain symmetry. Black root rot fungus can kill Japanese holly as it approaches ten years, and the fungus that infects this plant is especially fond of heavy clay soils. Plant your hollies high, such as in a raised bed, as a means of preventing fungal attack. Nematodes can wreck Japanese hollies in sandy soils.

Companion Planting and Design
Use an upright form such as 'Hetzii' as a hedge, or 'Sky Pencil' for a vertical accent. Low growing varieties should be grouped together in mass plantings or used as a ground cover. Dwarf forms such as 'Soft Touch' can be planted as an edging in the flowerbed.

Our Personal Favorites
The standard workhorse varieties are 'Compacta' and 'Green Luster'. From the Piedmont southward, dwarf yaupon (*I. vomitoria*) is happy in sunny, hot beds.

Dwarf Nandina
Nandina domestica

When, Where, and How to Plant

Plant dwarf nandinas from spring to fall. Move established nandinas in late fall or in spring before growth begins. Their best winter leaf color appears when they are planted in a sunny, well drained location. They adapt to shade and dry sites and can be planted near the roots of shade trees, but fine-textured soils like clay loams will literally suck the water out of the rootballs of potted plants. See planting recommendations, on page 176. Water thoroughly at planting, then mulch.

Growing Tips

The first two to three weeks after planting is critical to the survival of a shrub. Water deeply every third day for the first several weeks in warm weather; don't let the shrubs wilt first. After the new roots catch, nandinas are on their own. They are tough, low maintenance shrubs. Fertilize in fall or spring with a general garden fertilizer like 4-1-2 analysis at $1/4$ cup per plant. They are not heavy feeders.

Care

Thin mature plants in spring. Dwarf nandina is vulnerable to a virus disorder that causes some plants to be stunted and twisted—although the same or another virus may be responsible for the red color we enjoy in the species. In case the plant looks miserable, just dig it out and replace it with a healthy specimen. Don't plant nandinas, or for that matter most ornamentals, in wet, sticky, clay soil. Rainy seasons can encourage leaf spots; just remove spoiled leaves with a good shearing and thinning.

Companion Planting and Design

A mass grouping of these small evergreen shrubs fronted by an edging of variegated liriope or pansies is a car-stopper in winter. They are a substitute for winter flowers in borders.

Our Personal Favorites

'Harbour Dwarf' and 'Fire Power' give the most winter color. The ground cover variety 'San Gabriel' has delicate, needle-like leaves.

Dwarf nandin pictured above is hard to beat! It's a virtually pest-free, "no maintenance" ornamental. These are compact plants with dense foliage that can glow brilliant red if you plant cultivars like 'Fire Power' and 'Gulf Stream'. Dwarf nandinas maintain the look of the species nandinas with their compound pointed leaves, though they may reach only two to three feet in height. Unlike the common, tall, old-garden nandinas that produced clusters of red berries just in time for the holidays, the dwarf nandinas are nearly fruitless—but what they lack in fruit and flowers they make up for in foliage color. The winter color of dwarf nandinas is superior to that of other shrubs in winter. The lack of berries should calm the concerns of environmentalists who fear the spreading of common nandina into Carolina woods.

Bloom Period and Seasonal Color
Few flowers are produced, but foliage compensates fully.

Mature Height × Spread
2 to 3 ft. × 2 to 6 ft.

False Cypress

Chamaecyparis obtusa 'Nana Gracilis'

If you like dwarf conifers, you will find that the diversity in this false cypress group is truly outstanding. Chamaecyparis is largely made up of Japanese natives, which include Hinoki cypresses and numerous varieties of the species C. pisifera. These evergreens perform exceptionally well in Carolina landscapes, and the striking color and form they add to a winter garden are unsurpassed. These slow growing shrubs have soft, compressed foliage that can be a rich green to golden color. Dwarf Hinoki, 'Nana Gracilis', has tufted, dark green foliage and a pyramidal shape. It is a choice plant for most residential homeowners who need the vertical accent provided by a pyramidal shrub. Another exciting variety is 'Golden-thread', or 'Mops'. Its fine-textured foliage is a bright yellow in spring and winter.

Other Common Name
Hinoki Cypress

Bloom Period and Seasonal Color
No significant flower color.

Mature Height × Spread
6 to 10 ft. × 3 to 4 ft.

When, Where, and How to Plant

Plant any time during the year as soil conditions permit. These shrubs are not difficult to transplant; move established plants in fall or in early spring, maintaining an intact rootball if possible. They adapt to a wide range of soil types. Most prefer moist, slightly acidic soil that drains well. Plant in full sun to partial shade. Water well to settle the soil. Spread 2 inches of mulch then apply several more gallons of water. Water twice a week for the first month. See tpae 176 for more planting tips.

Growing Tips

Hinoki cypresses are slow to establish and can suffer in dry soils during the first growing season. The family is native to bog areas, and the plants love moisture. There is no benefit to fertilizing the first year. Apply a slow-release fertilizer in spring each year after planting. Reapply mulch as often as necessary to enrich the soil and reduce the need for watering.

Care

Prune in late spring, using hand shears. Proper spacing is dependent on the chosen cultivar. Most Hinoki cypresses reach their mature height within fifteen years. Toby reports he has had no pest problems with them over the years, although mites are common on narrowleaf evergreens. Insecticidal soaps make good miticides. Hold white paper under branch tips and tap them. If little black dots start moving on the paper, you've got bugs.

Companion Planting and Design

Hinoki cypress can be planted in partial shade and look good with hostas and many other perennials. You can grow them in planters or as accents in foundation plantings. Some choice cultivars have a low, spreading habit that makes them useful in borders, in rock gardens, and as specimen plantings. Use the golden cultivars as specimen shrubs. The 'Boulevard' variety is popular for its unique, blue-gray foliage.

Our Personal Favorite

'Nana Gracilis' has dark green color and fine, soft foliage.

Forsythia

Forsythia × intermedia

When, Where, and How to Plant

Plant forsythias any time the soil can be worked. Even the smallest specimens will take off once the roots establish. Provide full-sun locations with good drainage. Forsythias adapt to a wide range of soil types and will tolerate dry sites if watered during the first growing season. They will establish more quickly if you first unravel the potbound roots. Some root-pruning is helpful. Space forsythias 6 to 8 feet apart. Water every three days for the first two weeks.

Growing Tips

Water routinely the first season; afterward, these tough shrubs will take dry soil very well. Forsythias benefit from monthly fertilizing with a water-soluble fertilizer until the shrubs have attained a decent size. Continue fertilizing through September. After the first two seasons, fertilize after flowering subsides. Forsythias are low maintenance shrubs at maturity.

Care

Prune forsythias immediately after they flower. Cut the entire plant back to a height of 15 inches to force long, flowing, graceful branches to develop. This plant can look tortured if it is sheared like a boxwood. Pests are only a minor concern. Occasionally forsythia will succumb to a bacterial disease known as crown gall. Symptoms appear as golfball-sized galls on the lower half of branches. Prune these away by removing the affected branches; spray the plant with a copper fungicide then disinfect your pruning shears. If the galls occur on the roots, the plant will die.

Companion Planting and Design

Forsythia has an erect to arching habit and is best planted in masses in borders. Do not use forsythia as a foundation shrub; it can spread to great size. Redbud and Yoshino cherry trees are great companions unless clashing colors set your teeth on edge.

Our Personal Favorites

For very large, golden flowers plant 'Karl Sax' as a specimen shrub. Cultivars such as 'Lynwood Gold' are great for borders and cut flowers.

Few shrubs herald the coming of spring like forsythia. By January, this fast growing, deciduous plant is raring to go. Yellow star-like flowers shine sporadically during warm spells. When the soil temperatures rise sufficiently in late winter, hardy forsythias explode into bloom, and in a matter of days the leafless branches are aglow with one-inch, golden flower clusters. Many transplants from "Up North" complain about the poor flowering of our forsythias in the Carolinas—Toby's response to them is, "Count the blossoms in my garden!" Any shrub that is as cold hardy and resilient as forsythia has earned a spot in Carolina gardens. Many traditional gardens feature this spring gem. Entire branches can be cut early and brought into a warm room where the blossoms will open within a few days. Watch for deer damage, and apply a repellent if necessary.

Other Common Name
Yellow Bells

Bloom Period and Seasonal Color
Bright yellow flowers in late winter.

Mature Height × Spread
6 to 10 ft. × 6 to 10 ft.

Fothergilla

Fothergilla gardenii

When azaleas are everywhere during April, "witch alders" offer a breath of fresh air. This native deciduous ornamental boasts showy two-inch, white, "bottlebrush" flowers and dazzling fall colors from yellow to orange-red. What a terrific break it is to find a native plant nursery that offers fothergillas. This shrub is a relative of witch hazel and exhibits some of the same traits, particularly pest resistance, shade tolerance, and fall coloration. Dwarf witch alder is a low, mounded shrub. Where it gets at least a half-day of sun, dense twigs produce a profusion of oblong, airy blooms in late spring. This shrub deserves a place alongside your azaleas to brighten up a woodland garden. For years, Jim enjoyed 'Mt. Airy' that flourished on the drip line of a great old American holly in his Piedmont garden. It liked the afternoon shade.

Other Common Name
Dwarf Witch Alder

Bloom Period and Seasonal Color
White spring blooms; vivid fall coloration.

Mature Height × Spread
4 ft. × 5 ft.

When, Where, and How to Plant

Container-grown dwarf witch alder can be planted in spring, fall, or late winter. It grows relatively fast in moist, acidic soils, tolerating full sun to partial shade. Small container-grown plants are a little slow to take off until well established. This species is native to our coastal plains, where it can be found growing by ponds or bogs. Fothergillas require growing conditions similar to those of the azaleas: well-drained, acidic soils. Compost or sphagnum peat moss improves the soil and keeps the roots moist as well. Apply a 3-inch layer of pine-needle mulch. For planting how-tos, turn to page 176.

Growing Tips

Keep the soil moist but not soggy throughout the first growing season. During extended dry periods, lay out a soaker hose for daily watering. Watering in the driest part of summer will benefit fothergilla, although they are amazingly tolerant of dry conditions. Add mulch annually to keep the soil moist. Apply a specialty slow-release fertilizer in spring at the drip line and beyond. Keep fertilizer away from the root collar at the base of the plant. Water the day before you fertilize to avoid injury to drought-stressed plants.

Care

Thin selectively in the early years to train the shrubs into a pleasing open form. Most pruning should be delayed until after the blooming period. Prune in late spring to remove old branches or rangy shoots. They are disease free but will lose a branch occasionally due to stem borer. Dwarf fothergilla is a little less cold hardy than the other native, *F. major.*

Companion Planting and Design

This plant is a good companion for rhododendrons and azaleas in partial shade. Plant it in front of a gold threadleaf cypress, loropetalum, or other evergreen hedge so the blossoms pop out.

Our Personal Favorite

Toby reports the cultivar 'Mt. Airy' has been a delightful addition to his perennial border. It should perform well in your garden, too.

Gardenia

Gardenia augusta

When, Where, and How to Plant

Plant in spring and early summer. Gardenias grow in a wide range of soils, but they do best in moist, loamy, well drained soil with a pH of 5.0 to 6.0. Plant in a site protected from cold winter winds and early morning sun, which can cause foliage to sunburn. Sunlight is important for flowering, but modest blooming occurs in a half-day of direct sun. When setting out plants, do not disturb the rootball unless it is rootbound. If you have any questions about how to plant gardenias, turn to page 176 for some hints.

Growing Tips

This shrub prefers moist soil and benefits from a drip irrigation system or at least a soaker hose. Fertilize your gardenias twice each year with a complete garden fertilizer such as 10-10-10 analysis at a rate of 2 tablespoons per foot of height. One application is needed in early April and a second in mid-June. For darker green foliage, an iron-rich fertilizer can be substituted for one of these applications.

Care

Prune cold-damaged twigs in March. Immediately after it flowers, prune selectively with hand shears to maintain the natural shape. Dwarf gardenias require little pruning, but some twig thinning or deadheading of faded blossoms is in order at times. White flies and wax scales may appear. If untreated, leaves turn black from sooty mold fungus. Use horticultural oil sprays or weekly insecticidal soap treatments to manage white flies.

Companion Planting and Design

Gardenias make wonderful specimen plants anywhere their fragrance can be appreciated. Groupings of the dwarf, cold tolerant shrub 'Kleim's Hardy' are great for borders, and single plants make good accents in foundation plantings.

Our Personal Favorites

'Chuck Hayes' is cold hardy and may rebloom in autumn; it's great for cut flowers. 'Grift's Select' is also gaining popularity.

However much it may be maligned, there is an advantage to the hot, wet climate in the Carolinas. Gardenias will grow here! Gardenias are one of our most valued landscape ornamentals, especially in the eastern half of the state. They bloom in profusion, emitting a sweet fragrance that brings the ambience of the Old South to our gardens. This delightful evergreen has distinctive dark green, glossy foliage. The beautiful two- to three-inch-wide, pristine white flowers resemble the waxy flowers of Southern magnolia. With the introduction of new cold-tolerant varieties, it isn't unusual to find gardenias in gardens west of the Piedmont. This native of China has found a place in the hearts of Southerners for more than a century. Jim remembers prom corsages of gardenias and his mother floating gardenia blossoms in a shallow bowl of water.

Other Common Names
Cape Jasmine, Hardy Gardenia

Bloom Period and Seasonal Color
Pure-white blooms in late spring and early summer.

Mature Height × Spread
3 to 6 ft. × 3 to 5 ft.

Hydrangea
Hydrangea macrophylla

Carolina gardeners know the big-leaf French or florists' hydrangeas as the large blue-flowering shrubs found in old gardens or at farmhouses, but few are familiar with the new selections of lacecap hydrangeas. Unlike the large blue types, lacecaps have an umbrella-shaped flower structure with rings of large showy flowers surrounding a center of bead-shaped blossoms. Unlike the voluptuous French hydrangeas, this group of deciduous shrubs offers both a touch of nostalgia and a sleek, contemporary look to the garden. Lacecaps are moderate- to fast-growing shrubs. Their large, dark green foliage offers great texture for a background or mass planting. Plant the variegated kinds in a shade garden that needs a touch of light accents. Another advantage of the lacecaps is that the airy blossoms deliver multiple bloom flushes periodically until frost.

Bloom Period and Seasonal Color
Pink, blue, and red to pure white blooms in summer.

Mature Height × Spread
5 to 7 ft. × 4 to 8 ft.

When, Where, and How to Plant
Only container-grown lacecap hydrangeas are available at nurseries. Plant them from spring through summer. Most lacecap hydrangeas prefer a partial-shade location protected from afternoon sun. To avoid leaf wilt in hot weather, plant in moist soil or where irrigation is available. Though hydrangeas prefer moist soil, they also need good drainage. Once the plant is set in the hole and the soil firmed-in around the ball, the top inch or so of the roots should be visible. Cover these roots with 2 inches of loose mulch and water well. In poorly drained conditions, plant above grade in a berm or well-prepared bed containing copious amounts of organic matter.

Growing Tips
Irrigation is necessary during the summer months. In spring when new growth is several inches long, fertilize lacecaps with a general garden fertilizer.

Care
Prune lacecap hydrangea immediately following the bloom period. This ensures more flowers and keeps viable young wood actively growing. Hard cold may kill the flower buds of hydrangeas formed the previous fall. Some tip pruning may be necessary following the winter season as tender growth is burned by exposure to cold. French hydrangea needs a protected location when planted in the western Piedmont or mountains. There, give hydrangea crowns extra protection from cold in late December with a deep mulch of leaves or pine needles. Remove this deep mulch layer as new growth resumes. Groom by removing weak or dead twigs annually. There are no pests. Hydrangea cuttings will root easily for new plantings, but young plants will need protection from rabbits.

Companion Planting and Design
Plant lacecaps in groups of several shrubs for a border. Use them as accents with fine-textured shrubs. Plant in cutting gardens alongside daylilies. Interplant with the summer flowering *H. arborescens* 'Annabelle' or *H. paniculata* 'Tardiva' for seasonal color. Add repeat blooming mopheads, 'Penny Mac' and 'Endless Summer' to your hydrangea collection.

Our Personal Favorites
'Blue Wave' is a three-time winner of Royal Horticultural Society Awards; or try 'Nikko Blue'.

Indian Hawthorn
Rhaphiolepis indica

When, Where, and How to Plant

In coastal regions, plant container-grown Indian hawthorn anytime the ground is workable. The mountain region is borderline (too cold) for this plant. Plant in full sun or partial shade. Indian hawthorn performs best in fertile, fast-draining soils. This shrub prefers a slightly alkaline soil, so add limestone if needed to bring the pH to 6.5. After removing the plant from its container, score the rootball and fray out circling roots. Irrigate every three days after planting for two weeks then apply a water-soluble fertilizer with a 1-2-1 analysis. Mulch well in sandy soils.

Growing Tips

Irrigate during dry periods in the first growing season. This is especially important in coastal gardens. Drip irrigation and mulching will be necessary where hawthorns are planted in open locations at the beach. Fertilize in May with 10-10-10 analysis fertilizer.

Care

Prune lightly in late winter to remove damaged foliage. This shrub flowers on old wood, so delay most of the pruning until blooming is over. If you have Indian hawthorns growing in full shade, the plants will get leggy and need shaping periodically. Rejuvenate old plants by pruning back to 1 foot in late winter. In the Piedmont, occasional harsh winters can burn the foliage and kill Indian hawthorns in exposed locations. There are no pests to control, provided you plant in well-drained soils and buy healthy plants.

Companion Planting and Design

Use Indian hawthorn in raised planters where it will cascade gracefully over the sides or as a low-growing street buffer. Use it as a great drought-tolerant plant for seaside gardens alongside juniper, oleander, and pittosporum. 'Gulf Green' planted in groups is good for borders and beds.

Our Personal Favorites

'Pink Lady' has survived our Zone 7 weather. Look for leaf spot-resistant varieties, such as 'Eleanor Tabor'.

Gardeners on the coast should not be without Indian hawthorn. This shrub is the coastal equivalent of the Piedmont's Kurume azaleas, as it flourishes in hot locations where azaleas wither. There are cultivars that will survive the harsh winters in the central Piedmont, but in general this shrub is best suited to mild-winter areas. It flowers later than azaleas and can extend the bloom season. It has rounded, dark green, leathery leaves and dense clusters of fragrant pink or white flowers. Its slow to medium growth rate qualifies it for low-maintenance landscapes. Indian hawthorn prefers well-drained, fertile soil but tolerates drought and salt spray. It forms a compact mound. The hybrid hawthorn R. × delacourii is known for having an edge in winter hardiness. Look for cultivars that resist leaf spot.

Bloom Period and Seasonal Color
Pink or white flowers in late spring.

Mature Height × Spread
4 ft. × 4 ft. or more

Lilac
Syringa × hybrida

When growing up in the mountains or foothills of the western Carolinas, seeing a shabby lilac bush somewhere on the homeplace was inevitable. The common lilacs (S. vulgaris) of past eras were marvelously fragrant but tall and ungainly. After the spring flush of flowers had faded and powdery mildew had set in, the shrubs were "ugly as sin!" You might say they were the only kind of shrub a grandmother could love. Well, there is good news for gardeners who must have lilacs to be happy—the kind called "Persian lilacs" will perform better in our gardens. Like the common lilac, the Persian group has a fragrance with few horticultural rivals. Its flower heads are much smaller than those of the common variety, and the shrub itself is smaller, making it an attractive candidate for landscapes.

Bloom Period and Seasonal Color
White, blue, or lavender blooms in late spring.

Mature Height × Spread
3 to 8 ft. × 4 to 6 ft.

When, Where, and How to Plant
Persian lilacs are usually sold in 3-gallon containers. Many gardeners buy them in bloom to be sure of the color. Keep them in the container, watering daily, until the blooms are spent and you can prune them off. Plant in full sun with good air circulation to diminish the chance of powdery mildew disfiguring the foliage. It is important to lime the soil before planting. On clay soil, mix 3 cups of pelletized dolomitic limestone with the backfill to bring the soil pH level up to 6.5. Two cups would be sufficient on sandy soils.

Growing Tips
Trickle water slowly around the rootball of your newly planted lilac approximately one minute for each inch of diameter of the rootball. Repeat three times the first week, twice the second week, and then once a week until the shrub's roots are established. In the spring following planting, apply slow-release nursery fertilizer at a rate of $1/2$ cup per 10 square feet under the canopy and a little beyond. Rake back the mulch, spread the fertilizer, then replace the mulch, keeping it away from the base of the plant.

Care
Overgrown lilacs can be pruned back severely in late winter, but doing 20 removes flower buds for the upcoming season. Powdery mildew presents a problem for Persian lilacs, particularly in shaded areas; select disease-resistant cultivars. Suckers arising anytime from the root collar area should be removed. Lilac hornets chew and remove the plant's bark for their nests; an insecticide spray may be warranted.

Companion Planting and Design
Persian lilacs with low-growing evergreens hiding their bare legs make a good combination. Plant by a patio window where the fragrance can be enjoyed. As a specimen, the Japanese tree lilac *S. reticulata* is a show-stopper in Zones 6 and 7. For its first several years, it looks more like a shrub than a tree.

Our Personal Favorites
'Miss Kim' and 'Blue Skies' are favorites. The Descanso hybrids perform well in our warm climate. 'Lilac Sunday' resists powdery mildew and blooms reliably.

Loropetalum
Loropetalum chinense var. *rubrum*

When, Where, and How to Plant

Loropetalum can be planted any time it is available and when attention can be given to watering. For winter plantings, allow one month in the ground for root growth before the soil freezes. In the western Carolinas, plant in spring when apple trees begin blooming, and only in protected areas. The mountains are too cold for loropetalum to retain evergreen foliage, and this shrub's hardiness at upper elevations is not well documented. It thrives in moist, well drained soil, regardless of soil type. The plum-to-burgundy foliage will show up best when it is planted in a sunny location, but it will handle partly shady sites just fine. When planting, mix a slow-release nursery fertilizer into the soil. For planting tips, turn to page 176.

Growing Tips

Spring plantings need ample water. Water every three days for the first two weeks, then weekly until dry weather arrives. Add a 2- to 3-inch mulch layer. Wait three to six months to fertilize spring-planted ornamentals to allow sufficient root growth. Fertilize annually in spring with a nursery special fertilizer (3-1-2 ratio).

Care

Loropetalum may need some pruning after the second season to keep it shaped and to control height. Prune in late spring or after the spring bloom period. Some thinning may be needed to groom the plant. Prune back to within 1 foot of the ground if a small shrub is desired. Winter in Zone 7 can be hard on loropetalum; remove injured twigs. Late-summer fertilization can make it cold-sensitive.

Companion Planting and Design

This shrub can be espaliered and planted as a standard in the garden. Use it in small groups for an accent with coarse-textured evergreens in the background.

Our Personal Favorites

For fabulous burgundy foliage in summer, try 'Sizzling Pink'. 'Zhuzhou Fuhsia' is cold hardy with abundant flowers and little dieback.

Modern loropetalum is a showy evergreen shrub with burgundy leaves. In spring, its wide-spreading branches light up with feathery, hot pink flowers. Blooms occur sporadically during the summer as growth continues. This plant is a vigorous grower and will thrive in sun or partial shade. In full sun, its small leaves will turn a dark green, but as autumn arrives, shiny plum-colored foliage appears. In Toby's garden, it is magnificent just in time for Christmas. The standard white-flowering loropetalum has been used for decades as a hedge or screening plant. In early spring, this Asian cousin bears blooms resembling the spider-like flowers of witch hazel. Its roundish green leaves are small and leathery. Both types are pest free in most gardens.

Other Common Names

Fringe Flower (not to be confused with fringe tree), Pink Loropetalum, Ribbon Flower

Bloom Period and Seasonal Color

Pink blooms in spring.

Mature Height × Spread

8 ft. × 6 ft.

Mountain Laurel
Kalmia latifolia

This large, robust, attractive native shrub may be the most underrated broadleaf evergreen. In May, mountain laurel features beautiful 4-inch flower clusters in pure white, deep pink, near red, or maroon-banded colors. Magnificent specimens are found along the roadside on the Blue Ridge Parkway, and occasional colonies can be found as understory plants along creeks in Zones 7 and 8. Modern propagation techniques have made many new hybrids available, including a miniature form. Mountain laurel is often found in large groves in the wild and is terrific when planted in masses. Young plants are symmetrical and densely branched. Older plants develop character with an open branch structure and gnarled, reddish trunks and limbs. The most important reason for planting it is its outstanding display of flower clusters in spring. Its attractive, lustrous, dark evergreen foliage is delightful year-round.

Bloom Period and Seasonal Color
White, pink, near-red, and maroon-banded blooms in late spring.

Mature Height × Spread
7 to 15 ft. × 3 to 5 ft.

When, Where, and How to Plant
Spring is ideal for planting balled-and-burlapped plants. Spring and fall plantings of container-grown shrubs are successful. This evergreen will grow in sun or shade, depending on summer temperatures. A partially shaded location is ideal. Once established, mountain laurels are more drought tolerant than rhododendrons, but well-drained soil is critical to their survival. Loosen the roots of container-grown plants before transplanting. In heavy clay soil, prepare a raised bed for drainage. Plant atop the soil, not in a hole. Build up around the rootball (not on top) with native soil amended with organic matter. In sandy soil, mix organic matter into the entire bed. Most soils in the Carolinas also need additional phosphate. Water thoroughly, then water every three days for three weeks. You can find more planting hints on page 176.

Growing Tips
These shallow-rooted plants should not be allowed to dry out—but do not over-water, as this causes root rot. Frequent shallow watering may be needed during summer dry spells, since this shrub has few feeder roots. Mountain laurels are light feeders, and plants that are kept well-mulched should not need fertilizing in the early years. When fertilizing, use an organic product or a specialty azalea fertilizer.

Care
Pruning is seldom needed on mountain laurel. Trim lightly after bloom time if desired. Early spring pruning reduces flowering in May. Dormant pruning stimulates dense, well branched plants. Leaf spot affects the attractiveness of the foliage but is not life-threatening. Root rot is life-threatening in clay soils, so plant "high." This shrub is insect resistant, but deer will browse the flower buds.

Companion Planting and Design
Mountain laurel is an excellent plant for naturalizing and performs well on the woodland edge. Underplant with Japanese plum yew and ground covers. For small gardens, consider the miniature 'Elf'. Few plants hold up in shade like this ornamental.

Our Personal Favorite
Colorful new growth and pinkish flowers make 'Olympic Fire' a winner.

Oak Leaf Hydrangea

Hydrangea quercifolia

When, Where, and How to Plant

Plant oak leaf hydrangea year-round as soil conditions permit. (That means when the ground isn't frozen.) Oak leaf hydrangea is a wonderful shrub in the landscape and is very durable, even when planted by a novice gardener. Place in a sunny to partially shaded spot in moist, fertile, well drained soil. Its fibrous root system tends to sucker and spread, making oak leaf hydrangea a candidate for mass plantings on banks. If the native soil is friable (loose like coffee grounds), no soil amendments are necessary. Mulch will keep the roots cool. For some more planting how-tos, turn to page 176.

Growing Tips

Water routinely after planting. Irrigate 3 times the first week, twice the second week, and then once a week until the roots are established. Oak leaf hydrangea likes moist soil but not soggy sites. Water generously during the first and second growing season. Water during a drought if leaves wilt. This shrub will tolerate dryness very well after it is established. Oak leaf hydrangeas are not fussy about fertilizing. In spring, drill a slow-release fertilizer (analysis 12-6-6 or equal) at the rate suggested by the product.

Care

Oak leaf hydrangea is carefree. Pruning is rarely needed unless space is limited. In spring, prune to remove sucker growth at the base of the plant, and remove the oldest branches every other year. Cut back spent blooms in winter after they deteriorate. Mulch heavily and annually if it's placed in woodland garden sites.

Companion Planting and Design

Plant on the edge of a treeline or use for a screen. Plant compact cultivars if your garden space is limited. Good companions are cherry laurel, plum yew, and fine-textured shrubs. The exfoliating bark and persistent dried flower clusters add winter interest.

Our Personal Favorites

'Snow Queen' is renowned for its huge, erect, white, cone-like blooms. 'Pee Wee' is a fine dwarf.

Oak leaf hydrangea is one of the finest native shrubs, with large leaves that resemble those of red oak. To some it may appear plain, but to the landscape designer it has a distinct beauty all its own. During June, oak leaf hydrangea displays large showy panicles of white flowers that later fade to a soft rose color. The plant's coarse leaves are loosely arranged and provide the woodland garden a lush, almost tropical appeal. This deciduous shrub has outstanding exfoliating, cinnamon-colored bark on spindly, crooked stems. As the plants mature, their wide-spreading branches form an open canopy in light shade. Every gardener with enough space would do well to plant the native ornamental oak leaf in a shade garden. It is easier to grow than the highly hybridized garden hydrangeas.

Bloom Period and Seasonal Color

White blooms fading to dusty rose in late summer. Persistent dried flower heads.

Mature Height × Spread

6 ft. × 8 ft. (wider in very old specimens)

Oleander

Nerium oleander

Oleanders are a gorgeous but tender evergreen shrub—commonly seen in the coastal region but rarely elsewhere in the Carolinas. They are hardy throughout Zone 8, providing a tropical accent as a specimen plant in the landscape. With its lustrous, narrow, green leaves and clusters of 1-inch single or double blooms, oleander blooms heavily spring through summer. Gardeners in Zone 7 learned a hard lesson when most of the "cold-hardy" oleanders perished overnight one winter in the mid-1980s. We now know to grow them in containers so we can bring them indoors. The dwarf forms are most suited to mass plantings. The wide range of colors and tolerance of droughty conditions make them superb for difficult seaside landscapes.

Bloom Period and Seasonal Color
White to pink, red, and salmon blooms in summer.

Mature Height × Spread
4 to 12 ft. × 6 to 10 ft.

When, Where, and How to Plant
Plant container-grown oleander in spring or fall. In areas colder than Zone 8, it may not survive winter if planted outdoors. This showy ornamental prefers strong sunlight and does quite well as a street shrub; it will bloom freely if established in a sunny spot. It is not particular about soil, even tolerating salty conditions. Limestone is not needed, but a small handful of superphosphate is beneficial added at planting. Review the planting tips in the introduction if you want more planting guidance.

Growing Tips
Once established, oleanders are quite drought tolerant. Consistently wet soil encourages lush growth and fewer flowers. Scatter a general garden fertilizer, such as 10-10-10 analysis, six weeks after planting and each spring thereafter. A couple of inches of compost or mulch will conserve moisture and encourage new roots in sandy soils.

Care
Protect young plants for the first couple of winters in Zone 8a. An application of a wilt-proofing spray and a windscreen constructed around the plant in January will help it through cold weather. Alternatively, protect the crown with a deep mulch of pine straw and depend on new canes to form and bloom. Prune for height control; do this while the plant is dormant and before growth begins in spring. Thinning to maintain the form, and removal of small suckers from the base is recommended. To rejuvenate, cut old canes to the ground. This interesting shrub has virtually no pests other than an occasional caterpillar. In shade, oleander is leggy and produces few flowers. **Warning:** Please warn children to eat no part of the plant, as it is very poisonous. Be careful that livestock does not have access.

Companion Planting and Design
Plant oleander where you can view it often while it is in bloom. Use it as a hedge, as a backdrop for perennials, or as an accent shrub in large gardens. White-flowered and double yellow plants are delightful in small gardens.

Our Personal Favorites
Choose cold hardy oleanders, 'Hardy Red' and 'Hardy Pink'.

When, Where, and How to Plant

Plant anytime soil conditions allow; early fall is ideal. Pieris thrives in part shade. It grows best when planted in well drained, acidic soils with a pH near 5.5. A soil rich in organic matter is best. It is short-lived in wet sites; in heavy clay soil, prepare a raised bed. Loosen the roots and cover with native soil mixed with some organic matter. Most Carolina soils lack phosphorus, which can be added per soil test recommendations at planting time. After planting, always water well and apply mulch. Specific planting advice can be found on page 176.

Growing Tips

Irrigate your plantings for the first three summer seasons. Andromeda is very shallow rooted and should not be allowed to dry out. Water weekly during summer months when rainfall is sparse. Keep in mind that raised beds dry out much faster than native soil. To avoid over-watering, irrigate when the top 3 inches of soil are dry—excessive soil moisture encourages root rot diseases. Feed with a 14-7-7 or similar analysis plant food, applied in early April.

Care

Prune pieris to shape or to remove an occasional dead branch. Cut back individual stems immediately after flowering in spring. Excessive watering and poor soil drainage can bring phytophthora root rot; there is no treatment for infected plants. Twig dieback can appear in early summer and should be pruned out immediately. Lace bugs can be a serious pest, turning the leaves grayish. Use an insecticide spray in mid-April and September to control. Try to take out the first generation before they multiply.

Companion Planting and Design

Pieris are wonderful additions to woodland edges or as specimens by the front door. Plant them in mass groupings near a water feature. Interplant with a ground cover, azaleas, or rhododendrons.

Our Personal Favorites

'Variegata' has year-round interest. In sunny locations, 'Compacta' is hard to beat.

Whether you know it as andromeda or pieris, this mounding shrub features chains of lightly fragrant spring flowers that cascade over the plant's spreading branches. Its reddish-bronze new growth unfurls into lustrous evergreen foliage. A common name for pieris is lily-of-the-valley shrub, as it has tiny clusters of urn-shaped flowers that resemble those of that popular ground cover. This durable woody ornamental begins blooming before winter passes. Cool weather sustains the flowers and extends the floral display into spring. Most cultivars exhibit white flowers, but a few feature pink flowers. Yet another variety, 'Mountain Fire', sports fiery-red new growth. New introductions have transformed this plant into a harbinger of spring. Whether planted in a container or the garden, it is a real beauty. Northeastern flower shows often force this shrub to flower in March for their display gardens.

Other Common Names
Japanese Andromeda, Lily-of-the-valley Shrub

Bloom Period and Seasonal Color
White or pink blossoms in late winter.

Mature Height × Spread
4 to 6 ft. × 4 to 6 ft.

Pittosporum

Pittosporum tobira

This evergreen shrub is hardy only in the warmer regions of the Carolinas, from Raleigh and Columbia eastward. It grows in many forms depending on the cultivar. Pittosporum is distinguished by its lustrous, leathery leaves and full, rounded appearance. Where winter temperatures drop below 15 degrees Fahrenheit, the plant must be placed in a sheltered location or grown as a container plant to be taken indoors where it can be enjoyed indoors during the winter months. Whitespot pittosporum makes a fine houseplant as well as an attractive landscape specimen. All the pittosporum shrubs are tidy and have dense foliage that extends to the ground. In coastal counties, overgrown specimens can be limbed up to make small multi-trunk trees.

Other Common Name
Japanese Pittosporum

Bloom Period and Seasonal Color
Creamy white, fragrant flowers in spring.

Mature Height × Spread
10 to 15 ft. × 12 ft.

When, Where, and How to Plant
Plant in late winter or spring. Except near the coast, fall plantings in exposed sites are subject to winter injury. In Zone 8a gardens, give pittosporums a south-facing exposure where they are protected from winter winds. Either full to partial sun or partial shade is fine, but the dwarf and variegated forms need a shady location. Pittosporum requires a well-drained soil with a pH range of 5.0 to 6.0. Page 176 has some helpful shrub planting advice.

Growing Tips
In sandy soils, water pittosporum weekly during the first growing season. Once established, it is drought resistant. Fertilize in March and July, using a 5-10-10 fertilizer at the rate of 1/2 cup per plant, or 1 ounce per foot of height on mature shrubs. In Zone 8a, where cold weather may harm pittosporum, withhold fertilizer and water in early fall to increase cold hardiness.

Care
Allow plenty of growing room and you will not have to shear this lovely plant. For a sheared hedge, begin pruning in spring while the plants are still young. On more mature plants, control the height by removing new growth before leaves mature. Pittosporum is usually pest free, but near the coast, scale may become a problem. Consult your local County Cooperative Extension Office for advice.

Companion Planting and Design
Grow pittosporum as an informal screen. Pittosporum tolerates salt spray and is popular for coastal landscapes. Plant near a patio to enjoy the aromatic, citrus-scented flowers. 'Variegata' is great for floral arrangements and accents.

Our Personal Favorite
The dwarf variety 'Wheeler's Dwarf' forms a dense mound without pruning. It is perfect for landscaping large open areas.

Plum Yew
Cephalotaxus harringtonia

When, Where, and How to Plant

Plant plum yew in spring in Zone 7 or fall in colder zones. It prefers a location where there is some shade from the summer sun for better year-round color. Don't be reluctant to it plant in shade gardens. Though growth is best in moist soils, plum yew will survive dry summer conditions. These shrubs don't like wet feet; they prefer well drained, moist, fertile soil like that preferred by rhododendrons. Plant high to prevent root rot disease, and give them plenty of room to grow. Prepare the soil using 1/3 organic matter by volume for enrichment. Dig a wide planting hole and spread out plum yew's fleshy roots, position it in the hole, backfill, and water as you replace the soil.

Growing Tips

Water well for the first two summers during dry periods. When established, the plants will thrive in dry shaded locations. Fertilize with an organic fertilizer every other spring to keep the best foliage color. Maintain a layer of mulch to help retain moisture. Apply 3 inches of compost annually, and discontinue fertilizing once they're established.

Care

Remove upright-growing shoots to maintain the spreading form. Prune in late spring to control height or to groom the plant. Browning foliage is a sign of winter injury or too dry soil. Keep plum yew mulched and watered in periods of drought.

Companion Plant and Design

Japanese plum yews are suitable for grouping in a foundation planting or planting on the edge of a woodland garden. They are beautiful by a shaded water feature. Good companions are azalea, fothergilla, and upright conifers for shrub borders.

Our Personal Favorites

Toby's original plants were 'Duke Garden' yews. 'Fastigiata' is a narrow grower to 10 feet, the perfect fit for a small garden.

Toby has admired Japanese plum yew since he first laid eyes on the giant shrubs in the Sarah P. Duke Gardens at Duke University. Soon afterward, he acquired several rooted cuttings, and the specimens thrived in light shade in his entrance planting. Jim first saw it at the Atlanta Botanical Garden and recognized its suitability as a substitute for the yews (Taxus) that are so popular in more northerly states. The dark green, prostrate form and fine texture of plum yews make them versatile in the landscape. Plum yew is said to be an evergreen with an identity crisis. It is neither yew (Taxus) nor Japanese yew (Podocarpus), though all have dark needle-like foliage and upright growth. The popularity of plum yew will continue to grow as people discover they are care-free and perfectly happy in shady nooks.

Other Common Name

Japanese Plum Yew

Bloom Period and Seasonal Color

No flowers; deep green foliage.

Mature Height × Spread

2 to 6 ft. × 5 to 10 ft.

Pyracantha

Pyracantha coccinea

Pyracantha is a handsome, practical evergreen. It serves as an ornamental shrub or as an impenetrable thorny hedge. (Sometimes a shrub that will discourage intruders is useful when designing a "security landscape.") The narrow, dark green leaves of this vigorous grower often hide the stiff 1- to 3-inch barbs that can make you dread a pruning job. In the Carolinas, a favorite use of pyracantha is as an espalier on stark, blank walls—despite the daunting task of training this determined grower. Pyracantha is adored for its clusters of showy yellow, orange, or scarlet berries. Songbirds feast on the pea-sized fruit and find this rangy ornamental a haven for nesting. Mockingbirds and robins stuff their craws with so many berries that they can barely fly. Screech owls have been known to take up residence in the densely twigged firethorns. Jim recently learned that gardeners are making jelly from the berries.*

Other Common Name
Firethorn

Bloom Period and Seasonal Color
White blooms in spring; orange-red or yellow fruit summer to fall.

Mature Height × Spread
6 to 15 ft. × 6 to 10 ft.

When, Where, and How to Plant
In the Piedmont and foothills, plant pyracantha in spring. In the eastern Carolinas, plant anytime the ground can be prepared. Large container-grown trellised specimens are the best ones to purchase if you are going to espalier this ornamental. Pyracantha transplants with some difficulty. It prefers full sun for berry production. Plant in well-drained soil or dry sites with a pH of 6. Loosen the roots of container-grown plants. Dig a wide, shallow hole 3/4 as deep as and three time as wide as the rootball. Mix bark soil conditioner into the backfill and firm it around the roots. Settle the soil by slowly trickling water for about 30 minutes. Mulch to a depth of 2 inches, at least 3 inches from the base of the plant.

Growing Tips
Water weekly during dry spells for the first or second season. Fertilize using a slow-release product in March at a rate of 1/2 cup per 10 square feet, but only if the plant seems to need it. Fertilizing in fall can subject this shrub to winterkill.

Care
Prune wild shoots to train or to groom the plant. When planted in close quarters, pyracantha needs constant pruning; do so in spring after the flowers or berries are showing. In hedges, remove errant shoots as needed. Severe pruning should be done in March. Lace bugs and aphids are often present but are rather benign. Spray with an appropriate insecticide or horticultural oil in May and again in August. Prune out twigs that are killed by fire-blight disease. Make your cuts on green wood so you don't spread the blight to other branches. A lack of berries is often due to improper pruning practices, overfertilization, or winter injury. To prevent cold injury, avoid hard fall pruning.

Companion Planting and Design
Train a pair of robust pyracanthas into a wonderful garden gate. For foundation plantings, use a compact variety or the low, dense species, *P. koidzumii* (though this species is less cold hardy).

Our Personal Favorite
Pest- and fire-blight-resistant 'Mohave' bears huge masses of orange-red berries.

Rhododendron

Rhododendron spp.

When, Where, and How to Plant

Plant container-grown rhododendrons anytime except during hot, dry weather, and plant field-grown rhodies from December though April. The secret to success is to recreate the plant's native habitat. This means planting in partial shade where there is well-drained, moist, acidic soil. An east- or north-facing exposure in a woodland garden or foundation planting is ideal. Rhododendrons do well in our native soils, which are generally acidic. Test soil drainage by digging a foot-deep hole and fill it twice with water. It should drain within twenty-four hours. Otherwise, plant in raised beds. See the introduction for specific planting instructions

Growing Tips

Water new plants every third day for the first three to four weeks. Water weekly or when the soil feels dry to the touch during the first two growing seasons. Once established, the plants are fairly drought tolerant and durable. Do not overwater—root rot is the primary killer of rhodies. Rhododendrons are not heavy feeders and extract most of their nutrients from natural mulches such as shredded leaves, compost, or pine needles spread 2 inches thick.

Care

Prune in late winter to control height. Avoid shearing. Apply a systemic fungicide after pruning. Sudden wilting of a branch in summer may indicate borers or twig dieback fungus. Twig dieback is recognized by curling leaves and off-colored foliage; prune out such a branch. Prevent root rot with a fungicidal soil drench when there are large numbers of plants in the same bed. Remove rhodies that defoliate heavily in summer. Keep raised beds moist using soaker hoses. In hot, dry gardens, try mounting misting heads above your rhodies to keep plants cool and moist.

Companion Planting and Design

Use as a background hedge for finer-textured ornamentals. Rhodies are too large for foundation plantings. The dwarf cultivars offer new possibilities. PJM rhodies are underrated.

Our Personal Favorite

The lustrous foliage and large flower trusses of 'Scintillation' are simply incredible.

Rhododendrons have been called the "Crown Jewel of the Garden," the standard by which many gardeners unfairly rate other flowering shrubs. Rhododendrons are members of the same family as mountain laurel and heather. Azaleas are a subclass within the genus Rhododendron. One does not have to travel to distant estate gardens to see marvelous specimens. There are many fine collections in the mountain regions and throughout the Piedmont. Great numbers of tourists flock to the Smokies annually to see the lavender-pink blooms of our native Catawba rhododendron (R. catawbiense). Since the mid-1800s when the Ironclad hybrids were introduced, gardeners have searched for cultivars for the hot, humid Sunbelt. A love affair with this evergreen shrub can be bittersweet. Without proper planting and variety selection, many rhododendrons are destined for a short life.

Bloom Period and Seasonal Color

Flower trusses in myriad colors in late spring.

Mature Height × Spread

2 to 10 ft. × 2 to 10 ft.

Rose of Sharon

Hibiscus syriacus

Rose of Sharon, often called althea, is a deciduous member of the mallow family, as its funnel-shaped blooms clearly indicate. One of Toby's childhood memories is of swinging on his grandparents' porch in Statesville, NC, admiring the lavender-pink summer flowers of this multi-branched shrub. He confesses that he never developed an appreciation for rose of Sharon until decades later when he noticed a neighbor's border blooming in July. Only a precious few shrubs have the stamina to bloom in the twilight of summer. Multitudes of flowers give rise to brown capsules that hang on through winter. Rich green foliage and loosely upright branches give it a unique form. National Arboretum hybrids are sterile and do not contribute to the abundance of unwanted seedlings that naturalize from the old-fashioned variety.

Other Common Name
Althea

Bloom Period and Seasonal Color
Large flowers in white, lavender, pink, and red in summer.

Mature Height × Spread
8 to 12 ft. × 6 to 12 ft.

When, Where, and How to Plant
Plant this deciduous shrub anytime from late fall until spring. Rose of Sharon's flowers are single, double, or semidouble; it is best to buy blooming plants to ensure the form you prefer. Rose of Sharon tolerates half-shade conditions but flowers best in direct sun. It accepts a wide range of pH and soil types but flourishes in moist, fertile soil. For hedges, space plants 5 or more feet apart. Plant container-grown shrubs no deeper than originally grown at the nursery. Prepare a wider planting hole with a dusting of limestone and 10-10-10 analysis fertilizer. Water thoroughly before mulching. Water twice weekly to keep the top 3 inches of soil moist for four to six weeks.

Growing Tips
Water during prolonged dry periods and keep the plantings mulched for weed control. Irrigate the shrub during the dry periods and while they are blooming. Fertilize with a bloom-booster product in late spring.

Care
If it is growing wildly, cut back twigs to four buds in March. Remove large branches at the base with a pruning saw. Rose of Sharon can be pruned severely at maturity for height control. Allow specimen shrubs to grow as small trees by limbing up. The large flowers will attract bees and beetles to the huge volume of pollen and nectar; don't apply insecticides except when Japanese beetles devour leaves. Beware—the abundant flowers produce legions of seedlings that should be destroyed or transplanted in late spring.

Companion Planting and Design
Gardeners will frequently plant a hedge or screen of one of the inexpensive varieties. Use as a specimen for late summer color. Underplant tree-form plantings with low-growing annuals, perennials, or spreading holly shrubs. Don't use this big plant in foundation plantings.

Our Personal Favorites
Triploid, seedless USDA hybrids, are outstanding and have Greek goddess names—'Minerva', 'Aphrodite', and 'Helene'. The pure white, 4-inch flowers of 'Diana' remain open at night.

Waxmyrtle

Myrica cerifera

When, Where, and How to Plant

Plant container-grown waxmyrtle in spring, summer, or fall. Avoid planting when the soil is too wet to handle. They tolerate full sun to partially shaded locations in any type of soil. When planting several plants as a hedge or screen, rototill and plant in a slightly raised bed. Loosen potbound roots and shake off most of the soil. Prepare individual holes 3 to 4 times as wide as the rootball. Pack soil firmly around the sides of the rootball. Water well before and after mulching to settle the soil. Mulch 4 inches deep, staying clear of the crown. Water twice weekly for the first month.

Growing Tips

Water newly planted waxmyrtle with a water wand for ten minutes three times weekly. Do this until the shrub's roots are established, generally in three to four weeks, or when new growth is evident. This plant enjoys moist soil, so be generous with water in dry weather, but it will not tolerate "wet feet" from poor drainage. It is a heavy feeder, so fertilize yearly for the first four years. Thereafter apply a slow-release nursery fertilizer each spring.

Care

It tolerates heavy pruning in early spring before new growth emerges or in midsummer. Waxmyrtle does not like to be sheared. Heavy leaf drop can occur in winter in the western Carolinas. Twig dieback caused by a fungus is common during wet summers but not serious. Apply a fungicide if you prune heavily in summer. Waxmyrtle produces suckers from the base; remove them or let it be, if you desire a hedge.

Companion Planting and Design

Plant waxmyrtle in sun for a wonderful evergreen privacy screen. Use the compact varieties for a tall border. Their scented green foliage can be appreciated as a specimen tree form in a small garden. It is much too large for foundations.

Our Personal Favorites

'Don's Dwarf' and 'Fairfax' are more compact. 'Emperor' is gorgeous where it has room to grow.

Waxmyrtle may be known best as bayberry since it produces heavy crops of aromatic gray berries used in candle making and relished by wild birds. This native evergreen grows where most landscape shrubs would fail. Waxmyrtle is tolerant of a wide range of planting sites from moist clays to sand dunes on the coast. It is the designers' choice for informal privacy screens and tall hedges. Its beautiful evergreen to semi-evergreen scented foliage resembles that of willows. Its leaves are olive green and loosely arranged on the stems. The plant is a strong and fast grower, yielding multi-trunked shrubs, which can be limbed up to form specimen trees. The upright growth habit serves the gardener well as a windbreak. This native can be found growing throughout the eastern Carolinas in sunny or shady gardens. Too bad it isn't cold hardy in mountain landscapes and is susceptible to ice storm damage.

Other Common Names
Southern Bayberry, Waxberry

Bloom Period and Seasonal Color
Non-showy flowers in spring.

Mature Height × Spread
5 to 20 ft. × 5 to 10 ft.

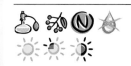

Witch Hazel

Hamamelis virginiana

One of the best plants to help achieve your goal of a twelve-month garden is witch hazel. This deliciously sweet-scented native bears twisted, creamy yellow flowers along naked stems in late fall. The ribbon-like flowers of this multi-stem beauty are not its only interesting feature—its golden fall foliage is also impressive. In the wild, witch hazel is a slow grower, reaching eight to twelve feet in height with a similar spread. It is well-adapted to ordinary garden soils provided they are enriched with organic matter. "Early settlers used the forked branches of witch hazel for divining rods," write Tripp and Raulston in The Year in Trees. Though its name has an eerie history, this rugged and pest-free ornamental is perfect for the woodland garden.

Bloom Period and Seasonal Color
Creamy yellow, red, or orange blooms in late fall to winter.

Mature Height × Spread
8 to 12 ft. × 8 to 12 ft.

When, Where, and How to Plant
Purchase witch hazel in bloom and plant in spring or late fall, but avoid planting within a few weeks of the ground's freezing. Witch hazels prefer moist soils and partial shade but will adapt to a wide range of soil types. Morning sun or a semi-sunny location is ideal. A full-sun site is acceptable only if the plant is mulched well or irrigated during dry periods, especially in August and September. Enrich the soil with copious amounts of compost or soil conditioner. Highly organic soils that are well drained are witch hazel's natural soil preference. Position the shrub in a wide shallow hole that is 3 times as wide as the rootball. Fold back natural burlap into the planting hole if planting a balled-and-burlapped specimen. Firm-in the roots with the amended soil, and water regularly during the first two months. This native will appreciate a 2-inch layer of mulch or leaf compost.

Growing Tips
Irrigate the newly planted shrubs during the first two summers. A soaker hose or, even better, drip irrigation is useful. Clay soils absorb only 1/4 inch of water per hour, so hand watering is an inefficient method of irrigating moisture-loving natives in big gardens. Fertilize witch hazels in the spring with an organic fertilizer or finished compost.

Care
Prune these shrubs after they bloom in late winter to open up the plants or to control their size. They are best left in a natural shape. Keep them mulched and pay attention to soil moisture during the active growth periods. Good leaf mulch does wonders for stimulating root activity. This is important in the early years of development for woody plants.

Companion Planting and Design
This native is striking in bloom when planted in front of an evergreen border of American hollies. Good companions are rhododendrons, fothergilla, loropetalum, and winter flowering bulbs. The red-flowering 'Diane' makes a good specimen plant.

Our Personal Favorite
To extend the flowering season, select the Chinese hybrid 'Arnold Promise' for its yellow blooms in early spring.

Yaupon Holly
Ilex vomitoria

When, Where, and How to Plant

Plant year-round as soil conditions permit. Plant potted yaupon hollies early in fall to allow time for root establishment before winter. In western North Carolina, wet clay soils and winter weather can injure fall plantings if they are put in too late. Site in full sun to partial shade. These evergreen shrubs are tolerant of extremes in planting sites, although they do prefer hot locations. Yaupons are found thriving in dry as well as extremely wet sites. Planting location will depend on the form and variety you choose. Loosen the roots of this vigorous grower after removing the plant from the pot. Dig a planting hole twice the diameter of the rootball and equal to its depth. There is no advantage to amending the soil unless drainage is poor. Work the soil in around the roots, firming with the native backfill. Apply a 5-gallon bucketful of water twice weekly for a month.

Growing Tips

Occasional watering will help yaupon through the first summer when planted in coastal sands. Fertilize in spring with a complete garden fertilizer, and water during drought. Mulch yaupons in the warmer months.

Care

These shrubs are tolerant of severe pruning. Shape the large shrub forms into small trees, topiaries, or formal "green meatballs." Dwarf yaupon needs nothing more than an occasional light shearing, and some grooming if cold damages the branch tips. Many horticulturists are reluctant to recommend yaupon in Zone 7. There are no pests.

Companion Planting and Design

Native yaupons can be limbed up to create trees or espaliered on a south wall. Dwarf and cultivars are terrific foundation shrubs when used in groups. Upright and weeping yaupon holly forms can be used as specimen accents.

Our Personal Favorites

The compact form of 'Schillings Dwarf' yaupon is useful in foundations. For lots of red berries and cold hardiness, 'Shadow's Hardy Female' may be worth a try.

Legend has it that Native Americans used the leaves to make a black tea to induce vomiting (hence "vomitoria"). Yaupon holly was Toby's top pick for foundation plantings until the winter of 2000 threw them into a tailspin. Unlike the Japanese hollies, which they resemble, yaupons cannot survive a mild fall followed by a deep freeze. East of Charlotte and south, most recovered after a severe spring pruning, but many skeletons were replaced in the Piedmont. We can't write off this shrub just yet, because it tolerates drought and neglect. Yaupon holly survives coastal conditions, and it does not succumb to pests, root rot, or nematodes. This evergreen species offers great versatility and is available in a variety of plant forms. The shiny, dark green, narrow leaves and clear gray stems of the species are adorned with bright-red berries. They are tough cookies!

Bloom Period and Seasonal Color
Small white flowers in spring; winter berries.

Mature Height × Spread
3 to 16 ft. × 3 to 16 ft.

Trees *for the Carolinas*

In studies of residential real estate values, tree-filled building lots bring market prices twenty to thirty percent higher than similar lots without trees. Strategically placed trees can significantly reduce the cost of cooling a home by providing much-needed shade during the summer months. Trees are nature's air-conditioners, reducing ambient heat as they shade homes and transpire moisture. In addition to the natural beauty they provide, shade trees can be a financial asset.

With increasing concerns for air quality, the public should recognize that trees provide a cost-effective way to clean the air in urban communities. Carbon dioxide production is a major factor in global warming. A single mature tree consumes thirteen pounds of carbon dioxide every year.

The Value of Trees

It is hard to imagine living in a neighborhood without trees. Trees make our environments more pleasant and add seasonal beauty. In the Carolinas, trees display unique arboreal interest through all four seasons. Autumn color in the Carolinas is spectacular, particularly in the Piedmont and mountains, and winter snowstorms light up our evergreens on hillsides and mountain ridges. Our spring-flowering bulbs are enhanced by the blossoms of native and introduced trees. Trees produce berries that attract birds and wildlife to our home landscapes. Evergreen trees are important nesting sites for birds, doubling as windbreaks and privacy screens.

Spring announces its arrival in our states with a parade of redbuds, Japanese cherries, saucer magnolias, and, of course, dogwoods in full, resplendent bloom. In early summer, 'Royal Purple' smoke tree and 'Forest Pansy' redbuds steal the show with their fabulous burgundy leaf color. Fall echoes the floral display of spring with dazzling colors of other hues. The fall show that envelops the Carolinas begins in early October on the lofty peaks of the Blue Ridge and Great Smoky Mountains and gradually wends its way across the Piedmont to the Coastal Plains. The seasonal spectacle of our hardwood trees ensures that tourism will always contribute to the economy of the Carolinas.

Japanese Maple

Selecting a Tree

A tree should be selected not only for its form but also for a number of other characteristics as well. Some varieties grow upright or round. Others are columnar like cedar, pendulous like weeping cherry, or vase-like, like elm and zelkova. There are deciduous and evergreen species. Deciduous trees, those that drop their leaves in autumn, are often selected because they offer summer shade and allow the winter sun to warm our houses. The largest specimens, like the oaks,

Pink Dogwood

are known for their long lives and majestic form, while others provide outstanding fall color and ornamental appeal. Still others, like the ginkgo have an ancient history.

What Trees Offer

Shade trees can frame a house the way a beautiful frame enhances a lasting work of art. Evergreens block objectionable views and divert strong winds. As a group, evergreens can add color to an otherwise bleak winter landscape, and they generally grow slowly. Although they never lose all their leaves, pines shed needles or leaves each year in spring or fall, gifting you with coveted "pine straw" mulch. People commonly plant evergreens too close to the house. Ask the question, "What is the mature spread?" and plant accordingly.

During the dreary winter months, many ornamental trees provide colorful berries for our enjoyment and sustenance for birds. The seedpods and berries that follow the handsome flowers are a special treat in the garden. Boughs laden with snow provide a "photo op" for gardeners anxious to capture a cardinal feasting near a window. *Prunus mume*, the Japanese flowering apricot, is a winter gem that bears fruit in years where no late frosts occur.

One often overlooked characteristic of deciduous trees is exfoliating bark, such as is seen on river birches. The cinnamon-colored, mottled bark of crape myrtle is most appreciated in the winter garden. Research the subtle seasonal characteristics of landscape trees before you plant, and site them where their traits can be appreciated.

Beauty Close to Home

Many Carolina gardeners are passionate about dogwood, the North Carolina state flower. Dogwood is a native flowering tree whose spring, fall, and winter beauty is unsurpassed. A fungal disease, dogwood anthracnose, threatens the dogwood's survival in mountain and upper Piedmont landscapes. New disease-resistant dogwood hybrids offer hope that this deciduous tree will be found in our gardens for many decades to come.

Thinking Ahead

Trees can be the biggest investment in landscape installations. They are relatively expensive at the nursery, and species with long, brittle limbs can incur expenses following storm damage. With a little forethought, you can avoid making costly mistakes when selecting and planting trees. Ask yourself why you need a tree for a particular location. Is shade your primary goal? What about privacy? Are there height restrictions in the space? If a tree produces fruit or drops twigs, would it create a hazard or maintenance concern? Do you desire pretty flowers, or is a conifer acceptable? Many trees attract wildlife; are you prepared for the litter that accompanies critters?

Saucer Magnolia

You can consult with a county forester, city arborist, or a County Cooperative Extension Agent for lists of trees for special situations. They can guide your tree selection by considering your particular soil types and environment. Keep in mind that your tree can become a liability for a neighbor or the public at large. Branches hanging over the property line and into rights-of-way can be pruned without your permission. A hazardous tree can fall, creating insurance nightmares. Many municipalities have tree ordinances that specify which tree species can be planted by streets and that stipulate restrictions for protecting valuable trees.

Variety Is the Spice of Life

Not all trees are created equal. There is as much difference between species of trees as there are breeds of dogs, and selecting a tree for the home landscape requires thoughtful preparation. Architect Frank Lloyd Wright once said, "Form follows function." This is a good rule to remember when selecting a tree. Select the right form (size and shape) to complement the desired function, and you will reduce maintenance costs in the long run. It is sad to see a tree topped or removed at its prime due to poor planning. Worst-case scenarios occur with street plantings where large trees obstruct power lines, requiring utility companies to disfigure specimen trees in order to keep power flowing to communities.

In the mid-1990s, Extension Agents in fifteen counties across North Carolina participated in an urban tree evaluation program. The evaluation hoped to promote tree planting diversity for difficult sites such as highways and beneath utility lines. Sixty-eight varieties were planted over a three-year period in differing environmental situations. Most were given minimal maintenance and limited irrigation. Notable trees in the original plantings included franklinia, 'Celestial dogwood'™, Chinese wingnut, and Carolina silverbell.

Results from the tree evaluation were published as "Ten Top Performers." Most of these trees have been mainstreamed into the nursery trade since the study. The list includes:

Corneliancherry dogwood (*Cornus mas*)
Chinese fringetree (*Chionanthus retusus*)
'Norwegian Sunset' maple (*Acer platanoides*)
'Pacific Sunset' maple (*Acer trucatum*)
'Autumn Blaze' Freeman maple
    (*Acer × freemani*)
Lacebark elm (*Ulmus parviflora*)

Fruitless sweetgum (*Liquidumbar volundiloba*)
'Wada's Memory' magnolia (*Magnolia robus*)
'Blieriana' plum (*P. × blieriana*)
'Royal Burgundy' flowering cherry
    (*Prunus × serrulata*)

The study narrowed the field from literally hundreds of possible landscape candidates to a few of the best. Before you rush out and purchase these trees, however, understand that they were chosen for their average survivability over a wide range of environmental conditions. Many of these trees are limited in availability, and a few may have growth habits that will not serve all needs.

An Important Consideration

Though trees are resilient and durable, their durability can be undermined by human activity, especially through root disturbance and improper pruning. Most trees don't have taproots. Instead they develop an extensive surface network of lateral and feeder roots. Most of their roots live in the top eighteen inches of soil. It is very easy to disturb trees by trenching, grading, backfilling, and landscaping within the drip line of mature specimens. (Now you know why most developers strip building sites up front; conservation comes with a price.)

Much has been written on pruning. Proper pruning prevents wood decay and keeps a tree healthy. It is necessary to remove branches or make pruning cuts at a natural juncture, such as the branch collar or another branch union. There is no good reason to top a tree. Proper tree selection and thinning by a certified arborist should keep your tree healthy and attractive. (See pruning information in the appendix.) For long-term nutritional needs, it is important to follow soil test recommendations for fertilizing mature trees. While we know that trees can benefit from fertilization when nutrients are deficient, numerous studies provide strong evidence that fertilization decreases a trees resistance to insect pests. Too much nitrogen can result in a weak branch structure or encourage hungry insects like aphids or scale.

How to Plant a Tree

After you have selected the right tree for the right site, plant it so the tree will establish quickly and grow into a thing of beauty. The planting hole should be wide and shallow rather than deep and narrow.

- Kill grass within a circle about six feet across and till or spade it to a depth of 6 inches.
- Spread limestone and superphosphate if called for by soil test.
- Amend clay or sandy soils by adding organic soil conditioner (1/3 the amount of existing backfill) over an area 4 feet across.
- Dig a planting hole to the depth of the rootball then put 2 inches of amended soil in the bottom.
- Break up any large clods and remove stones, roots, and debris.
- Inspect the rootball and cut roots that encircle it. If a mat of roots has formed on the bottom of the rootball, prune off the mat.
- Set the tree in the center of the hole, oriented so the best side faces where it will be seen most often.
- Shovel the conditioned soil around the rootball. Firm it down with your shovel handle.
- The backfill should come up to the soil line on the tree and taper down.
- Trickle water around the rootball for an hour or so until it begins to run off.
- Mulch three to four inches deep over the tilled area.
- Drive two steel fence posts into the soil on opposite sides of the rootball.
- Fasten twine or cotton cord to the posts near the bottom of the tree. Leave a little slack. On large trees, use wire cushioned with pieces of water hose or, better still, use canvas straps and tree guying kits available at garden shops.
- Water twice weekly for a month then monthly unless rain does the job for you.

The noteworthy trees on the following pages are personal favorites and comprise by no means an exhaustive list of good-quality trees offered by nurseries.

American Holly

Ilex opaca

Throughout the Carolinas and up the Eastern seaboard, American hollies grow in the wild. This wonderful native evergreen has a rich history, and it has been a symbol of friendship for centuries. The genus Ilex has been hybridized repeatedly and offers some of the finest woody ornamentals for landscaping. More than 300 varieties of I. opaca have been named, and over sixty of these are commercially available. This is the stately holly that evokes memories of Christmas Past with berries on the mantel. Individual trees may be either male or female, and berry production depends upon having both within the range of foraging bees. Small yards call for female trees, but male trees earn the space they occupy in large landscapes by providing season-long foliage color.

Bloom Period and Seasonal Color
White flowers in spring and red berries in fall and winter.

Mature Height × Spread
45 ft. × 15 to 25 ft.; taller in moist woodlands where trees must reach for the sun.

When, Where, and How to Plant
Balled-and-burlapped specimens should be planted in late winter and spring. Container-grown trees can be planted in spring and in the fall. Summer planting should be avoided if possible. Plant in full sun or part sun. American hollies prefer a well-drained, moist soil. They will tolerate dry sites if irrigated during establishment. Hollies grow relatively slowly in early years, but they need ample space. Rake the mulch twice yearly to kill weeds. Though holly trees are pH-adaptable, add lime to poor soil.

Growing Tips
There is no need to fertilize annually. Fertilize every few years if need is indicated by soil tests. Epsom salts or azalea fertilizer may help deepen foliage color. Add more mulch every summer to established trees to lessen drought stress. Don't be alarmed if your tree loses its leaves in early spring; they are being pushed off by emerging leaves. Fallen leaves from holly trees are slow to decay. You may wish to rake and pile them with green matter to make compost. Remember to wear gloves!

Care
Prune sparingly only in the winter because flowers and berries arise from previous season's growth. Groom and shear after the berries are visible in July. Don't expect berries on a female holly for a couple of years after planting since the plant's energy will go into getting it established. Leafminers are recurring pests on this plant; control with a systemic insecticide application in May. Native holly can be transplanted in winter after root-pruning in fall. Winter weather will often temporarily scorch the leaves.

Landscape Merit
Plant as a large specimen tree or in groups for a dense privacy screen. A woodland setting is a perfect location but requires frequent watering the first year to overcome root competition from older trees.

Our Personal Favorites
Superior selections include 'Jersey Knight' and 'Jersey Princess'. 'Canary' has yellow berries. 'Greenleaf' and 'Carolina No. 2' rank high for the south.

Bald Cypress

Taxodium distichum

When, Where, and How to Plant

Fall or winter, after the needles have dropped, is the best time for setting out cypress trees. The rapid growth of container-grown specimens can overtake established trees growing nearby. Ideally, cypress should be planted near a pond, stream, or swale where its roots can take up water; plant cypress near a water faucet or sprinkling system. However, it can tolerate dry sites. A full sun location is best. Add plenty of organic soil conditioner to the excavated soil before backfilling and increase the mulch layer to 4 or 5 inches deep. Keep the trunk free of mulch.

Growing Tips

Young cypress trees don't need staking or tying for support, unless you risk setting out container-grown plants during the summer. Cypress trees rarely need supplemental fertilizer; their decaying needles, dropped from their gracefully descending limbs, supply much of their nutrient needs.

Care

Be careful not to injure the tip of the upright "leader," because its loss can result in lopsided growth. Under no circumstances cut the top out of a cypress tree or limb it up until the tree is twenty or more years old. The beauty of cypress is symmetry, and a chain saw can mutilate it. Years later, when the lower branches have begun to look ragged, you can limb up the tree gradually, removing a limb or two each year until you can walk beneath the canopy. Leave a stub 1/2 inch in length. Don't paint it or apply tar; let nature heal the scar.

Landscape Merit

Cypress looks best when planted alone or in "groves" of 3 to 5 trees, spaced irregularly, 30 to 40 feet apart. Once the trees have grown enough to be limbed up, plant grass beneath the canopy to make a serene, shaded glade.

Our Personal Favorites

'Shawnee Brave' has a pyramidal form. 'Heritage' foliage has a more open spread. A recently introduced pond cypress, 'Debonair', matures at a smaller size than the bald cypress.

One of the few deciduous conifers, and a swamp citizen, this native tree makes an imposing specimen in large landscapes. It has been typecast as a swamp tree since it grows well in shallow water where it pokes up characteristic knobby "knees." But bald cypress also grows well in ordinary garden soil with no more water than is needed by deciduous yard trees . . . and its roots rarely develop knees. In yards, the trees grow moderately fast with a typical "Christmas tree" shape. Sun penetrating the lacy foliage helps lawn grass grow beneath the canopy, and the dropped needles don't have to be raked away. A related smaller species, pond cypress (T. ascendens) makes a good landscape tree but is seldom offered by nurseries.

Bloom Period and Seasonal Color

Brilliant light green in spring with color shift to cinnamon color at leaf drop.

Mature Height × Spread

100 ft. × 50 to 75 ft., depending on the cultivar.

Carolina Hornbeam
Carpinus caroliniana

This native tree, to paraphrase the late comedian Rodney Dangerfield, "Don't get no respect." It is no showboat, but for a small, slow-growing tree, it has few rivals. Red tinges its small, serrated leaves in spring. Pendent white bloom clusters, shaped like rattlesnake buttons, come in early summer. Other species have showier blooms and fall foliage color, but none has the slow growth, strong wood, dense branching, and small mature size of hornbeam. Jim reports that he planted a hornbeam in full sun in his Piedmont garden and watched it for twenty years. In that time it grew about fifteen feet tall and equally wide, with very closely spaced, muscular-looking branches all the way to the base. Hornbeam resists damage from ice or wind storms.

Other Common Names
Ironwood, Musclewood, Blue Beech

Bloom Period and Seasonal Color
Pendent white blooms in spring; unremarkable yellow to red foliage in fall.

Mature Height × Spread
30 ft. × 30 ft.; understory trees grow twice as high.

When, Where, and How to Plant
Start with a container-grown plant less than 4 feet in height and transplant it in fall or winter for best results. Spring or summer often bring dry weather, and skipped watering results in the tree's death. Hornbeam isn't at all particular about where you plant it; the tree thrives in full sun or all-day filtered shade. In the wild, it is usually found in moist bottomlands. Shaded locations beneath taller trees result in taller and spindlier growth.

Growing Tips
Maintain a 3- to 4-inch mulch to the drip line of new trees, avoiding the trunk. Don't try to open up young trees by removing branches. They don't need it. During drought, let a sprinkler run beneath your hornbeam; let it trickle for an hour or two once a week.

Care
Part of hornbeam's beauty is its remarkable bark. Protect it from damage by antler-rubbing deer, lawnmowers, and weed eaters. Beware of vegetation around trees that attract people with weedeaters who don't know that a single lashing of the tender basal bark can kill a young tree. Remove all grass and weeds, particularly bermudagrass and tall fescue, which compete with young trees for nutrients and water. Hornbeam has very few insect or disease problems.

Landscape Merit
In sunny locations, a fringe of dwarf flowering shrubs and azaleas around a hornbeam can make a pretty composition. The columnar forms adapt well to small yards, especially as privacy screens. In a woodland edge situation or beneath taller trees, hornbeam reaches for the sun and is sparsely branched with smooth, mottled, grey bark sculpted like the biceps of a weight lifter.

Our Personal Favorite
There are no generally available named varieties of hornbeam. The variation in seed-grown trees is considerable, so shop carefully for a tree with good form that is not rootbound.

Carolina Silverbell

Halesia tetraptera

When, Where, and How to Plant

Carolina silverbell can be planted successfully between November and March, preferably before the ground freezes in winter. Plant it in rich, moist, well-drained soil. Because dropping blooms make a slippery surface, plant your silverbell at least 10 feet from a walk or patio. It will grow slowly in full sun and is happier in partial shade. Follow the general planting instructions (page 221), but increase the amount of organic soil conditioner to $1/3$ of the backfill. Water well and finish by covering the top of the exposed roots with enhanced soil. Consider the generous layer of mulch as obligatory, not optional, since it reproduces the forest duff where silverbell grows naturally.

Growing Tips

The key element to maintenance is moisture. Water newly planted trees twice weekly for the first month, and later during periods of drought. Well-mulched native trees need very little fertilizer. In fact, you can kill a young tree during the first several years by overfertilizing with granular plant food that is high in ammoniacal nitrogen. Apply a slow-release fertilizer only when the tree is looking pale and puny.

Care

Train silverbell to a desirable form. As the tree matures, prune out weak branches or the weakest side of a fork with bark trapped in the "vee." Angular fruit may form on the tree, adding more seasonal interest. There are no serious insects or diseases to justify spraying. Winter cold is needed for the best flower display. Other silverbell species are better adapted to coastal areas.

Landscape Merit

As a lawn tree or accent specimen, Carolina silverbell makes a beautiful picture when planted with spring-flowering bulbs, saucer magnolias, fothergilla, and Kurume azaleas. It offers a low-maintenance alternative to the Japanese cherry or Bradford pear found in most residential landscapes. Silverbell's sparse branches allow sunlight to reach lawn grasses below.

Our Personal Favorites

The two-winged *H. diptera* is a compact species that blooms profusely. 'Rosea' is pink-flowered.

This attractive native understory tree is a gem, a small, deciduous tree that grows in moist, rich soil along streams and coves in the western regions of the Carolinas. The name "silverbell" comes from the early spring clusters of white, bell-shaped flowers that adorn this rounded tree. They display well against its apple-green leaves. Carolina silverbell assumes an open form in woodlands but can become an impressive tree in woodland edges where it has room to bush out. It does well on the north side of a house or in the afternoon shade from a large oak tree. Most ornamental trees prefer drier soil, but this beauty will thrive in the moist soil that goes with sprinkler systems. Many garden centers offer small container-grown seedlings that will transplant.

Bloom Period and Seasonal Color

In spring, white flowers with golden centers followed by attractive, angular fruit.

Mature Height × Spread

25 to 70 ft. × variable spread (depending on variety and planting site)

Colorado Blue Spruce

Picea pungens 'Glauca'

Although a slow grower, Colorado blue spruce is worth planting in large gardens across the mountains and in counties of the Foothill region of the Carolinas. When selecting a blue spruce, choose the grafted cultivars that have the startling silver-blue color—the color is what attracts most gardeners to this stately pyramidal evergreen. A group planting of blue spruces can be a striking landscape feature. Unfortunately, the farther east you go, the less blue color you see on the blue spruces. They have difficulty with hot summer weather and the heavy clay soils in the Piedmont. The heat-tolerant cultivar 'Foxtail', with its bushy blue branch tips, has the best chance for survival. When placed appropriately, Colorado blue spruce can make a landscape come alive. Gardeners in Zone 8 would be happier with a pine species or Arizona cypress.

Bloom Period and Seasonal Color
Year-round silvery blue foliage

Mature Height × Spread
60 ft. × 20 ft.

When, Where, and How to Plant

Plant field-grown spruces in the dormant season from November to March. Plant container-grown trees in spring or fall. Seedlings are available from mail-order nurseries but may vary in color. Blue spruce needs full sun, or at least six hours of direct sun. It appreciates moist soil. Avoid poorly drained soils since the trees are vulnerable to root rot diseases. Follow the general planting directions, including 8 inches of loosened soil outside the rootball in which new roots can forage. Water every three days for the first two weeks if there is no rain. Apply a 3- to 4-inch mulch layer.

Growing Tips

Water during the first two seasons is important to keep blue spruce thriving. Irrigate every three weeks or more during a drought. To maintain good color, use a slow-release fertilizer every year in March. Maintain a 3- to 4-inch mulch layer to the drip line of individual trees.

Care

To shape, shear in mid-June after new candles form. Remove only $1/3$ of the new candles, or remove entire branches that are crowded. Don't limb up spruces, though, because it ruins their appearance. In dry locations, spider mites can become a nuisance. Spraying with hose-pressure water during July and August helps control mites and cools the tree. Spruce spider mite and adelgids (white bark aphids) can be controlled with a miticide treatment. Beware: oil sprays can remove the blue color. The spruces are deer-resistant.

Landscape Merit

Blue spruce is a major player in the winter landscape. Grow it as a specimen or in a grouping for screens and accent. 'Montgomery Dwarf' can be grown in planters and used as temporary plantings like dwarf Alberta spruces.

Our Personal Favorites

'Hoopsii' blue spruce is a priceless find with consistent blue color. In Zone 8, *Cupressus arizonica* var. *glabra* 'Blue Ice' and 'Carolina Sapphire' mimic blue spruce color and handle heat well.

Crape Myrtle

Lagerstroemia indica

When, Where, and How to Plant

Plant balled-and-burlapped crape myrtles in early spring and container-grown specimens in spring or fall. Transplant established plants in late winter or in spring. Sow seeds of dwarf crape myrtles in late spring. Without ample sun, expect sparse flowering and powdery mildew disease. These trees like moist, slightly acidic soils (pH 5.5) and good soil drainage. In heavy clay soils, plant the rootball 1/3 above the soil. Pull conditioned soil up around it. Apply a full 5-gallon bucket of water, then layer 3 to 4 inches of hardwood or bark mulch. Fertilizer planting tablets can be used with large specimens.

Growing Tips

Until established, crape myrtles require 1 inch of water per week during the first summer. Water neglect can result in tree loss. Though drought-tolerant when established, crape myrtle needs irrigation during the flowering period and prolonged dry periods. Fertilize as new growth begins following soil test recommendations. A nursery fertilizer is acceptable; use according to directions.

Care

For more blooms, remove fading flower clusters before the seedpods form in late summer. If you don't remove the seedheads, prune them off in March. Do not over-fertilize or prune hard in the fall. Topping, known as "Crape Murder," will ruin the form. Train into a small single or multi-trunk tree, pruning to expose the attractive trunk; remove basal suckers. Blackening leaves in summer indicate aphid infestation, and Japanese beetles crave the new growth. Consider tolerating moderate damage rather than applying insecticides.

Landscape Merit

Plant shrubby varieties in groups, and large varieties as specimens with ground covers to accentuate their trunks. For a contemporary look, use in wide entrance plantings or courtyard gardens. Read labels carefully; some crape myrtles grow into significant trees, others grow more horizontally than vertically, and a few are true genetic dwarf shrubs.

Our Personal Favorite

Select mildew-resistant cultivars. The National Arboretum introduction, the robust and white-flowered 'Natchez', is mildew-resistant; its hybrids bear Indian names.

Crape myrtles make dramatic landscape trees, the glory of summer in the South. Because of their long bloom period, they are called the "flower of one hundred days" in China. In July, their terminal flower clusters are dense with brilliant, ruffled petals. They are most impressive when grown as multi-trunk specimens. Like birches, their peeling bark reveals mottled patterns of tan, twisted, muscle-like wood. The Japanese variety L. fauriei 'Fantasy', a J.C. Raulston Arboretum introduction, has outstanding, dark red bark and pure white flower clusters. Like clothing, crape myrtle is available in small, medium, and large. It makes an excellent large shrub for the winter bark color. Crape myrtles thrive in hot, sunny locations and will grow in almost any type of soil. Their fall coloration is spectacular—but short.

Other Common Name
Japanese Crape Myrtle

Bloom Period and Seasonal Color
Late-summer blooms in white, lavender, red, and pink; orange or red fall foliage.

Mature Height × Spread
Standards 15 to 30 ft. × 16 ft.; dwarf varieties 4 to 8 ft. × 6 ft. or less

Cryptomeria
Cryptomeria japonica

Cryptomeria, or Japanese cedar, a cousin to the giant sequoia, is quite different from our native red cedars. Soft sprays of foliage appear in spirals along drooping branches. The individual needles of juvenile Japanese cedars are spinelike and prickly. As the tree matures, the older needles, held closely together, look like fingers on the wide-spreading branches. Old specimens have attractive reddish-brown bark that peels off in long shreds. Once newly planted trees are established, they will shoot up quickly, producing two to three feet of tender growth in late summer. In the fall, the needles of cryptomeria turn brownish red but are replaced by fresh, dark green needles in the spring. It is puzzling that so few people are using Japanese cedars for screening purposes since they have few pests.

Other Common Name
Japanese Cedar

Bloom Period and Seasonal Color
Dark green foliage in spring; brownish red in fall.

Mature Height × Spread
60 ft. × 30 ft.

When, Where, and How to Plant

Plant cryptomeria any time the ground can be worked and the tree watered. Cryptomeria thrives in a sunny location with deep, rich, moist soil. In well-drained soils, plant at the same depth the trees were grown in the nursery, slightly higher in clay loam soils. A neutral pH is acceptable for this evergreen, so a little liming or the addition of wood ashes is encouraged. Spread out the loosened roots of container-grown plants in the planting hole. Firm the soil around the roots and pour a 5-gallon bucketful of water over the rootball. To prevent winter winds from toppling the new installation, stake fall-planted Japanese cedars.

Growing Tips

Unlike most conifers, Japanese cedars cannot tolerate long periods of drought. Keep them mulched and watered for the first two years, and you will be amazed at the rich, new growth in the late summer months. Apply slow-release nursery fertilizer as needed.

Care

Japanese cedars grow moderately fast after establishment. Keep their growth in bounds with light shearing. Cutting the central leader (trunk) is not recommended; it will ruin the shape of the tree. Cryptomerias are resistant to pests. As they age, the lower branches will die and must be removed. Underplant them with small shrubs at that point. Mites and twig dieback are possible if the tree is stressed. Japanese cedar's greenery is attractive for decorating.

Landscape Merit

Cryptomeria is a viable alternative to Leyland cypress, though cryptomeria spreads wider. Plant it as a tall screen; it makes a fine specimen accent and can survive in shaded gardens. Cherry laurels and rhododendrons are fine companions. There are some marvelous miniature varieties for foundations.

Our Personal Favorite

'Yoshino' has blue-green summer foliage and is widely adapted.

Deodar Cedar

Cedrus deodara

When, Where, and How to Plant

Container-grown specimens can be planted from spring through early fall. In the western half of the Carolinas, plant only in the spring after the soil warms. Provide plenty of space for its canopy to spread. Full sun to a half-day of shade in a moderately dry site is ideal. In colder regions, provide some protection from winter winds. Add fertilizer planting tablets to the planting hole, or add $1/2$ cup of superphosphate. Water thoroughly and mulch well.

Growing Tips

Water newly-planted deodar cedars three times the first week, twice the second, and weekly for two months until they begin growing strongly. Once established, they are tolerant of dry soils. More fertilizer will not be necessary until the spring of the second growing season. A general garden fertilizer can be applied in the spring every two or three years. These evergreens grow relatively fast once they become acclimated to a new site.

Care

Do not prune or stake unless there is good reason to do either. As deodar cedar matures, some lower limbs inevitably die, probably because of heavy shading from the upper canopy. This is normal; remove the dying limbs to make lawn-mowing easier. Forget growing grass inside the drip line of this evergreen—leave it mulched. Harsh winters and deodar weevils can take the tops off these trees. In mountain counties, anti-transpirants can be applied during the first few winters to reduce water loss and subsequent drying out of the plant.

Landscape Merit

Unequivocally a specimen tree due to its size, deodar cedar's fine texture and needle-like leaves are a pleasing backdrop for broadleaf shrub borders. Weeping blue atlas cedar is a better choice for city landscapes; it can be planted as a screen growing on a trellis.

Our Personal Favorite

While 'Shalimar' is the most cold-hardy, a dwarf form would be a better buy.

Mention "cedar" in the Carolinas and most residents think of the rows of lanky Eastern red cedars that line farm fencerows or the dark conical evergreens that dot our roadsides. Experienced gardeners know that those cedars are actually junipers. The "true cedars" that thrive in our hot, wet climate include deodar cedar and two somewhat similar but lesser-known species, cedar-of-Lebanon (C. libani) and atlas cedar (C. atlantica). Deodar cedar is a marvelous tree for the landscape on larger properties where evergreens are not cramped for space. Mature specimens look like distant mountains on the horizon. These trees mature at 70 feet, often with flattened tops, the result of being frozen back during severe winters. Deodar cedar has a wide-spreading pyramidal form and makes a emphatic landscape statement wherever it is planted.

Bloom Period and Seasonal Color
Grayish-green foliage year-round; decorative cones at maturity.

Mature Height × Spread
70 ft. × 40 ft.

Flowering Cherry

Prunus spp.

Starting with a few sparse blooms, Japanese flowering cherry quickly bursts into a light-pink wash of color that dominates the April landscape. Except for the grafted weeping cultivars, most Japanese cherry trees are upright in form. Sterile and fruitless, this outstanding ornamental produces either double or single flowers. The large double pink blooms of 'Kwansan' are very popular in the western Carolinas, while 'Yoshino', the white-flowering variety seen at the nation's capitol, is the one that thrives in the East. Unfortunately, these trees often fail to harden-off properly for the winter, resulting in twig dieback and a short life expectancy in Zone 7b and south. The weeping Higan cherry is a large, long-lived tree that is popular with landscapers in the Piedmont. These seedling trees are not grafted.

Bloom Period and Seasonal Color
April blooms in white and shades of pink.

Mature Height × Spread
15 to 35 ft. × 25 ft.

When, Where, and How to Plant
Flowering cherry trees are cold-sensitive and should be planted in the spring before bud swell. Balled-and-burlapped trees can be planted any time during the dormant season. Trees planted in summer are subject to invasion by borers and decline from heat stress. Find a protected site out of the south sun where the soil drains well. Excellent soil drainage is imperative because root rot diseases are acute in heavy soils. This tree benefits from being planted on a berm. In friable soils, dig a hole twice as wide as the rootball and half as deep. In mass plantings, bury perforated plastic drainpipe every 6 feet for drainage. Keep the soil moist through spring. Give flowering cherry trees plenty of space, 20 feet between them. Non-grafted trees appear to be better adapted to mountain climates, as graft unions may be sensitive to damage from freezing.

Growing Tips
Watering is a must during the early years and during drought; apply 10 gallons of water per week. The soil must drain well, or the tree will die from "wet feet." Fertilize in mid-March and prune during the dormant season or in early August.

Care
Heavy fertilization or pruning in the fall may encourage late-season growth, increasing the chances of winter injury. Remove sucker growth at the base of the tree and at graft union. Remove webworms, tent caterpillars, and Japanese beetles by hand or chemically. Consult your Extension Agent for advice on controlling borers. Avoid pruning during the borer season.

Landscape Merit
Flowering cherry is best used as a specimen tree or as part of a formal landscape design. Plant to soften the lines of a large house. What landscape could not benefit from the unique cascading form of a Higan cherry, 'Pendula' (*P.* × *subhertella*) 'Autumnalis' offers a long flowering period.

Our Personal Favorites
'Okame' grows quickly, blooms early, and is heat tolerant.

Flowering Crabapple

Malus sp.

When, Where, and How to Plant

Plant container-grown crabapples in late winter, spring, fall, or just about any time the soil is prepared and water can be provided. Locate a spot where there is plenty of sun and good air circulation. The soil must drain well to prevent shallow roots or, even worse, root rot. Dig a hole that is equal in depth to the rootball and twice its width (see tree-planting instructions (page 221). Use the soil from the hole for the backfill. Plant high in clay soils. Spread 3 to 4 inches of mulch over the tilled area out to the dripline. Water well.

Growing Tips

Water weekly the first month and biweekly thereafter until the tree is firmly established, which usually happens after one growing season. Slowly trickle water from a hose for a half hour. Fertilize crabapples between February and April; use a 10-10-10 analysis at a rate of 1 pound per inch of trunk diameter.

Care

During the early years, some light pruning will be needed to train the tree. Once it begins to mature, pruning is a must for the best flowering appeal. Prune in late summer to prevent switches of suckers forming at pruning cuts. Farmer wisdom describes pruning crabapples "so a bird can fly through the canopy." Prune back to the main trunk or to the branch's point of origin. Reduce apple rust and apple scab diseases by planting only disease-resistant cultivars.

Landscape Merit

Use flowering crabapple en masse in large yards and parks. Flowering crabapples also make good specimen trees, especially the columnar and weeping forms. Avoid planting by a walk or patio where the fruit can create a hazardous mess.

Our Personal Favorites

'Narragansett' is a disease-resistant selection from the National Arboretum. Plant small-fruited 'Red Jade' for birds.

Noted for its beauty when in spring bloom, the crabapple is wrongfully maligned for premature leaf drop caused by chronic leaf spot diseases. Today these diseases are avoidable, and more disease-resistant introductions, such as 'Donald Wyman', appear every year. Growth habits vary from rounded to upright to weeping. As evidenced by their popularity in the Midwestern states, these trees are extremely cold-hardy. Like their close cousins the apples, crabapples grace landscapes in every county in the Carolinas. This bears testimony to their tolerance of a wide range of soils, including heavy clay. Though the flowering period is ten days or less, the trees don't succumb to borers and short-life problems as do Japanese cherries and purple leaf plums, and they offer a bonus: colorful, edible fruit.

Bloom Period and Seasonal Color
White, pink, and rosy-red blooms in spring.

Mature Height × Spread
10 to 30 ft. × 10 to 25 ft.

Flowering Dogwood
Cornus florida

Across much of eastern North America, the dogwood may be the most popular flowering tree. In fact, dogwood is the state flower of North Carolina. Dogwood deserves the accolades it receives from its admirers. It makes a beautiful understory tree. When planted in a shady area, it will grow an open framework. The blooms will have a layered effect. Though white or pink blooms mean spring to Southerners, we also enjoy the early and intense red fall color they add to our autumn palette, arriving slowly in October with the finale by mid-November. Because of the big scare over the fatal "dogwood blight" (Discula destructiva), it is reassuring that new disease-resistant introductions are on the market—most notably the 'Stellar' series and many fine cultivars. Check with the NCSU Arboretum in Asheville and the South Carolina Botanical Garden for advice on preventing and fighting dogwood blight.

Bloom Period and Seasonal Color
Spring blooms in white or shades of pink; red foliage in fall.

Mature Height × Spread
20 to 30 ft. × 20 to 30 ft.

When, Where, and How to Plant
Unlike most deciduous trees, dogwood plants best in spring rather than fall. Purchase healthy grafted trees and leave the seedlings in the woods. Plant in well-drained, highly organic, acidic soil. Nursery-grown dogwood tolerates sun or partial shade. However, planting in full sun predisposes the tree to borers and other stressers (see general tree-planting instructions, page 221). The top of the rootball should stand 5 inches or more above the soil line, even higher in poorly drained soils. Pull conditioned soil up around it and add 3 to 4 inches of mulch. Water well following planting and twice each week for one month.

Growing Tips
Use a hose with a slow trickle to water new trees until the water runs off the saturated soil. Repeat twice the first week and weekly thereafter until the tree is firmly established (usually one growing season). In full sun, dogwoods will grow a dense, oval canopy and will need mulching and regular watering during periods of drought. Fertilize every two years with a 12-4-8 analysis using 1 pound per 100 square feet, but only if necessary. Rake the mulch aside, spread the fertilizer, then replace the mulch.

Care
Prune immediately following bloom. Remove crossing branches and some inner branches to promote an appealing shape and good airflow. Avoid pruning during borer season in June and July. Borers threaten weak or scarred trees under stress; holes in the bark the size of pencil points indicate their presence. Prevent borers by making proper pruning cuts and avoiding weed-eater and mower injuries. A borer spray treatment in June is beneficial. Spotted leaves indicate the presence of spot anthracnose, an unsightly and debilitating disease.

Landscape Merit
Plant in groups for a truly spectacular spring accent. This native understory tree is perfect for the woodland garden. Use as a specimen in mixed borders of spring-flowering bulbs, perennials, and ornamental shrubs such as azaleas.

Our Personal Favorites
'Cherokee Princess' and 'Cherokee Brave' (mildew-resistant) are wonderful trees.

Flowering Pear

Pyrus calleryana

When, Where, and How to Plant

Plant flowering pear during fall or late winter. Container-grown trees can be planted whenever the ground can be prepared. This tree needs room to grow since it's not small. Find a full sun location that has good drainage. Any type of soil is fine. Loosen the roots of pot-grown plants and straighten them out in the planting hole. Water well and apply a 3- to 4-inch layer of mulch. Avoid planting when the soil is too wet to work (especially in clay soils).

Growing Tips

Using a handheld, open-ended hose, water newly planted trees for ten minutes every third day until you see signs of new growth. Watering is essential for newly planted trees during the first two summers. Once the roots are established, water deeply every seven to ten days. Overfertilization in the early years contributes to weak branch structure. Use a slow-release, 12-6-6 fertilizer at the rate of 2 cups per 100 square feet over the root zone. Apply in April every three years, spreading it under the tree's canopy and just beyond. Maintain a ring of mulch over the root system to help conserve moisture.

Care

Bradford pear grows rapidly with few pest problems. It is resistant to fireblight disease, the most destructive disease of pears. Prune blackened twigs in early summer. Any other pruning should be performed in summer or late winter. Avoid mature branch-splitting by removing double leaders on young trees.

Landscape Merit

Flowering pear makes an excellent specimen tree for fall color and is an excellent background tree. Many are planted closely to make tall privacy screens, anticipating that every other tree will be removed later to allow expansion of those remaining. The spring color is especially attractive in bulb beds, but the display can be cut short by spring frosts. Its "smelly" flowers bother some people.

Our Personal Favorite

'Cleveland Select' (also known as 'Chanticleer') is the best variety for durability in storms. It is the variety to use for small spaces.

For more than two decades, 'Bradford' pear was the darling of Carolina landscapers. Its reputation as a durable landscape tree is now tainted because of damaging storms and hurricanes striking the Carolinas. Most major cities have banned this tree as a street tree. Despite its brittle wood and poor branch structure, 'Bradford' pears continue to be planted like there's no tomorrow. Flowering pear is a hard tree to resist at the nursery—it has dazzling white blooms, lustrous green foliage, and formal structure. Its exceptional red fall color is second only to our glorious red maples. Our advice is to plant a symmetrical specimen as a temporary landscape fixture, or opt for the recently introduced cultivars, such as 'Cleveland' that has a stronger, ladder-like branching habit.

Other Common Name
Callery Pear, Bradford Pear

Bloom Period and Seasonal Color
Clusters of white flowers each spring; red foliage in fall.

Mature Height × Spread
45 ft. × 20 ft.

Fruitless Sweet Gum

Liquidambar styraciflua 'Rotundiloba'

Carolina gardeners find few good things about our native sweet gums. In fact, most curse these trees and their spiny gumballs, which are messy and dangerous underfoot. Relegate this common hardwood tree to a natural area where the gumballs will not be a source of aggravation. There is a premier cultivar for sweet gum lovers! 'Rotundiloba', named for its distinctive rounded leaf lobes, has all the beauty and luster of the species but is sterile and doesn't set fruit. 'Rotundiloba' is columnar when young but takes on a pyramidal shape as it matures. A moist woodland garden would be ideal for this stately tree. The wonderful fall color and large glossy leaves are memorable. Buy your tree in the fall to get the color you want.

Other Common Name
Rotundiloba

Bloom Period and Seasonal Color
Unimpressive green blooms in spring; brilliant yellow and dark burgundy fall foliage.

Mature Height × Spread
50 ft. × 20 to 25 ft.

When, Where, and How to Plant
Plant fruitless sweet gum trees in late winter or early spring. Container-grown specimens can be put in the ground almost anytime, provided they can be irrigated. Most 'Rotundiloba' sweet gums are sold in large containers. They tolerate a wide range of soil conditions, though they prefer a moist, well-drained site. Plant in a sunny place for the most intense fall color. Set the tree at the same level it was in the container, or a few inches higher, and free up the circling roots. Water deeply with a garden hose set at a slow trickle. Mulch in a radius 3 feet around the trunk; add mulch yearly to maintain a 3- to 4-inch layer.

Growing Tips
Water weekly for thirty minutes or until the soil is saturated. In nature, the tree grows well with no special attention because it thrives in leaf litter mulch. Fertilize with a 16-4-8 nitrogen fertilizer every three years in March. Rake the mulch aside, spread fertilizer, and replace the mulch.

Care
After the first year, prune your new tree to train it; eliminate double leaders and very narrow branch crotch angles. Prune outside the branch collar and always prune back to a side limb. No specific pests are known. Wash minor pests off the tree with a garden hose. In dry or upland sites, drought can be its biggest enemy; mulch plantings and irrigate in August. Given plenty of room, your 'Rotundiloba' will need little maintenance other than leaf raking in fall. Limb breakage is common where ice storms occur.

Landscape Merit
'Rotundiloba' grows into a large specimen tree and should be planted at least 20 feet from a house. It can be used to provide welcome shade for a patio or deck, or spaced closely as a tall screen.

Our Personal Favorites
Plant 'Rotundiloba', unless you have a use for thousands of gumballs. 'Starlet', a variegated (but fertile) sweet gum, attracts attention.

Ginkgo
Ginkgo biloba

When, Where, and How to Plant

The best time to plant your ginkgo is from November through March. A tree that has been dug while dormant, heeled in, or well-rooted in a container may be planted at any time. Ginkgos like full sun and fertile soils for fastest growth. Once established, they will adapt to poor, dry soils, but they will grow very slowly. Avoid planting when the ground is frozen or muddy. On burlap-wrapped rootballs, cut the twine from around the trunk but leave the natural burlap on the ball when you plant. There is no need to loosen the roots; they will grow through the burlap. Water well by pouring on 5-gallon bucket of water at planting.

Growing Tips

Water your ginkgo tree with a slow trickle from a hose for a period of time equal to one minute per inch of diameter of the rootball twice a week for the first month and every two weeks thereafter. Do this until the tree is firmly established, which usually takes one growing season. When in doubt, check the soil moisture before watering by digging down through the mulch into the back-fill soil. Fertilize in March using a fertilizer high in nitrogen, one with a 3-1-2 or similar ratio.

Care

The best feature of your new ginkgo is that it is virtually pest and maintenance free. Ginkgos need very little pruning, but if it is needed, prune in winter or summer. A bonus with ginkgos is that autumn cleanup is not an arduous task.

Landscape Merit

These large, stately trees are used as specimen plants for a formal accent in the garden. Their open canopy casts fragmented shadows on the ground below, which is ideal for many shade-loving perennials.

Our Personal Favorite

Ginkgo is no small tree. Consider the narrow 'Fastigiata' in small landscapes.

Ginkgo is a native of China with ancestral ties to conifers. It is an excellent, slow-growing landscape tree with brilliant yellow fall color. Its distinctive fan-shaped leaves are two to four inches wide and bear a resemblance to those of maidenhair fern, the tree's namesake. The leaves drop abruptly and can be quickly add to the compost pile. Plant only male ginkgo trees; females produce large, foul-smelling fruit that are rather messy to handle, but considered a delicacy in Asia. Ginkgo tolerates urban conditions and is acclaimed as a street tree. The finest old specimens are scattered across the Carolinas from town squares to grand Southern estates. And yes, this is the plant that serves as a source for the ginkgo "health supplement."

Other Common Name
Maidenhair Tree

Bloom Period and Seasonal Color
Yellow foliage in fall.

Mature Height × Spread
70 ft. × 60 ft.

Hybrid Holly
Ilex 'Nellie R. Stevens'

A conical hybrid holly, 'Nellie R. Stevens' has become a favorite among landscape designers for formal hedges and screens. This magnificent holly is stately in appearance as it grows rather quickly to twenty-five feet at maturity. The foliage is narrow, compact, and glossy dark green. The bright-red fruits are not as prominent as they are on some of the American hollies, but the plant's rapid growth rate is a true advantage. 'Nellie R. Stevens' combines the beauty of its English holly parentage and the drought-tolerance of the Chinese holly family. Certainly it is a shrewd choice for a screen or a specimen evergreen tree. It is arguably the most popular of a large group of hybrid hollies that range in height from dwarf shrubs to tall trees.

Bloom Period and Seasonal Color
Dark green, lustrous foliage with red berries at maturity.

Mature Height × Spread
20 to 25 ft. × 10 to 15 ft.

When, Where, and How to Plant
Plant container-grown holly any time the ground permits. Large balled-and-burlapped plants meant for hedges should be planted in late winter through spring. To ensure compact foliage, plant in a full-sun location or one that gets at least six hours of sun. It adapts to clay soils, but avoid poorly drained conditions. Set the rootball slightly higher than the original grade (rootballs often settle in too deeply with large, heavy plants). Backfill halfway, firm-in the soil, and add 5 gallons of water. After the water drains out, finish backfilling, mulch, and water again.

Growing Tips
Water 'Nellie R. Stevens' during dry periods in the first two seasons, setting a sprinkler to deliver 2 inches of water per week over the rootzone. Mulches and soaker hoses are wonderful for irrigating thoroughly in hot summer weather. Once established, the plants tolerate drought extremely well but will grow slowly. Apply a slow-release fertilizer in spring or early fall. Don't overfertilize, or you will be pruning regularly. Keep your holly mulched.

Care
Stake new specimens over 5 feet tall for four to six months. Heavy pruning should be done in late winter or early summer. For specimens, limb up the lower branches of older trees to expose the smooth gray trunk. Shaping is important during the early years, particularly if the tree is grown singly as a specimen tree. Old foliage that has dropped should be raked up before reapplying mulch. Few pests other than scale insects bother this holly.

Landscape Merit
Planted 5 to 6 feet apart and left unpruned, a row of 'Nellie R. Stevens' hollies makes a fine impenetrable screen. Plant as an anchor for the corners of a two-story house, or as landscape specimens. Give 'Nellie' room to spread out; this is a tree, not a shrub.

Our Personal Favorite
Where smaller specimens are needed, consider 'Mary Nell' or a newer cultivar of red holly.

Japanese Maple

Acer palmatum

When, Where, and How to Plant

Plant Japanese maple trees any time from November through April. These grow well in a range of soils, provided the soils are not water-logged; they prefer moist, rich soils. Filtered shade is preferred to direct sun—some maples will sunburn. Heavy shade will cause the tree to grow spindly and perform poorly. When planting small container-grown trees, free up the roots before planting. Water regularly each week for the first month, trickling slowly from a garden hose for thirty minutes.

Growing Tips

Irrigate the root zone every week if there isn't sufficient rainfall. Water deeply in the summer. Until maturity, most trees benefit from irrigation during the dry months of summer. Maintain 2 to 3 inches of mulch across a minimum diameter of 3 feet; increase the size of the ring with time. To speed growth or compensate for nutrient deficiencies, apply a slow-release fertilizer in spring every three to five years to accelerate growth.

Care

Keep an eye out for Japanese beetles and spray when they first appear. Chronic leaf-tip burn, though not life-threatening, is worse in hot, dry sites. Avoid chronic leaf spot by choosing disease-resistant cultivars; apply fungicide as a last resort. Limb up the trees or thin the interior branches for an open form. Always remove dead twigs. As with all maples, summer pruning minimizes sap "bleeding."

Landscape Merit

Plant Japanese maple as an accent or in small groves to create a Japanese garden. Grow dwarf forms in foundation plantings. Plant them in concrete or lightweight containers that can withstand freezing and thawing. Place the lacy-leaf 'Dissectum' in close quarters where the lacy foliage can be touched. When planted at curbside, these low-growing trees will not interfere with power lines.

Our Personal Favorites

Both fall color and brilliant spring foliage are features of 'Bloodgood'. 'Sango Kaku' has reddish bark. The paperbark maple, *A. griseum*, grows into a startlingly beautiful specimen for close up viewing.

Few ornamental trees are as useful for landscaping as the Japanese maple. The outstanding features of this tree are its small size, intricate foliage, and its varying leaf types, colors, and shapes. From the seedlings to the grafted cultivars, the Japanese maples are superb trees. In spring, the leaves burst into color with intense red hues that later fade to green. The grafted cultivars like 'Bloodgood' maintain a steady burgundy color throughout the growing season. The Japanese maple captures the essence of fall color with a brilliance that is unparalleled by other small deciduous trees. The slow-growing threadleaf varieties are the "Rolls Royce" of maples. Though somewhat pricey, a lacy-leaf 'Crimson Queen' is worth every penny. Shop the nurseries in August when true leaf color can be assessed.

Bloom Period and Seasonal Color
Red foliage, spring through fall.

Mature Height × Spread
4 to 30 ft. (depending on cultivar) × 6 to 20 ft.

Lacebark Elm
Ulmus parvifolia

In the mid-1990s, seventy promising tree varieties were planted at fifteen locations across North Carolina as part of an Urban Tree Evaluation program. Emerging from the five-year study with a stellar performance was the lacebark elm. This medium-sized tree with small, lustrous green leaves has an upright-spreading form reminiscent of the American elms that once lined the streets in major cities. Lacebark elm is, however, resistant to the fatal Dutch elm disease that destroyed many of our stately American elms. It is a versatile species suited to home or municipal plantings. The trunk of mature specimens has an interesting bark pattern formed as small chips flake away to reveal rusty brown patches. Lacebark elm is destined to be a major player in the twenty-first century. However, this tree drops plenty of seeds; you'll either be picking them up, pulling up seedlings, or mowing them down.

Bloom Period and Seasonal Color
Inconspicuous flowers in spring; yellowish or reddish-purple foliage in fall.

Mature Height × Spread
40 to 50 ft. × 40 to 50 ft.

When, Where, and How to Plant
Plant a container-grown tree any season the soil is workable and the tree can be irrigated. A balled-and-burlapped tree should be planted during the dormant season. Lacebark elm is easily transplanted and adapts to extremes in pH and soil type. The best growth is achieved in moist, well-drained, fertile soil. A sunny location provides the best site, though a half-day of morning shade is acceptable.

Growing Tips
Watering is important during the first two summers to keep a young tree healthy. Irrigate deeply every ten days when the weather is hot and dry. Don't let the new foliage wilt. Fertilize the second spring with 12-4-8 analysis or a slow-release fertilizer. Fertilize thereafter as needed for good growth, and reapply mulch to replenish the area over the root zone.

Care
Lacebark elm is a low-maintenance tree with no serious pests. Flat greenish-white seeds the diameter of garden peas are borne in clusters by late summer. These may self-sow in mulched beds. This could be a minor inconvenience, but they are easily removed by hand. (Share the offspring with a friend.) This tree endures urban soil and grime extremely well. All elms sustain branch damage in ice storms. Avoid injury from mowers and weed eaters; canker disease can invade wounds and kill young trees.

Landscape Merit
Lacebark elm makes a fine specimen shade tree and can be planted in groups for screening. While it is intended as a replacement for native American elms, lacebark elm has a distinctive appearance due to its small leaves and broad crown. It is fast becoming a staple street tree since its leaves do not scorch during extended dry weather.

Our Personal Favorites
Paired plantings of the cultivar 'Allee' are found in commercial plantings throughout the Piedmont. Also, 'Athena' has been widely publicized. The most cold-hardy variety for Zone 6 is 'Dynasty'.

Leyland Cypress
Cupressocyparis × leylandii

When, Where, and How to Plant

Plant in early spring or late fall to avoid cold damage to foliage. Grow in well-drained soils in full, open sun. Partial shade is acceptable provided there is strong afternoon sun. Shady locations cause leylands to become top heavy and more likely to topple in windstorms. Stake a leyland cypress taller than 5 feet on the windward side; this is crucial on banks or other windy locations. When used for hedges, space leyland cypress 5 to 6 feet apart and plan to remove every other tree when their branch tips begin to touch. Topping results in coyote-ugly trees, but if you need them to screen an even uglier neighborhood scene, you can tolerate the decapitation.

Growing Tips

Leylands prefers moist soil, so water diligently, especially in the first summer. Fertilize the second spring after planting; apply a slow-release fertilizer in September to increase the growth rate. It is common to have interior foliage turn brown and drop as new growth appears.

Care

Leyland cypress can be topped or pruned moderately in late winter or spring. Do not remove more than $1/3$ of the foliage in any one season. Shear hedges to manage plant height, but for most plantings, just leave them alone and remove them when they look unsightly. Horticulturists are concerned about cypress canker; the fatal disease begins with the sudden death of a lower branch (see page 255 for more about cypress disease prevention and remedies). Keep an eye out for bagworms; their presence can be life-threatening to leylands.

Landscape Merit

It is a beautiful evergreen for commercial hedges and for tall screens used as a sound barrier by a noisy street. It is most preferred as a specimen plant that can be enjoyed for its soft, rich foliage. Don't overuse leyland cypress! Consider mixed evergreen plantings to add diversity to your garden.

Our Personal Favorites

Enjoy the more colorful, compact forms of 'Monca' and 'Irish Mint'.

In urban counties across the Carolinas, leyland cypress has become a household word. Few conifers grow so vigorously when planted as a privacy screen. It has a columnar form similar to our native red cedars, but a softer, more pleasing appearance. Leyland cypress is a hybrid of two Pacific Coast species, Monterey cypress and Alaska cedar. It was introduced to North Carolina in the mid-1970s and was an immediate hit with nurserymen who needed a hedge-plant alternative to our ailing redtip photinias. Once established, leylands can grow three feet each year and eventually become very large trees—much too large for yards. Leyland cypress is experiencing a rash of problems brought on by disease and insect pests. One concern is long-term survival and subsequent maintenance issues. Oh, the perils of overplanting!

Bloom Period and Seasonal Color
Flowers are generally absent on these hybrids that keep green foliage year round.

Mature Height × Spread
50 to 80 ft. × 8 to 12 ft.

Live Oak

Quercus virginiana

This signature evergreen tree of coastal counties has horizontal branches often festooned with Spanish moss and resurrection ferns. Near the coast, as with the above tree at Middleton Place in Charleston, the limbs of older trees are so long and heavy that they descend to touch the ground; but in the lower Piedmont, old live oaks form a dense canopy, broader than tall. Live oaks usually remain sound until a great age, unlike some of the faster growing oak species. Before you plant, be aware that within an average life span this tree will have time to grow huge and will change the appearance of your landscape like no other tree. Literally, it will define your home to such a degree that neighbors will point out your place as "the home with the big live oak in the yard."

Bloom Period and Seasonal Color
Winter, when other plants drop their leaves, is when live oaks show off brilliant fall colors

Mature Height × Spread
100 × 100 ft., often shorter and broader. Don't plant in small yards.

When, Where, and How to Plant
Oaks are relatively difficult to transplant. If you can find a live oak nearby, ask for acorns and plant them in the ground or in 1-gallon containers as soon as they ripen. If grown in containers, they'll need transplanting to a permanent site the following spring. If dealing with a started tree, be sure to prune off girdling roots. Container-grown trees can be transplanted at any time but fall and winter are best.

Growing Tips
Keep string trimmers away from young trees and mulch around them to prevent grass from competing. Don't attempt to train your tree. It will probably lean and branch unpredictably, which will add to its charm. Water transplanted trees twice weekly for a month, then weekly thereafter. The small, spoon-shaped leaves of live oak drop gradually each winter and are replaced by glossy new foliage.

Care
One way to reduce a live oak's need for care is to plant seedlings from trees that have prospered in your area for several generations. This is important all over the Carolinas, but especially in the Piedmont where tolerance to winter cold and clay soil is critical. Oak wilt can affect live oaks. Chestnut blight can also be a problem on oaks near the coast; call in a certified arborist at the first sign of decline. Don't permit tree trimmers to touch your tree; who knows where their saws have been.

Landscape Merit
No need for a supporting cast. A live oak is a show in itself. Azaleas thrive beneath its drip line if not too close to the trunk. Inject color into the picture by hanging baskets of variegated foliage plants out near branch ends. Darlington and water oaks can be planted in Zone 7 for the same look as live oak but better cold hardiness.

Our Personal Favorites
Any adapted live oak will do. They are always grown from seeds, and variability is inescapable. In southern talk, "You pays your money and you takes your chances."

Longleaf Pine

Pinus palustris

When, Where, and How to Plant

Plant container-grown longleaf pines or loblolly pines any time soil conditions allow. Position pine trees 75 to 100 feet from your home; a hurricane or strong wind following a soaking rain can knock them over. Bare-root seedlings may be available for planting woodlots. Plant seedlings immediately upon receipt, or heel them in and plant in very early spring. When planting a row, space the trees 20 to 25 feet apart unless a wind or privacy screen is desired.

Growing Tips

Water weekly until the tree is firmly established. On a dry, sandy planting site, water more often during the first growing season. Seedlings planted in quantity have to get by on rainfall. Ninety percent survival is typical. If trees lack normal color in summer, feed young trees with controlled-release fertilizer in spring before new shoots begin to form. (Results may not show for months.) Broadcast the fertilizer at the drip line and several feet beyond. After a few seasons, these trees rarely need fertilizing, which can produce weak growth.

Care

Stake trees that are over 6 feet in height to prevent wind from uprooting them. Prune any time except when new growth is developing—wait until new candle shoots harden-off. Longleaf pine can be limbed up to allow planting under the canopy, but don't cut the leader or a distorted tree will result. The large cones are a nuisance when the trees are planted in a lawn, but they are easy enough to gather for disposal or use in crafts. Sometimes the pine beetle attacks trees. Promptly remove any trees infested with bark beetles.

Landscape Merit

Plant Southern Indica azaleas in the shade of longleaf pines. Longleaf seedlings resemble clumps of ornamental grass. Groupings create a fine screen, and single trees are quite handsome. Japanese black pine and mugo pine offer variety for Carolina gardens that lack space for the larger species.

Our Personal Favorite

Improved seedling selections are available at most coastal nurseries.

Let's hear it for longleaf pine, the North Carolina state tree and one of the most distinctive Southern pines. It is appreciated most for its twelve-inch needles that provide the marvelous mulching material we southerners call pine straw. As the tree approaches twenty years in age, the coarse, scaly bark becomes a prominent feature; the mature trunk shows off rough plates of bark. In sandy coastal soils, this beautiful tree produces a deep taproot with well-developed laterals and will survive flooded soils. In Piedmont clay soils, longleaf pine has relatively shallow roots like other shade trees and can topple in high winds. Ice storms are longleaf pine's biggest threat. Healthy pines are fine shade trees, adding both beauty and winter interest.

Bloom Period and Seasonal Color
Lush green needles in spring; huge cones drop by winter.

Mature Height × Spread
80 ft. × 25 to 40 ft.

Red Buckeye
Aesculus pavia

Red buckeye is a Carolina native worth acquiring. Some landscape plants have to be pampered after they are established, but this small tree does not. The red buckeye is always a pleasure to behold during spring bloom with clusters of red flowers standing erect like a candelabrum. It is a small, open-growing tree with a tropical look. Small, glossy, brown nuts called "buckeyes" ripen in October. Though the buckeyes are poisonous, the Native Americans used to soak and grind them for flour meal. Another interesting member of the family is the bottlebrush buckeye, Aesculus parviflora. It is a widespreading shrub that produces long, showy, white flower panicles. Both of these buckeyes are terrific low-maintenance ornamentals for landscapes across the Carolinas, and both attract butterflies, particularly swallowtails.

Bloom Period and Seasonal Color
Clusters of red tubular blooms in April and May.

Mature Height × Spread
15 to 25 ft. × 20 ft.

When, Where, and How to Plant
Plant red buckeye in the dormant season; the nuts can be planted in late fall. Even container-grown plants will occasionally die if transplanted soon after they leaf out in spring. Red buckeye is best situated as a specimen tree. It will have better looking foliage where the soil is moist or where it will enjoy part shade, perhaps on the edge of a forest where the roots can enjoy a humus-rich soil that drains well. Do not disturb the roots of container-grown plants unless the plants are heavily rooted or potbound. Position the rootball slightly higher than grade. Firm the soil around the rootball. Water well to settle the soil. Mulch with leaf compost or aged hardwood mulch.

Growing Tips
Water weekly for the first month and regularly in dry periods during the first summer. Keep newly planted specimens well watered the first growing season, with weekly irrigations again during late summer. Buckeyes are quite drought tolerant once established, but expect some non-life-threatening leaf scorch or defoliation in very dry periods. Apply slow-release fertilizer every four years if the leaf color is abnormal due to nutrient deficiencies.

Care
Water weekly for the first month, and regularly during dry periods the first summer. Few native trees are as adaptable or as pest free as red buckeye. Pruning is usually not necessary unless desired for cosmetic reasons. In woodland plantings, wrap a foot-long strip of hardware cloth around the lower trunk to protect the tree from rabbits and voles. The nuts of buckeyes are reported to be poisonous and should not be eaten, so keep this in mind if young children play in your garden.

Landscape Merit
Plant red buckeye in front of an evergreen hedge or in a border of rhododendrons. This native is right at home in a woodland garden as an understory tree.

Our Personal Favorite
For nice fall foliage, plant *A. parviflora* 'Rogers' in groupings.

Redbud

Cercis canadensis

When, Where, and How to Plant

Transplant seedlings during the dormant season before the buds swell. Plant container-grown trees in spring or fall. Redbuds grow in moist soils from clay to loam, and in light shade to full sun. They are at home on the fringes of a woodland garden where they are protected from the afternoon sun. Though they are fairly adaptable, avoid water-logged locations. Pack backfill firmly around the sides of the rootball. Water well, then cover the exposed roots with a 3- to 4-inch layer of mulch.

Growing Tips

Water twice weekly for the first six weeks and, after that, during prolonged dry weather. As long as the leaves are a rich green color, do not be concerned about fertilizing. Redbuds are legumes and extract nitrogen from the air with the help of beneficial soil organisms. They form hundreds of seedpods which drop and release seeds. Seedlings by the score follow; discourage them by stirring the mulch or adding a layer.

Care

In the spring following the first full growing season, apply a slow-release fertilizer under the dripline at an estimated rate of 1 cup per 10 square feet. Do not fertilize for another two or three years. Redbud adapts with little care. Prune wild shoots arising from the trunk, and to shape the young tree. On occasion, a fungal twig dieback may occur; prune out the individual branch promptly. There are no serious pests, but the tree is short-lived.

Landscape Merit

A backdrop of evergreens helps the redbud's magenta flowers to leap out visually. With a height to 25 feet, redbud is recommended as a good choice for planting under power lines. Consider planting a specimen, such as the Chinese redbud or the weeping Texas cultivar 'Traveler'.

Our Personal Favorites

'Forest Pansy' is the rage because of its burgundy spring leaves. 'Appalachian Red', which has rosy-colored blooms, and 'Alba', with white flowers, are also special.

Redbuds in full bloom are among the most striking sights of spring. With flowering dogwoods growing alongside them, what a sight! Redbud's magenta or white pea-like flowers herald the arrival of spring and often burst into bloom slightly before dogwood. This small, vase-shaped tree forms a dense, round canopy of heart-shaped leaves by early summer. 'Forest Pansy' gets high marks for its burgundy spring foliage. When limbed up, redbud creates a marvelous oasis for outdoor lounging when you want to be shielded from the summer sun. Multi-trunk specimens of the outstanding Cercis reniformis 'Oklahoma' roundleaf redbud are real show-stoppers; this species is rated higher than the Eastern redbud by some authorities. The J. C. Raulston Arboretum in Raleigh has the largest collection of redbuds in the world.

Bloom Period and Seasonal Color
Spring blooms in lavender, magenta, or white.

Mature Height × Spread
25 ft. × 20 to 30 ft.

Red Maple
Acer rubrum

Red maple is the star of southern maples. This native tree reaches a mature height in a relatively short period of time. Its strong, upright growth habit and broad spreading crown make red maple a near-perfect shade tree for suburban landscapes. Its striking gray bark and medium-sized, three-lobed leaves with red petioles makes it easy to identify in our forests. Place red maple as a specimen tree where there is ample room, certainly not closer than twenty feet from the house. Homeowners with smaller yards can use the columnar and compact forms such as 'Armstrong'. The latest introductions include exquisite cultivars, such as 'October Glory', with lustrous crimson leaves that hold later than those of most maples.

Bloom Period and Seasonal Color
Brilliant red or orange fall foliage; distinctive red flowers in very early spring on some cultivars.

Mature Height × Spread
50 to 60 ft. × 50 ft.

When, Where, and How to Plant
Red maple trees are available as both container-grown and balled-and-burlapped specimens. Plant balled-and-burlapped trees in winter or early spring if they are heeled in and irrigated properly. Plant container-grown trees any time the soil can be prepared. Red maple grows in a wide range of soil conditions but performs best in moist locations in full sun or light shade. Stake it if you have planted it in a windy location or if it is quite large. Mulch with 3 to 4 inches of leaf compost or aged hardwood. Maple's shallow root systems may "heave up" walks and driveway pavement. It is difficult to garden under red maples due to exposed roots and heavy shade

Growing Tips
There are few challenges in getting red maples to grow other than summer and fall irrigation. Water regularly during the growing season for the first two years, using a soaker hose or a slow trickle from the garden hose for at least thirty minutes. For the first two months, irrigate twice a week; after that, every ten days. Fertilize your tree every three years in March or November. Prune during the late summer months.

Care
Try to develop a strong framework with a single trunk and branches growing perpendicular to the trunk. As the tree matures, remove weak branches and limbs or leaders with narrow crotches at the trunk. Prune during the summer if possible. Pruning while the trees are dormant is also acceptable, but the trees may bleed sap profusely. Ignore chronic leaf spots if they appear.

Landscape Merit
Some use red maple in an allée to line a driveway. Plant it as a specimen to frame a house or on large lots in groups of 3 to 5 trees, spaced 30 feet apart, to make a shaded grove with fall color impact.

Our Personal Favorites
Pyramid-shaped 'Red Sunset' has wonderful orange-red fall color. 'Summer Red' produces red leaves on new growth with persistent color in cooler climates.

Red Oak
Quercus rubra

When, Where, and How to Plant

Plant red oak in winter from containers or as acorns. The absence of a taproot makes transplanting easier, especially with smaller trees. When transplanting, leave $^1/_3$ of the rootball above grade and backfill up to the former soil line. Leaving several inches above ground helps avoid drainage problems after the tree settles (see page 221). Red oak adapts to a range of environmental conditions and tolerates moist clay soils as well as dry areas. It prefers slightly acidic (pH 5.5 to 6.5) loamy soils and full sun. Stake larger specimens for six months. Water deeply at planting and mulch 3 to 4 inches deep out to the drip line.

Growing Tips

Water deeply every ten days the first growing season. Red oak can be fertilized any time in late winter to early spring after it is established. It is best to have the soil tested prior to fertilization. If possible, allow leaves to accumulate under the tree.

Care

Red oak has few pest problems but is subject to oak wilt. Do not prune young trees except to remove narrow angled branches and broken twigs. Prune trees with double leaders (twin trunks) to one central leader. Protect existing oaks during construction projects so that soil is not compacted beneath them or piled over the root system. Drive steel fence posts around the drip line and have the bulldozer operator sign an agreement that he will honor the off-limits area. Old, weak trees are best removed since they are subject to windfall.

Landscape Merit

Red oaks are good choices for urban landscapes such as homes, parks, streets, and commercial sites. Their height allows for shrub underplantings. Plant them well away from structures.

Our Personal Favorites

Both Southern and Northern lines of red oaks grow well from seedlings. Shumard oak, *Q. shumardii*, is attractive and durable. The most popular variety for fall color and rapid growth is the pin oak, *Q. palustris*. Clemson horticulturists rate English oak as outstanding.

Red oak is an excellent landscape tree that grows rapidly and tolerates urban conditions well. It is not uncommon for a properly planted red oak to add two feet in height in a year. These trees mature into symmetrical specimens with rounded crowns, adding a majestic touch to any landscape planting. Tender reddish buds open up in spring. During the summer months, the large pointed leaves of the foliage are a lustrous dark green, but they change to a deep red in autumn. In older trees, the black, deeply fissured bark adds texture to the landscape. Many older neighborhoods have mature white oak trees that are in stages of decline due to old age and urban stress. The rapid-growing red oak makes a good replacement.

Bloom Period and Seasonal Color
Red buds in spring; red foliage in late fall.

Mature Height × Spread
75 ft. × 35 ft.

River Birch

Betula nigra

Many people think river birch needs a wet site to flourish, but if you allow enough space for this beautiful native tree, you can enjoy its marvelous features practically anywhere in the home landscape. 'Heritage'®, a cultivar that will tolerate our summer heat, loses tattered bark in slabs to reveal peach-colored inner bark. However, hot, windy locations may cause summer leaves to drop. 'Dura-Heat'®, a vigorous grower, has better retention of its rough-textured, dark green leaves. Most birch trees are grown as multi-trunked specimens whose exfoliating bark looks especially nice in the winter landscape. Allow a few growing seasons for peak bark color. Don't waste your time trying to grow northern white birch in the Carolinas, it thrives in cooler climes to the north.

Bloom Period and Seasonal Color
Non-showy brownish catkins and yellow fall foliage; year-round peeling bark.

Mature Height × Spread
40 ft. × 28 ft.

When, Where, and How to Plant

Plant container-grown birches anytime but summer. Small specimens establish quickly and frequently outgrow larger trees in a few years. Plant at least 25 feet from a structure or patio. Provide a moist site with at least a half-day of sun. No soil amendment is necessary. After planting, water at a slow trickle for twenty minutes, or pour 5 gallons of water from a bucket. Layer with 3 to 4 inches of mulch to the drip line. Birches' shallow, exposed roots can hinder mowing a lawn or be in danger near septic fields.

Growing Tips

Water newly planted trees twice the first week, then weekly thereafter for ten weeks. Water during dry periods to avoid heavy leaf drop. In deep, rich soils, fertilizer is not necessary during establishment. In other soils, fertilize every three or four years to keep lush green foliage. Scatter 10-10-10 fertilizer or use fertilizer spikes at the drip line. After the tree reaches desired height, stop fertilizing except for maintenance applications. Young trees grow fast after the second season.

Care

In summer, remove suckers at the base of the trunk. Prune in late summer since the cuts will close quickly. "Limb up" the trees to maintain easy passage under foliage. Unlike white birch, river birch does not have problems with bronze-birch borers. Control aphids if heavy leaf drop occurs. Ice storms are the enemy of their brittle wood. Note: pollen and seed drop occur for a few weeks in spring. Be prepared to remove seedlings in mulched beds.

Landscape Merit

The graceful branching habit of river birch is most appealing in natural areas and informal settings such as a courtyard. Plant for winter interest. Use along the perimeter of your property in beds of ground covers and low growing, shade tolerant evergreens.

Our Personal Favorite

'Dura-Heat' is an improvement over the standard 'Heritage' river birch for dry areas. Seedling river birches seldom show the attractive peeling of bark featured by improved cultivars.

Sabal Palmetto

Sabal palmetto

When, Where, and How to Plant

Plant container-grown plants in late spring or summer. They transplant easily from May to July in Zones 7 and 8. Give a palmetto plenty of space and a sunny location. It tolerates a variety of soil from clay to sand, and it loves moisture. Using a handheld cultivator, carefully loosen the roots of plants grown in pots. Work plenty of aged compost into the planting hole, especially in heavy soils or pure sand. Keep the roots moist during establishment, and mulch well. Palmetto is marginally hardy in the foothills region of the Carolinas.

Growing Tips

Keep palmetto well watered the first two summers until established; it will benefit from drip irrigation in dry summer weather. Fertilize every few years with a slow-release plant food. Spread mulch 3 to 4 inches deep in a circle around specimen palmettos.

Care

Old leaves deteriorate and stems should be sawed off close to the trunk. In Zones 7 and 8a, deep winter mulch applied within the drip line area will increase survival of seedlings during harsh winters. To protect young plants, place a 2-foot-high cylinder of welded wire fencing around them and fill it with leaves or pine straw; remove it in March. Pest problems are minimal, but palmetto weevil and palm leaf skeletonizer may warrant some control. Extremely cold winters sometimes cause leafburn.

Landscape Merit

Tolerant of salt spray, palmetto is an excellent street tree or specimen plant for the seaside. Use it as a tropical accent in a patio or terrace garden where it will create interesting shadow patterns against walls. Sabal palmetto is a different species from the low, spreading saw palmetto of coastal swamps.

Our Personal Favorite

Carolinians may wish to celebrate the part played by palmettos during Revolutionary War battles. Its durable trunks were used to absorb cannon fire. The trunk-forming windmill palm, *Trachycarpus fortunei*, is graceful and cold-hardy to 0 degrees Fahrenheit.

This Southeastern native is one of the hardiest palm species known. Once established, it can withstand temperatures of 10 degrees Fahrenheit. Palmetto is known by its straight or slightly curved single trunk covered with persistent leaf bases and fan-shaped foliage. Palmettos are seldom seen in Piedmont landscapes because the fronds can freeze back, though they typically recover. Juvenile palmettos resemble shrubs, but they can be expected to grow to a height of 30 feet or more. Dwarf palmettos (S. minor) are very hardy even into Piedmont North Carolina; their blue-green foliage adds a tropical look to landscapes. Another interesting compact palm is the very hardy needle palm, Rhapidophyllum hystrix. Jim reports seeing it as far west as Anderson, S.C. Both will adapt to the drier soils found across the Carolinas.

Other Common Name
Cabbage Palm

Bloom Period and Seasonal Color
Large clusters of tiny flowers at maturity.

Mature Height × Spread
20 to 50 ft. × 6 to 10 ft.

Saucer Magnolia
Magnolia × soulangiana

Saucer magnolias have one major flaw: they don't stay in bloom long enough. When they are at the zenith of their early spring glory, they create a magnificent spectacle, and gardeners rush to nurseries in search of this large-flowered beauty. The latest introductions are quite floriferous and flower sporadically throughout the growing season, especially with adequate rainfall. During the primary bloom period, the six-inch white or pinkish-purple fleshy flowers burst open before leaves emerge. Unlike the evergreen Southern magnolia, the coarse-textured leaves of saucer magnolia do not litter the landscape. Multi-trunk specimens have smooth gray bark and make outstanding garden accents. The best thing about this hardy magnolia is that recent cultivars such as 'Verbanica' and 'Brozzoni' require very little work to stay in full splendor.

Other Common Name
Tulip Magnolia

Bloom Period and Seasonal Color
White, and pink to purplish flowers in early spring.

Mature Height × Spread
35 ft. × 12 to 20 ft.

When, Where, and How to Plant

Saucer magnolia may be planted from containers anytime from late winter to fall. Plant balled-and-burlapped trees while they are dormant. Grow in partial shade or full sun. Moist soil will ensure strong, rapid growth. Trees that are planted in sheltered sites often escape late-spring frosts that periodically spoil the floral display. Thoroughly loosen the roots of plants grown in pots. Prepare a wide, shallow hole 3/4 as deep and 3 times as wide as the rootball. Firm soil conditioned with equal parts conditioner around the rootball. Water slowly, applying 5 gallons of water to settle the plant. Add 3 to 4 inches of mulch, keeping it away from the crown of the plant. Water every three days for three weeks. Avoid planting when the soil is frozen or when the soil is too wet to work.

Growing Tips

Irrigate saucer magnolias routinely during the summer and fall months until established. Flower buds form during the summer, and letting the trees go dry can affect next year's bloom. Apply a slow-release fertilizer in the spring after flowering commences, as directed by soil tests.

Care

Train single-trunk specimens in order to develop a strong framework of scaffold branches. Prune saucer magnolias while they are young and keep the basal suckers removed. Any cold-damaged twigs should be pruned off. Multiple-trunk specimens can be limbed up in summer or immediately following bloom. Leaf spots can occur during mild, wet springs. Caution: spent flower petals that drop onto walks can be slippery.

Landscape Merit

Saucer magnolia is spectacular in a courtyard or patio garden. It offers seasonal interest with its smooth gray bark that contrasts with the dark green foliage and ostentatious flowers. Saucer magnolias will grow large enough to provide appreciable shade. Underplant with ground covers or small perennials, such as dianthus.

Our Personal Favorites

'Jane', a late-flowering hybrid and a repeat-bloomer, and the 'Little Girl' hybrids are best for Zones 6 to 7.

Snowbell
Styrax japonica

When, Where, and How to Plant

Plant snowbell in morning sun or filtered shade, especially in Zone 8 gardens. This tree prefers a moist, acidic, well-drained soil; spade in copious amounts of organic matter or leaf compost with sandy soils; don't add limestone to the planting hole. Container-grown trees can be planted any time they can be kept watered, but preferably before summer weather begins. Water thoroughly immediately after planting, and weekly as needed for two months.

Growing Tips

Snowbell may be slow to establish, but after the first year it will do well with little attention if sited properly. It is important to water the tree in summer during the early years and routinely during periods of drought in subsequent seasons. Apply a slow-release or organic fertilizer in spring every few years. Keep your tree mulched with 3 to 4 inches of organic mulch for moisture retention. Do little pruning until its natural form develops.

Care

This tree has relatively small foliage, and plants growing around it do well in the filtered light cast on the ground. Never remove more than one quarter of the growth when thinning. Once established, it is practically carefree. It has been reported that some *Styrax* species are borer-prone; ambrosia beetle is the culprit. Check with the County Cooperative Extension Office for a recommended borer treatment. Diseases are not a problem. However, planting too deeply in poorly drained clay soil can spell trouble if you overwater.

Landscape Merit

Snowbell is a choice specimen tree for small properties or courtyard gardens where the delicate bell-shaped flowers can be appreciated. Its gray, smooth bark and wide spreading branches are set off well with a background of evergreen shrubs. Good companions are shade perennials, azaleas, and hydrangea.

Our Personal Favorites

'Emerald Pagoda' with its large, fragrant flowers is delightful. In mountain regions, plant the cold hardy fragrant snowbell, *S. obassia*. Jim reports success with the native *Styrax americanus* in his Piedmont garden.

One of the great discoveries by the late Dr. J. C. Raulston while on a plant collecting expedition to Korea was the *Styrax japonica* cultivar 'Emerald Pagoda' ('Sohuksan'). His glowing description says it all, "a fantastic, phenomenal, unparalleled small flowering tree." This tree has thick, emerald leaves and pendent, bell shaped, white-tinged-pink fragrant flowers in May. Though relatively unknown by most gardeners, snowbell is now showing up at most full-service garden centers. Its compact form and tolerance of shade give it an edge over many noteworthy candidates. While plantings of the common *Styrax* species have languished in the warmer Carolina climes, the Japanese snowbell has flourished. It is worthy of planting where it can be appreciated close up during its rather short blooming season in spring.

Other Names

Japanese Snowbell, Storax

Bloom Period and Seasonal Color

Pinkish-white flowers in May; yellow foliage in fall.

Mature Height × Spread

30 ft. × 30 ft.

Southern Magnolia
Magnolia grandiflora

Southern magnolia is a champion among fine evergreen trees. In the Carolinas, magnolias are valued for their large, shiny green leaves and ten-inch, creamy white flowers. The sweet fragrance of magnolia blossoms has long inspired songwriters. The large conical southern magnolia grows wild from the coastal counties through the Piedmont and well into the mountains. Most urban landscapes are too small for this big tree. For small yards, sweetbay magnolia, a much smaller tree, is a better choice. Many homeowners choose 'Little Gem' southern magnolia, thinking it is a dwarf shrub form—and it is not! It eventually grows into a mid-sized tree. It is precocious and blooms soon after planting. Hand-size flowers may appear again by September. The leaves and seedpods of magnolias are great for holiday decorations and quick down-home arrangements.

Bloom Period and Seasonal Color
Creamy white blossoms in late spring.

Mature Height × Spread
40 to 70 ft. × 20 to 50 ft.; 'Little Gem' is more compact.

When, Where, and How to Plant
Southern magnolia's fleshy roots make it sensitive to cold or dry conditions. Plant container-grown trees in late winter or spring or later. The foliage looks better when grown in partial shade. It grows naturally in rich, moist soil along river swamps or in deep woods, though it will tolerate drier sites. It thrives in high-organic soils with moderate fertility and a pH of 4 to 6. Break out the cottonseed meal and enrich the ground before planting. Spade in amendments, or till an area 4 to 5 times larger than the rootball (see page 221). Judge when and how much water you should apply; if it droops or turns color, you certainly irrigate.

Growing Tips
Water well during the first two seasons. Mulches and soaker hoses perform wonders. This tree likes organic fertilizers applied at the drip line in spring. Some landscapers mix equal parts by volume of cottonseed meal and 10-10-10 analysis fertilizer. Use 1 pound per inch of trunk diameter.

Care
Expect burned foliage after hard winters. Selectively prune overgrown trees in March and August. Prune back to make a bushier tree, or train a young magnolia for a full pyramidal shape. Allow lower branches to sweep the ground and hide the leaves and seedpods this tree drops. Leaf spots may appear if the tree is stressed by drought.

Landscape Merit
Stately southern magnolias add a feeling of grandeur to an estate. On a typical subdivision lot, plant the smaller 'Little Gem' as a specimen tree or a backdrop for small airy ornamentals such as butterfly bush, loropetalum, smoke tree, and Japanese maple.

Our Personal Favorites
The fabulous 'Bracken's Brown Beauty' is a small, dense, upright cultivar. 'Overton' reportedly matures at an even smaller size than 'Little Gem'. For mountain landscapes, check with the North Carolina Arboretum at Asheville for southern magnolias that are reliable at higher elevations. Or, look up the columnar sweetbay magnolia, *M. virginiana*, named 'Jim Wilson'. Honestly!

Zelkova

Zelkova serrata

When, Where, and How to Plant

Zelkova trees in 2-inch trunk calipers are available at garden centers in large containers. Check for girdling roots and free up the major roots. Plant zelkova when the ground is workable in fall or spring, certainly by May. Balled-and-burlapped trees are available during their dormant season, January through March. For maximum growth, plant in moist, deep soil and in sun or partial shade. Follow soil-test recommendations for new homesites. Zelkova's performance depends on its successful transplanting. If zelkova is planted properly, it will grow well with little care.

Growing Tips

Watering during the first two growing seasons is a must if the summers are dry. A soaker hose is a good investment. Decline of plantings can be related to poorly drained soils. In late September, apply fertilizer to help build a stronger root system, but fertilization is not necessary every year. Maintain a mulch ring out to the outermost branches. This discourages weeds and protects the thin-barked tree from weed-eater or mower injury. Don't heap mulch up on the trunk.

Care

Expect your zelkova to send out many branches from a short area on the trunk. Where these would lead to breakage in Bradford pears, the wood of zelkova is so tough that you needn't worry. Light pruning of weak twigs is important as the main scaffold limbs develop. Japanese beetles are occasional zelkova pests in the Carolinas—but even if you don't spray, beetle injury is of minor importance. Elm bark beetles may also show up but seldom cause the fatal Dutch elm disease.

Landscape Merit

Plant this specimen tree by a deck or patio to create the perfect place to enjoy a cold drink in the summer. Shade the southeast or southwest roof with Japanese zelkova and save a bundle on your power bill.

Our Personal Favorite

'Village Green' turns rusty red in the fall and is vigorous.

The new homebuyer would be well advised to plant a zelkova for fast shade and natural cooling. This large deciduous beauty grows to seventy feet, big enough to thwart the hot afternoon sun. First introduced as a replacement for the disappearing American elm, zelkova has moved from an urban street tree to suburban backyards. Its foliage closely resembles that of Chinese elm with its pointed tips and serrated leaf margins. What it lacks in fall color, zelkova balances with its rich green foliage, sturdy stature and its tough wood that resists damage from ice and wind storms. This wonderful care-free shade tree is a rapid grower and will reward you with two or more feet in height each season. Once established, your prized zelkova will do just fine in drier weather.

Other Common Name

Japanese Zelkova

Bloom Period and Seasonal Color

Dark green leaves in summer; yellowish-bronze to red fall foliage.

Mature Height × Spread

70 ft. × 50 to 60 ft.

Enviro Tips

For Safety and Success, Read the Label!

For many of us, it has become second nature to read the nutrition label before tossing anything into the grocery cart, but do you exercise the same care with garden chemicals? Fact is, pesticide labels are packed with great information that will not only keep you safe but will also help you get better results in the yard and garden.

The first thing to check is the signal word, which will be "Caution," "Warning," or "Danger" listed here in order of increasing toxicity. If you have a choice, select a product with a "Caution" label. And since garden chemicals aren't cheap, be sure you're getting the right product for the job. Read the label carefully to make sure that the insect, weed or disease problem will actually be controlled by the product. But that's only half the story. Be sure that it's safe to use on the plants. That lawn herbicide may work great on dandelions, but spray it on your flower or vegetable garden and you'll regret it!

When you are ready to apply, it's time for another close look at the label. The important questions are how to apply it and what kind of safety precautions to take. Follow the instructions carefully for the benefit of you, your family, your pets, and your plants. Become a label reader, and you'll be a safer, smarter, and more successful gardener.

Caring for Your Lawn and the Environment

Reduce runoff and trap pollutants with a healthy lawn! Use care when gardening so that you protect streams, rivers, lakes, estuaries, and coastal waters.

Fertilizer Facts

Fertilizer labels always display three numbers in the same order, (i.e., 10-6-4). These numbers represent the percent by weight of three important nutrients:

Nitrogen (N) – for green, leafy growth.

Phosphorus (P) – for root and bud growth.

Potassium (K) – promotes disease tolerance and drought tolerance.

Example: A 40-pound bag of 10-6-4 fertilizer is 10 percent nitrogen (4 pounds of N), 6 percent phosphate (2.4 pounds of P), and 4 percent potassium (1.6 pounds of K).

Fertilizer Rates

A typical lawn feeding is 1 pound of nitrogen per 1,000 square feet. Here are some common lawn fertilizer formulations and the amount of each needed to obtain 1 pound of nitrogen.

Fertilizer bag reads:	Amount needed for 1 pound of nitrogen*:
6-2-0	17 pounds
10-10-10	10 pounds
14-3-6	7 pounds
20-5-5	5 pounds
26-3-4	4 pounds
35-3-5	3 pounds

*Rounded to nearest pound

For other formulations, follow this example using a fertilizer labeled 24-6-6:

- The first number is the percent of nitrogen: Ñ 24%
- To find out how much total product it takes to apply 1 pound of nitrogen, divide the 1 pound by .24
- 1 divided by .24 equals 4.17. This is equal to a little more than 4 pounds of product.
- If your lawn is 5,000 square feet, multiply 4 pounds by 5. The result is 20. You would need a 20-pound bag of 24-6-6 to cover your lawn.

Nitrogen Fertilizer Guide for Lawns

Lawns need some nitrogen each year to remain dense and healthy. Many lawns will do fine with only 1 or 2 pounds of nitrogen per 1,000 square feet each year. This chart shows when and how much nitrogen to apply to your lawn, depending on the kind of grass you have.

Turf	Monthly application rates (month of application)		pounds nitrogen/ 1,000 sq. ft./yr.
Bahiagrass	1/2 (May)	1/2 (July)	1
Bermudagrass	1 (May)	1 (June)	4.0
	1 (July)	1 (Aug.)[b]	
Centipedegrass	1/2 (June)[c]		1/2
Fescue, Tall	1/2 to 1 (Feb.)	1 (Sep.)	2.5 to 3
	1 (Nov.)		
Kentucky Bluegrass	1/2 to 1 (Feb.)	1 (Sep.)	2.5 to 3
	1 (Nov.)		
Kentucky Bluegrass/ Fine Fescue	1/2 to 1 (Feb.) 1 (Nov.)	1 (Sep.)	2.5 to 3
Kentucky Bluegrass/ Tall Fescue	1/2 to 1 (Feb.) 1 (Nov.)	1 (Sep.)	2.5 to 3
Kentucky Bluegrass/ Tall Fescue/Fine Fescue	1/2 to 1 (Feb) 1 (Nov.)	1 (Sep.)	2.5 to 3
Kentucky Bluegrass/ Perennial Ryegrass	1/2 to 1 (Feb.) 1 (Nov.)	1 (Sep.)	2.5 to 3
St. Augustinegrass	1/2 (May) 1 (July)	1/2 (June) 1/2 (Aug.)[b]	2.5
Zoysiagrass	1/2 (Apr.) 1/2 (Aug.)[b]	1/2 (June)	1.5

Dates suggested are for the central Piedmont. For the west, dates may be 1 to 2 weeks later in the spring and earlier in the fall; for the east, 1 to 2 weeks earlier in the spring and later in the fall.

[b]In the absence of soil test recommendations, apply about 1 pound of potasssium per 1,000 square feet using 1.6 pounds of muriate of potassium (0-0-60), 5 pounds of potassium-magnesium sulfate (0-0-22), or 2 pounds of potassium sulfate (0-0-50) to Bermudagrass, Centipedegrass, St. Augustinegrass, and Zoysiagrass.

[c]Centipedegrass should be fertilized very lightly after establishment. An additional fertilization in August may enhance Centipedegrass performance in coastal locations. Avoid using any phosphorus on Centipedegrass after establishment.

Source: North Carolina Cooperative Extension Service.

Safe Use of Pesticides

Authors' Caution

Remember, it is a violation of state and federal laws to use any pesticide in a manner inconsistent with the label. Products mentioned in this book are used for the sole purpose of education and do not necessarily imply an endorsement. The use of pest controls must remain the choice of each individual gardener. It may not always be necessary to use pesticides to control insects or diseases. Consider the use of alternative means including resistant varieties, the use of botanical and microbial insecticides or soaps, the use of beneficial insects, mechanical means such as screening and handpicking, and improving cultural practices. If you decide to use traditional chemical pest controls, first consult your local County Cooperative Extension Service for correct pest identification and control recommendations. Once you have decided to use a specific product, you must read and follow label directions carefully.

Education on the Safe Use of Pesticides

A pesticide may be used only on the plants, animals, or sites named in the directions for use. You may not use higher dosages, high concentrations, or more frequent applications. You must follow all directions for use, including directions concerning safety, mixing, diluting, storage, and disposal. You must wear the specified personal protective equipment even though you may be risking only your own safety by not wearing it. The use directions and instructions are not advice, they are requirements.

Federal law does allow you to use pesticides in some ways not specifically mentioned in the labeling. Unless you would be in violation of the laws of your state or tribe, you may:

- apply a pesticide at any dosage, concentration, or frequency less than that listed on the labeling,
- apply a pesticide against any target pest not listed on the labeling if the application is to a plant, animal, or site that is listed,
- use any appropriate equipment or method of application that is not prohibited by the labeling,
- mix a pesticide or pesticides with a fertilizer if the mixture is not prohibited by the labeling. (Understand, however, that certain fertilizers can cause pesticides to precipitate.)
- mix two or more pesticides, if all of the dosages are at or below the recommended rate.

All pesticide labeling contains some instructions for storing the pesticide. These may include both general statements, such as "Keep out of reach of children and pets," and specific directions, such as "Do not store in temperatures below 32 degrees Fahrenheit."

Pesticide labeling also contains some general information about how to dispose of excess pesticide and the pesticide container in ways that are acceptable under Federal regulations. State and local laws vary, however, so the labeling usually does not give exact disposal instructions.

Storage and disposal statements usually appear in a special section of the labeling titled "Storage and Disposal."

root flare: The transition at the base of a tree trunk where the bark tissue begins to differentiate and roots begin to form just before entering the soil. This area should not be covered with soil when planting a tree.

self-seeding: The tendency of some plants to sow their seeds freely around the yard. It creates many seedlings the following season that may or may not be welcome.

semi-evergreen: Tending to be evergreen in a mild climate but deciduous in a rigorous one.

shade: An area of filtered light or partial darkness. Not all shade is equal; true shade-loving plants can tolerate morning sun in North Carolina conditions but wither if the shade period is reversed; dappled shade is preferred. The dry, shaded conditions under a maple are extreme compared to those under tall pines. Plants flourish in shade by a stream.

shearing: The pruning technique whereby plant stems and branches are cut uniformly with long-bladed pruning shears (hedge shears) or powered hedge trimmers. It is used when creating and maintaining hedges and topiary.

slow-release fertilizer: Fertilizer that is water-insoluble and therefore releases its nutrients gradually as a function of soil temperature, moisture, and related microbial activity. Typically granular, it may be organic or synthetic.

specimen plant: An ornamental shrub or tree used alone to create a focal point or accent in the landscape. Often, the plant has some unique features, such as showy bark, fragrant flowers, etc.

succulent growth: The sometimes undesirable production of fleshy, water-storing leaves or stems that results from overfertilization.

sucker: A new growing shoot; underground plant roots produce suckers to form new stems and spread by means of these suckering roots to form large plantings, or colonies. Some plants produce root suckers or branch suckers as a result of pruning or wounding.

supplemental irrigation: The recommended amount of water for gardens from May until September is 1 to 1¹/₂ inches per week. When rainfall is short or drought sets in, most plants benefit from watering weekly (less often for trees).

tuber: A type of underground storage structure in a plant stem, analogous to a bulb. It generates roots below and stems above ground (example: dahlia).

variegated: Having various colors or color patterns. The term usually refers to plant foliage that is streaked, edged, blotched, or mottled with a contrasting color, often green with yellow, cream, or white.

white grubs: Fat, off-white, wormlike larvae of Japanese beetles, May beetles, or June beetles. They reside in the soil and damage turf by feeding on roots until summer when they emerge as beetles to feed on plant foliage.

Public Gardens

Along the Carolina Coast

Airlie Gardens
Wilmington, NC
(910) 763-4646

Boone Hall Plantation
Mt. Pleasant, SC
(843) 884-4371

Brookgreen Gardens
Pawleys Island, SC
(800) 849-1931

Cypress Gardens
Moncks Corner, SC
(843) 553-0515

Elizabethan Gardens
Manteo, NC
(919) 473-3234

Greenfield Gardens
Wilmington, NC
(910) 341-7855

Magnolia Plantation and Gardens
Charleston, SC
(843) 571-1266

MIddleton Place
Charleston, SC
(800) 782-3608

Nancy Bryan Luce Garden
Moncks Corner, SC
(843) 761-8509

**New Hanover County Extension
Service Arboretum**
Wilmington, NC
(910) 452-6393

Orton Plantation Gardens
Wilmington, NC
(910) 371-6851

Roycroft Daylily Nursery
Georgetown, SC
(800) 950-5459

Tryon Palace and Gardens
New Bern, NC
(800) 767-1560

Of the Carolina Piedmont and Coastal Plain

Cape Fear Botanical Garden
Fayetteville, NC
(910) 486-0221

Chinqua-Penn Plantation
Reidsville, NC
(336) 349-4576

**Clemson University Sandhill Research
and Education Center**
Columbia, SC
(803) 788-5700

Daniel Stowe Botanical Garden
Belmont, NC
(704) 825-4492

Davidson College Arboretum
Davidson, NC
(704) 892-2596

De Hart Botanical Gardens
Louisburg, NC
(919) 496-4771

Edisto Memorial Gardens
Orangeburg, SC
(803) 533-6020

Fearrington Village
Pittsboro, NC
(919) 542-1145

Flora Macdonald Gardens
Red Springs, NC
(910) 843-5000

Francis Reidler Forest
Harleyville, SC
(843) 462-2150

Gardens of Greensboro
Greensboro, NC
(336) 373-2199

Hamlin Sensory Garden
Salisbury, NC
(704) 637-1881

Hatcher Gardens
Spartanburg, SC
(864) 574-7724

Hemlock Bluffs Nature Preserve
Cary, NC
(919) 387-5980

Hezeldan Alexander Homeside
Charlotte, NC
(704) 568-1774

Historic Bethabara Park Community/ Medical Gardens
Winston-Salem, NC
(336) 924-8191

Historic Mill Hill Plantation
Concord, NC
(704) 786-3900

Hopeland Gardens and Rye Patch
Aiken, SC
(803) 642-7630

Hurley Park
Salisbury, NC
(704) 638-5260

Iron Gate Gardens
Kings Mountain, NC
(704) 435-6178

JC Raulston Arboretum*
Raleigh, NC
(919) 515-3132

Kalmia Gardens of Coker College
Hartsville, SC
(843) 383-8145

Memorial Garden
Concord, NC
(704) 786-8009

Mordecai Historic Park
Raleigh, NC
(919) 834-4844

Municipal Rose Garden
Raleigh, NC
(919) 821-4579

NC Botanical Garden
Chapel Hill, NC
(919) 962-0522

NC Wesleyan College
Rocky Mount, NC
(252) 985-5100

NC Zoological Park
Asheboro, NC
(800) 488-0444

Old Salem
Winston-Salem, NC
(800) 441-5305

**Park Seed Co. Trial and
  Display Gardens***
Greenwood, SC
(803) 223-7333

**Reynolda Gardens of
  Wake Forest University***
Winston-Salem, NC
(336) 758-5593

Ribbon Walk
Charlotte, NC
(704) 365-9080

**Riverbanks Zoological Park and
  Botanical Garden**
Columbia, SC
(803) 779-8717

Robert Mills Historic House and Garden
Columbia, SC
(803) 252-1770

Rose Hill Plantation State Park
Union, SC
(803) 427-5966

Sarah P. Duke Memorial Gardens
Durham, NC
(910) 684-3698

Sandhills Horticultural Gardens
Pinehurst, NC
(910) 695-3882

SC Botanical Gardens*
Clemson, SC
(864) 656-3405

Swan Lake Iris Gardens
Sumter, SC
(803) 773-3371

Tanglewood Park & Arboretum
Clemmons, NC
(336) 778-6300

UNC-Charlotte Botanical Gardens
Charlotte, NC
(704) 547-2555

White Pines Natural Area
Raleigh, NC
(919) 833-3662

**Wing Haven Gardens and
  Bird Sanctuary**
Charlotte, NC
(704) 334-0664

WRAL Gardens*
Raleigh, NC
(919) 821-8555

Of the Carolina Mountains

Biltmore House and Gardens
Asheville, NC
(800) 432-2961

Blue Ridge Community College*
Flat Rock, NC
(828) 692-3572

Botanical Gardens of Asheville
Asheville, NC
(828) 252-5190

**Campus Arboretum of
  Haywood Community College**
Clyde, NC
(828) 627-4640

Cherokee Botanical Garden
Cherokee, NC
(704) 497-2111

Chimney Rock Park
Chimney Rock, NC
(800) 277-9611

Daniel Boone Native Gardens
Boone, NC
(828) 264-2120

Grandfather Mountain
Linville, NC
(828) 733-2013

N.C. Arboretum
Asheville, NC
(828) 665-2492

Pearson's Falls
Tryon, NC
(828) 749-3031

Wilkes Community College Gardens*
Wilkesboro, NC
(336) 838-6100

*All-America Selections Display Gardens

Bibliography

Publications

American Nurseryman Publishing Co. *American Nurseryman* (semimonthly publication). Chicago, Illinois.

Armitage, Allan M. *Herbaceous Perennial Plants*. Varsity Press. Athens, Georgia. 1989.

Bender, Steve and Felder Rushing. *Passalong Plants*. University of North Carolina Press. Chapel Hill, North Carolina. 1993.

Bir, Richard E. *Growing and Propagating Showy Native Woody Plants*. University of North Carolina. Chapel Hill, North Carolina. 1992.

Cathey, H. Marc. *Heat-Zone Gardening*. Time-Life Inc. China. 1998.

Clausen, Ruth Rogers and Nicolas H. Ekstrom. *Perennials for American Gardens*. Random House. New York. 1989.

Cox, Jeff and Marilyn. *The Perennial Garden*. Rodale Press. Emmaus, Pennsylvania. 1985.

Dirr, Michael A. *Manual of Woody Landscape Plants, Fifth Ed*. Stripes Publishing Company. Champaign, Illinois. 1998.

Eyre, Suzanne E. *Sunset National Gardening Book*. Sunset Books, Inc. Menlo Park, California. 1997.

Floyd, John Alex. *Southern Living Gardening: Trees and Shrubs*. Oxmoor House. Birmingham, Alabama. 1980.

Glenn, Walter and Lark Foster. *The Tennessee Gardener's Guide*. Cool Springs Press. Franklin, Tennessee. 1996.

Halfacre, Gordon R. and Anne R. Shawcroft. *Landscape Plants of the Southeast, Fifth Ed*. Sparks Press. Raleigh, North Carolina. 1992.

Harper, Pamela and Frederick McGourty. *Perennials*. HP Books. Los Angeles, California. 1985.

Heriteau, Jacqueline with Dr. Marc Cathey. *The National Arboretum Book of Outstanding Plants*. Simon and Schuster. New York, New York. 1990.

Heriteau, Jacqueline. *The American Horticultural Society Flower Finder*. Simon and Schuster. New York, New York. 1992.

Hunt, William L. *Southern Gardens, Southern Gardening*. Duke University Press. Durham, North Carolina.

Ladendorf, Sandra F. *Successful Southern Gardening*. University of North Carolina Press. Chapel Hill, North Carolina. 1989.

Lathrop, Norma Jean. *Herbs*. HP Books. Los Angeles, California. 1981.

Meredith Corporation. *Successful Rose Gardening*. Des Moines, Iowa. 1993.

North Carolina Association of Nurserymen, Inc. *Plants for Enjoyable Living*. Raleigh, North Carolina.

Tripp, Kim E. and J. C. Raulston. 1995. *The Year in Trees*. Timber Press. Portland, Oregon.

Associations

Carolina Gardener. Greensboro, North Carolina.

Wayside Gardens. Hodges, South Carolina.

Parks Seed Wholesale, Inc. Greenwood, South Carolina.

Plant Index

Featured plant selections are indicated in **boldface**.

Meet the Authors

Toby Bost

Born and raised in Piedmont, North Carolina, Toby Bost has served Tar Heel gardeners for 28 years. He is presently an Extension Agent with N.C. State University's Cooperative Extension Service where he dedicates his time to helping fellow gardeners conquer stubborn clay soils and grow healthy lawns and ornamentals.

Toby has received both local and national awards from the National Association of County Agricultural Agents for his gardening projects and publications including the Distinguished Service and Community Appearance Leadership Awards. He is also a member of the Garden Writers Association. He frequently appears on radio and television across the state where he readily shares insightful landscaping information. In the past twenty years he has recruited and trained more than 400 Master Gardeners in Cooperative Extension. Currently he provides training for Green Industry professionals seeking certification in myriad trade associations.

Toby and his wife, Becky, reside in Winston-Salem while 2 children are away at university. In his leisure time Toby can be found gardening at home or consulting with friends who benefit from his trouble-shooting skills.

Jim Wilson

Jim Wilson is best known for his ten years as co-host of the popular PBS television show, *The Victory Garden*. A lecturer and renowned writer, he is author and co-author of numerous books on a wide variety of gardening subjects, including *Landscaping with Wildflowers, Masters of the Victory Garden, Jim Wilson's Container Gardening, South Carolina Gardener's Guide,* and *Gardening Through Your Golden Years.* Jim has received several prestigious awards including election into the Garden Writers Association Hall of Fame. He has been named Garden Communicator of the Year by the American Nursery Association. In 1996, Jim was made a Life Member of the National Council of State Garden Clubs.

Jim has devoted his life to helping people understand and appreciate both the natural and designed landscape. He wants to instill in his audience the joy of working in the soil. He has achieved over half a century of gardening experience and considers it his privilege to apply his knowledge fostering intrigue, fascination and appreciation for the simple pleasures and complex inner workings of nature.